T0345744

IBUSE MASUJI: A CENTURY REMEMBERED
ANTONÍN LÍMAN

# Ibuse Masuji: A Century Remembered

**Antonín Líman**

Charles University in Prague
Karolinum Press 2008

For Eva and Tony

*The calligraphy on the book's cover is Ibuse's*
*celebrated translation of Yü Wu-ling's*
*Chinese verse: "Accept this cup and fill it to the brim;*
*they say flowers are torn down by the storm,*
*and human life is nothing but Farewells."*

*Photography: Ibuse in his native house in Kamo*
*in 1948. Courtesy of Asahi Graph, special edition,*
*June 25, 1992.*

Some parts of this book were originally published
by The Edwin Mellen Press, in *A Critical Study*
*of The Literary Style of Ibuse Masuji: As Sensitive as Waters*,
and were used with their kind permission.

ISBN 978-80-246-1452-6

# TABLE OF CONTENTS

## ACKNOWLEDGEMENTS

*I would like to express my sincere thanks to Tony Liman Jr. and David Aylward for a careful reading of the manuscript and valuable suggestions. My profound thanks go to Professor Isogai Hideo from Hiroshima University and his team (Aihara Kazukuni, Itô Shin'ichirô, Iwasaki Fumito, Maeda Sadaaki, Tanabe Kenji and Terayoko Takeo), who provided tremendous help with my research. I am also grateful to Professor Noji Junya from Hiroshima who gave me several rare first editions of Ibuse's works. A number of generous grants from The Japan Foundation and the SSHRC (Social Sciences and Humanities Research Council of Canada) enabled my research stays in Japan. I am also grateful to Mrs. Masumi Abe for checking my Japanese references and translations, and to my students Hanna Kozielska, Yuuki Hirano and Rachel Millard for revising bibliographic data in English. I'd also like to thank my editor, Ms. Renata Čámská at Karolinum for her meticulous and devoted editing of the text.*

*We grow to respect the sceptical mode as the strongest trait*
*of an enlightened modern consciousness.*[1]

Harold Kaplan

Few words have been more abused in the last century
than the word modern. Unless we define it with great
care, it may mean as little as the Heian catchword *imam-
ekashi.*[2] If by modern we mean a trendy, versatile style
of writing readily understood by the average reader, or
a thematic interest in fashionable current topics, then
Ibuse's writing is hardly modern. The term modern
and in a narrower sense, modernist, has acquired a special meaning in Europe after the first world war, where
it came to denote fairly exclusive poetry by Ezra Pound
or W. B. Yeats and experimental prose by James Joyce,
Virginia Woolf and Gertrude Stein. Lautréamont's
famous statement that poetry is a "fortuitous encounter on a dissection table of a sewing machine and an
umbrella" may have had a limited significance among
European avantgarde circles, but extreme modernist
theories like Marinetti's futurism or Tristan Tzara's

---

[1] Kaplan, Harold: *The Passive Voice: An Approach to Modern Fiction.* Athens,
Ohio University Press 1966, p. 5.

[2] Trendy, up-to-date.

dadaism were never succesfully transplanted to Japan. Stephen Spender offers a reasonable definition of modern art that would fit Japanese literature as well as European:

> Modern art is that in which the artist reflects awareness of an unprecedented modern situation in its form and idiom. The quality which is called modern shows in the realized sensibility of style and form more than in the subject matter.[3]

Art heralded as truly modern is often formally more conventional than its traditional models if it follows any current orthodoxy. For example, the proletarian novels of the thirties may have appeared as something startlingly new at the time - mainly thanks to the novelty of their subject matter in Japanese literature - yet with the passage of time and some objective distance one sees how shallow and uninventive they were in terms of "sensibility of style and form." I mean not only polish of style and poetic refinement, but an ability of the writer's language to express in a lasting manner the uniqueness of a so far unmapped consciousness. One would not mind a less refined language in the proletarian novels if it truly conveyed to us the workers' thoughts and actions and showed them as springing from the substance of their being. What they do most of the time, however, is to repeat stale ideological clichés and - even more unbearably - project the patronizing sentiments of intellectuals into working people's heads, disguised as their own thoughts and feelings.

[3] Spender, Stephen: *The Struggle of the Modern*. Berkeley, University of California Press 1963, p. 71.

That Ibuse's writing, especially in his later years, is characterized by a great deal of unromantic scepticism – Japanese traditional aesthetics would call it *shibumi* – is quite obvious. That many of his rustic or historical themes and most of his colourful, not to say eccentric characters are also a product of a truly enlightened consciousness is far less apparent.

In his native country, Ibuse's reputation rests on two commonly admired achievements: he is acclaimed as a popular writer (*shomin sakka*) on one hand and his writing is admittedly characterized by a unique style on the other. Most critics agree that his is one of the most original stylistic experiments in modern Japanese prose. But how are we to understand these two qualities – are they not contradictory? Ibuse's themes and settings may be drawn from common people's lives, and yet if they are conveyed by a highly stylized literary language, the writing will appeal only to a fairly narrow segment of the audience. This is a common dilemma of any serious writer's existence: how to compromise between one's own genuine social sympathies and the pressures of friendly côteries and other social groupings – and the awesome responsibility to a partly inherited, partly imported literary structure.

It is doubly difficult for a young writer in Japan, where beginning artists naturally band together and subscribe to an established social or artistic movement or create their own and publish group journals in which even the greatest Shôwa writers had once placed their maiden works. When many of Ibuse's literary friends joined the popular 'proletarian literature' movement in the late twenties and adjusted their artistic standards accordingly to get 'closer to the people', he kept writing the way he had started out, searching painstakingly for his own style. For this stubborn loyalty to high personal standards he had to pay a steep price: his leftist friends deserted him and he lost the opportunity to publish in their journals (*zasshi*).[4] Though Ibuse never went as far in his stylistic experiments as the European avantgarde, his bold experimentation with traditional prose techniques earned him a pejorative label of 'nonsense literature' from some critics and it took him nearly two decades to get rid of it completely. Of course when we get to his mature works all the linguistic innovations and experiments of his learning years are smoothly blended into what is sweepingly called "Ibuse's unique style." In such works as *Black Rain* (*Kuroi ame*, 1965) the artist has come full circle: he wrote a novel about the common people and their shattering experience, considered inexpressible by most, and he did it in a rich, precise language that lost nothing of its originality and yet can be readily understood and appreciated by the average reader. To trace the genesis and the development of this style is the main purpose of the present book.

In order to define Ibuse's overall artistic contribution and establish where his greatness as a prose writer lies, it might be helpful to separate the three basic components of great storytelling which in the more specialized genres tend to monopolize the overall narrative technique. In the Western tradition, one of the most common expectations from a good story is the thrill of its storyline and its dramatic suspense, usu-

[4] *Zasshi* or *dôjin zasshi*, côterie journals.

ally carried by a fast moving linear plot; this is most pronounced in novels of the adventure or detective genre, whose authors are more interested in creating a sense of excitement and anticipation in their readers than appealing to their taste for sophisticated nuances of style or for subtle psychological delineation of character. Not only detective novels but an ever increasing number of contemporary bestsellers are written this way.

Japanese traditional aesthetics have never placed as much emphasis on linear plot, and the Aristotelian dramatic structure is by and large missing from the great classical *monogatari* such as *The Tale of Genji* or *The Tales of the Heike* and obviously from the more intimate diary (*nikki*) genre. From the Japanese point of view, the absence of a strong mechanical plot not only does not constitute a weakness, it can give a distinct advantage to even a modern novelist like Ibuse, since it allows more freedom in developping story and character.

The second important feature of an accomplished narrative is the psychological delineation of character. Again, the Western realistic novel of the 19th century as practiced by writers as diverse as Dickens, Balzac, or Tolstoy has established a certain shared tradition of psychological portrayal that does not necessarily correspond to traditional Japanese modes of character representation. Whereas the masters of 19th century European novels are interested not only in an introspective analysis of individual characters, but also in presenting the psychological implications of a complex interplay between individuals and their society, Japanese classical authors and their present day inheritors concentrate on the private emotions of a small circle of people, or simply on the private world of one protagonist – usually a thinly disguised persona of the author himself. Yet if the larger social scene and an objective understanding of the historical forces that dominate it are mostly missing from this lyrical, subjective tradition, it can present, by its closer focus and detailed concentration, a profound, lasting portrayal of human emotions that have little to do with the passing of social and historical forces. Since the rigidly controlled objective frame of Western realism never really came into existence in Japan, action and consciousness are only vaguely separated in this lyrical narrative tradition. There is not only an emotional closeness between fictional character and narrator, but an easy, fluid transition from the inner to the outer landscape and vice versa; unlike the 'rounded' character of the Western classical novel the Japanese lyrical character grows out of its natural setting that has more power to shape its emotional moods beyond intellectual control. If there are any formal parallels with the European novel, then we must look for them in the later, more specialized techniques of psychological description of Joyce or Proust. Although Ibuse breaks with the lyrical tradition in a number of ways – not least by his keen interest in larger historical issues such as the war and the atomic bomb and their impact on the communal mind – we shall see that this does not mean an automatic adoption of standard Western techniques: his solution is based on a selective adaptation of some native modes and a careful compromise with imported ones.

And third, we might talk about a specialization of yet another kind, about novels and stories in which the author's interest shifts from story, plot and character to the narrative technique itself, or to the craft of storytelling as such. In these novels, style moves to centre stage to become the main actor as it were, and human character is developed from within by modes of speech such as personal mannerisms, stylized elements of dialect, subtle inflections of dialogue and the like, rather than described from without by an omniscient narrator. Writers who work at this level are quite rare and seldom become popular in their own time. There are only a few artists in each generation who really understand and use to its fullest a language developed by millions of their countrymen.

This isolation of the various narrative components is of course too schematic as every serious writer tries to combine all three into one organic blend. It is rather a question of emphasis, especially during the formative years of a writer's career. The literature of writers who work at this level is always based on what de Saussure calls *parole* rather than on *langue* and makes conscious use of as many 'linguistic accidents' of their native tongue as possible. Working within the conventions of their language and yet constantly struggling to transcend them, they are "launching a relentless, bloody battle against their own mother-tongue,"[5] as Kamiya Tadataka defines Yokomitsu Riichi's literary efforts. Some of the resulting works are almost impossible to translate into another language, or at best can be translated only partially, while much of

[5] Kamiya, Tadataka: *Yokomitsu Riichi ron.* Tokyo, Sôbunsha 1978, p. 20.

their stylistic appeal remains locked in the original text. Such writers – say, Emily Brontë, Eudora Welty, William Faulkner or Ibuse Masuji – invariably come from a dense and secluded, not to say claustrophobic sociolinguistic environment. It is often an hinterland remote in terms of both economic and cultural communication with the 'Centre', be it London, New York or Tokyo. These writers grew up with the mixed feelings of being outsiders on one hand, and yet belonging to a local culture that has something special, a character more authentic than anything the metropolis can offer, on the other. Brontë's Yorkshire, Faulkner's and Welty's Mississippi and Ibuse's Bingo differ in so many respects and yet they have something essential in common. They all give their inhabitants a strong sense of belonging to a Place and its community which they come to love and to resent with almost equal intensity – a community that has existed for many generations without much change or outside intrusion until fairly recently. It is of course a community bound by common economic interest, and by shared traditions of custom and ritual. Above all – from a writer's point of view – it is a shared community of language. This language may be based not only on a distinctive dialect, but on a familiar lore of local yarns and anecdotes that give people individual colour and identity. These are often passed on from generation to generation. Because the circle is so small and the language so well understood, every speaker tries to add a bit of flavour to the highly ritualized speech patterns. In *The Departed Village*, R. E. Moreau puts it most succinctly:

Their ideas were limited, but they were expressed with a verbal piquancy that was laced with the distillate of past centuries.[6]

It is an almost fateful bond that ties our writers to their place. They know that what they are was made here, that the colours and shapes of this place, its trees and its people are forever imprinted in their minds. It is a basic blueprint of the world and a measure of the things in it. And precisely for that reason – since the reflection of their Place is so sharp and so deep in their minds, their concern about its inner tensions and contradictions so keen – they feel compelled to give it creative expression. Unlike the idyllic type of regional writer who writes from within, having a safe if fairly limited foothold inside the place he observes, writers of Welty's and Ibuse's kind work from a more complex position. They have acquired a formal education in the city and come to perceive their own creative existence as belonging to a larger artistic community. Through their basic experience they belong to their native place and it can give them what Welty describes as a writer's base of reference,[7] yet they do not belong to it as members of a critical community of city intellectuals. The strict laws of an artistic discipline have little to do with the everyday life of a rural community.

Furthermore, compared to Western Europe, Japan's industrial revolution occured very recently, or rather it was imported into a predominantly agrarian society.

---

[6] Moreau, Reginald Ernest: *The Departed Village: Berrick Salome at the turn of the century*. London, Oxford University Press 1968, p. 165.
[7] Welty, Eudora: "Place in Fiction." In: *Three Papers on Fiction*. Northampton, Smith College 1962, p. 11.

This agrarian culture, due to its insular isolation, relative scarcity of arable land, the need for cooperation in intensive wet-rice farming and a unique animistic relationship with the land, has created complex bonds of kinship and rich networks of peasant ritual. Although they have some parallels in pre-industrial Europe, they are more deeply rooted and persistent than similar rural patterns elsewhere. With a few exceptions – the genuinely urban writers like Kafû, Tanizaki or Mishima – the majority of Japanese novelists in the Taishô-Shôwa period cannot accept a clear separation and fully identify with either the rural or the urban mode. Rather, they perceive the conflict of values between the two as a painful unfinished process of transition, or better, a continuous *corso-ricorso* movement. This movement from country to city and back becomes their decisive experience – whether they face it as a dramatic theme in their writing as Ibuse did, or betray its traumatic effect by an overall anguish and discomfort in their personal life as did his pupil, Dazai Osamu. What makes the transition doubly painful for the post-Meiji Japanese is the fact that it is not simply a shift from their native countryside and its mentality to an urban atmosphere, but also from their country's native culture to an alien, imported one.

Yet if they cannot accept their Place as a gift anymore, writers of Ibuse's type are not inclined, like some country boys turned cosmopolitan, to rejecting it as an unseemly birthmark either. They feel they must translate its mixed blessing into their own words and communicate its story to the outside world. After all, it is the story they know best. What is even more important is that Ibuse managed to tell his story with a generous touch of that rarest of spices, so often missing from the grim cuisine of modern Japanese prose: a unique and subtle humour.

Since the imprint of Place is so crucial in Ibuse's work, I have tried to evoke its rich atmosphere in the first chapter, letting the author speak of it as frequently as possible through his essays and memoirs. It is an intrinsic part of Ibuse's life philosophy that he downplays dramatic events on the one hand and emphasizes what a contemporary Western reader might be tempted to pass over as marginal episodes or fleeting human encounters on the other. To impose too much of a Western biographer's sense of order and logic on Ibuse's own view of his life would distort the perspective – after all, it is the great respect for the 'insignificant' quotidian details of existence that give the author's life its distinctive charm. I tried to write a biocritical study that would look at this life with sympathy, and maintain critical objectivity when analyzing the author's texts. Having had the rare privilege of knowing Ibuse personally, I hope my recollections of him round out the portrayal of one of the most original and interesting men of letters in the 20th century.

*I was born on the 15th of February, in the thirty-first year of Meiji (1898).
It was the year when the third Itô cabinet was formed and fell, then the
first Ôkuma cabinet and soon after it the Yamagata cabinet; the same
year when Kôtoku Shûsui founded his study group of socialism…
It must have been a turbulent year in the political world.* [1]

Ibuse Masuji

But in Ibuse's native Kamo these distant events barely
made a ripple on the placid surface of village life.
Spread out along a shallow valley between two soft-
rounded hills, Kamo lies about twelve kilometers north
of the city of Fukuyama in the old province of Bingo,
or what is now known as Hiroshima Prefecture.

With its sixty households and one general store,
the Kamo-Awane[2] hamlet of his childhood must have
offered the typical view of a southern village: an
unrushed gathering of low-squatting thatched farm-

---

[1] Ibuse, Masuji: (hereafter IM), "Hanseiki." In: *Ibuse Masuji zenshû* (hereafter
*IMZ*), *vol. XIII*. Tokyo, Chikuma shobô 1974, p. 374. Another, more complete
*zenshû* was published by Chikuma shobô in 1996–1999. To distinguish between
the two, I am quoting the recent one in bold script. All quotations from Japanese
and other languages, unless the translator's name is stated, were translated by
the author.

[2] Kamo is the name of the whole village (Kamo township at present) and Awane
one of its administrative districts.

houses, some skirting the Kamo river in the middle of the valley, others near the foot or on the slopes of the surrounding mountains. Most properties were outlined, but not really closed off, by low, deep-ochre mud walls that give the visitor a feeling of warmth and cozy human scale. Those higher up the slopes were carved into the hillside and supported by high terrace walls on the open side facing the valley. The wealthier houses could be spotted at first sight by the tall, white storehouses (*kura*) in their courtyards.

To get to the Ibuse family house one passes a small roadside shrine in the village centre. Two man-sized statues and a stone lantern stand there side-by-side. The road forks here and these sculptures – one a jovial, rotund *Jizô* and the other an ancient, rugged piece of oblong rock – have been guarding this thoroughfare for many a century. On their foundation stones, several dates are carved. The oldest says: "At the time of the Kyôwa reign (1801–1803)," but that goes for the *Jizô* who is much younger; the rock may come from the dawn of Japanese history when monoliths of phallic shape were worshipped as symbols of fertility. From here, one fork of the road rises steeply for half-a-mile or so, all the way to a high stone wall that holds the slope. From the path that runs alongside, one can first glimpse the tall white *kura* and a large persimmon tree drooping over the mudwall built atop the terrace wall. Stepping into the sand-strewn square of the courtyard for the first time and taking in the elegant dignity of the ancient building and its garden, one cannot help thinking of Yasuoka Shôtarô's words: "Without the old home, there would be no Ibuse literature." Poet Miyoshi Tatsuji also felt the blessings of many generations of ancestors in Ibuse's writing and thought that without the aura of the old house such literature could never exist.[3] The house is large and solid, its structure almost massive. Yet since it has a clean functional shape and no unnecessary ornamentation, one gets an impression of almost religious austerity. When Yasuoka first came here, he thought this must be the local shrine. There is a pleasing contrast between the white sand in front of the porch and the smooth texture of its red-pine boards; the white paper of the four *shôji* is beautifully set off by the dark-stained timber of the front wall.

Behind the house, in a small plot shaded by the mountain, there is a neat row of carved tombstones; some of the weathered dates chiseled into the mossy rock are four centuries old. Ibuse's ancestors came to Kamo around 1570 from Shikoku, some years after the death of their liege lord, Ôuchi Yoshitaka[4], the *daimyô* of seven southern provinces. The author once told me with a smile:

> The man who founded this branch of our family seems to have spelt his name *I-bushi* and written it with the characters for wild boar and warrior (猪、武士)… But I guess he didn't want to look like a warmonger, and changed it to Ibuse.[5]

[3] Yasuoka talked about this in a lecture given at the University of Toronto in the spring of 1973. Miyoshi's comment is quoted in Kawamori, Yoshizô: *Ibuse Masuji zuimon*. Tokyo, Shinchôsha 1986, p. 203.

[4] Ôuchi, Yoshitaka, the most powerful daimyo of Western Honshû. Yoshitaka amassed a great fortune by trading with Korea and Japan and later in life became disillusioned with military exploits, making Yamaguchi Castle a centre of arts and culture; there he also met with Francis Xavier.

[5] I heard this story from Mr. Ibuse himself. Yoneda Seiichi relates the same in "Namae no koto." In: *IMZ XIV. Geppô* 14, pp. 7–8.

The characters he chose stand for 'well' (井) and 'lying low, hiding' (伏せる). Perhaps that is exactly how he felt, having fought the vengeful warlord Môri on the losing side. Young Masuji chose an even less martial-sounding variation for his given name, changing the *Masu* (満寿) of 'full, ripe age' into the *Masu* (鱒) of 'trout', so that we can read the characters 井伏 and 鱒二 as "Two trout lying at the bottom of a well." Given Ibuse's life-long interest in mountain streams and trout fishing, a most fitting name for the future writer.

By the small arbour in one corner of the garden, a huge jar of old Bizen ware stands casually – the simple, rustic type of pottery Ibuse favoured in his own home in Tokyo. Just like "old Kôtarô's jar" in *Black Rain* – "an enormous affair in Bizen ware" in which the old man kept live fish: "eels, sweetfish, trout or anything else one fancied."[6]

The mountain behind the house, actually a gently rounded hill of 250–260 metres, is wild only in comparison with the manicured garden. It has preserved many traces of human presence, some very ancient and no doubt mysterious to a young child. A few steps from the back porch of the house, a fort used to stand until the Civil Wars Period (*Sengoku jidai*, 16th century), when Lord Môri attacked it and razed it to the ground. It is said that the village was completely deserted at that point; man, woman and child having joined the mass evacuation to the nearby town of Fuchû. Higher up the mountain are even older remnants of antiquity

[6] IM: *Black Rain*. Trans. Bester, John. Tokyo, New York and San Francisco, Kôdansha International 1969, pp. 60–61.

– the prehistoric *kofun,* grave mounds dating from the Yayoi period (200 B.C.–250 A.D.). In an essay called "Until My Maiden Work" (*Shojosaku made*, 1970) Ibuse reminisces:

> When I was a child, a stone-mason by the name of Hama-yan lived in our neighbourhood. He did any kind of stonework, from stone-mortars to gravestones and *Jizô* statues, using boulders from the 'top of the mountain'. The left-over fragments and smaller pebbles were used as building material for the stone walls. For stepping stones and well-cribs he was using the flat slabs from the tombs…
>
> Every time Hama-yan brought down some rocks from the mountain, he would also fill a bamboo basket with the earthenware he found as he was unearthing the mounds. Once in a while he would happen on an ancient jewel – a *magatama* or a *kudatama* – and present them as an offering to the local temple. One day he gave me an earthenware bowl. I took it home and was just washing it by the pond, when my older brother (Fumio) spotted me and made me feel terribly guilty. (I think I was five or six that summer, my brother was home for his school vacations and loved to play the big brother with me):
>
> 'Hey you, stop that nonsense. If you keep playing with antiques, you'll never become a writer'…[7]

It is a pity that Fumio died long before he could read "The Master of the Old Curio Shoppe" (*Chinpindô shujin*, 1959), "Yosaku the Settler" (*Kaikon-mura no Yo-saku*, 1955) and many other wonderful stories in which the aura of these ancient mounds and the treasures

---

[7] IM: "Shojosaku made." In: *IMZ XXIV*. Tokyo, Chikuma shobô 1997, pp. 519–520. This text was published earlier under the title "Waga bungaku no yôranki" (The Cradle of My Literature) in: *IM shû, Geppô 17*. Tokyo, Shinchôsha 1970.

found in them play a central role. There were many attractions around the house – next to the mysterious relics on the mountain, the children could climb trees and spy on birds' nests. In those days, the mountain abounded not only with common birds like pheasants, turtle-doves and jays, but also with buntings (*hôjiro*), bulbuls (*hiyodori*) and dusky ouzels (*tsugumi*). They were not afraid to enter the garden, to bathe in its ponds or peck at the small, red fruit of the *nanten* tree.

Sometimes, as Ibuse recalls in "Birds' Nests" (*Tori no su*, 1950) even a shy kingfisher would alight on the lower branch of a pine tree and watch the pond with "a melancholy eye." In the same essay, he says:

> As a child, I loved to peek into birds' nests. Those little freckled eggs are not at all bad to look at. Should one call them 'charming' or 'elegant'? At any rate, I didn't know such words at the time, and just adored the eggs. The moment I spotted a nest in the branches of a tree, I would risk any danger to climb up and have a peek inside it. As long as the branches gave enough foothold, I felt confident to climb as high as one and a half to two meters.[8]

Years later, Ibuse wrote a brief essay about a poem by Kinoshita Yûji (a poet who used to live in the neighbouring town of Miyuki and joined him for many a fishing trip), called "A Lark's Nest" (*Hibari no su*); the poem goes:

> Found a skylark's nest
> No one knows about it yet
> It's over there
> By the old mill shack

[8] IM: "Tori no su." In: *Bamen no kôka*. Tokyo, Daiwa shobô 1966, p. 87.

Where the red roof of the clinic shows
In that wheatfield
Lined up in the nest
Five little eggs
I haven't told anybody yet...[9]

The essay is called "A Poem I Like" (*Watashi no sukina shi hitotsu*, 1970) and it is quite unusual, because Ibuse makes an involved critical comment on a piece of poetry – something he is usually quite reluctant to do. Here is why he likes the little poem so much:

Kinoshita Yûji says he wrote this poem for children but since it's plain enough to offer a shortcut towards understanding poetry, everybody can appreciate it. He makes no attempt to condescend to children and the poem gives such a pleasant feeling because it's not self-conscious at all. When I read it, I recall my own childhood. At one time a bunting built a nest on a tall *sazanka* tree growing from the ornamental hill in our garden and I climbed a pine-tree next to it to look inside the nest. Suddenly my heart began to beat faster. I thought: I won't tell a living soul about these eggs. No sooner did I get down from the tree, that I felt I must go up for another secret peek. Again I felt the same excitement. The freckled eggs looked as if they were thrown out completely at random, and yet they also seemed naturally lined up in a perfect, charming order. No one could have arranged them more elegantly, as they lay there with utter nonchalance.

Kinoshita writes: 'Lined up in the nest, five little eggs...' One imagines a sweet little child, barely able to

[9] Kinoshita, Yûji: *Hibari no su: Kinoshita Yûji jidô shishû*. Tokyo, Hikari shobô 1999, pp. 6–7.

count. The line 'five little eggs' focuses the image. The next one, 'I haven't told anybody yet' brings tears to your eyes.[10]

On Sundays young Masuji used to go fishing for crucian carp (*funa*) with a manservant called Yoichi, from whom he learned the angler's patience. Crucian carp has a small mouth and takes bait very gingerly, so the boy didn't catch much. Yoichi would sometimes pilfer some eggs from a duck's or pheasant's nest and make scrambled eggs over a campfire. When the strict family patriarch, Grandpa Tamizaemon (or Minzaemon), learned about that, the boy had to visit the local healer who'd exorcize his evil spirits, and then be shut up in the warehouse for "torturing weaker creatures." Even if Masuji did not catch too many fish on these Sunday excursions, his native landscape made a lasting imprint in his mind as he came to know intimately its fish, its birds, trees, even its local eccentrics to whom he'd return again and again in his stories. Could someone who had never climbed a tree have written the following passage about a birdcatcher from the story "Isle-on-the Billows"?

> The pine tree leaned slightly out from the cliff-face, but luckily its trunk was rough; he needed no special skill to climb a tree like this. He scrambled up, making sure the adult birds were not at home. Quickly he set his trap, smearing lime on some straw and spreading it round the nest. The nestlings' eyes were already open, their black feathers sprouting. At the light touch of Wabisuke's hand on their head, they stretched out their little necks

[10] IM: "Watashi no sukina shi hitotsu." In: *Tsuribito*. Tokyo, Shinchôsha 1970, pp. 55–56.

and squeaked with hunger. But it wasn't the chicks he was after, so after catching a pleasant whiff of their raw, slightly sour smell, he slid off the tree...[11]

Smell is the safest and least conscious link with one's forgotten past and it can evoke images of bygone time with amazing clarity. There are writers who depend more on their visual or auditory memory, but Ibuse ranks himself among those with a 'sharp nose':

> Among the many smells of my childhood, I recall most fondly the smell of rice being steamed, the fragrance of boiling *miso* soup and the smoke of the woodstove... In my old home in the country they prepared *misoshiru* by mixing old *miso* that passed through the heat and cold for at least three years with fresh 'one-year' *miso* half and half, and they'd strain it through a long, narrow bamboo sieve called *misokoshi*. In the evenings, when I played on the street with the children from our neighbourhood, I would always recognize the smell of cooking rice from our house. Soon after, the fragrance of boiling *miso* came wafting through the air...
>
> The smell of smoke rising from the woodstoves wasn't bad either. At a time when I had already resigned myself to never smelling it again, I became devoted to valley fishing and there in the mountain lodges I got an ample opportunity to experience it again. If you've never broiled your fresh-caught fish over a hearth, your eyes smarting from the smoke, you don't know what happiness is...

[11] IM: "Isle-on-the-Billows." In: *Waves*. Transl. Aylward, David and Liman, Anthony. Tokyo, New York and San Francisco, Kôdansha International 1986, p. 123.

I'll never be able to forget these three kinds of smell. Sometimes I even think: isn't my body made of these three fragrances and the water of my birthplace?[12]

He must have had a sharp nose indeed, since the children were playing in front of the *Jizô* statue by the shrine, which is at least a half mile away from the house. The games they enjoyed were not different from those of village children anywhere. The boys had their rougher pastimes like throwing stones and staging mock battles, or flipping *menko,* little coloured discs (known as tiddlywinks in the West), a much simpler game than the girls played. Perhap these plain toys required a greater imagination than computer games – Ibuse recalls that the boys called their 'big guns' Admiral Roshdestvenski, Commander Stoessel, or Lieutenant-Colonel Hirose, all popular names of the Russo-Japanese war.[13] As usual, the girls were excluded from the manly pastimes, and most of their games were too complex for the boys anyway. On some days they would play the *'Jizô-game'* (*Jizô san asobi*), a Japanese version of 'blind man's buff', at other times they played a difficult game called *'se-sse-sse',* which did not make much sense to the boys. Two girls would in turn stand face-to-face, clapping together their palms, once pointing up, once down and singing busily:

> *Se-sse-sse* – the first crest is a mandarin orange, the second one an iris, the third a wistaria, the fourth a peony, the fifth a mountain-cherry and the sixth a deep-dyed purple...[14]

[12] IM: "Nioi." In: *IMZ XII*, pp. 115–116.
[13] IM: "Menko." In: *IMZ XIV,* p. 198.
[14] IM: "Keirokushû." In: *IMZ IX*, pp. 253–254.

Ibuse remembered these 'meaningless' little songs well, and after half a century wove them deftly into the fabric of his major novel; in a world rendered empty by the bomb, they became a vital link with a more humane past:

Whenever a breeze sprang up [the leaves] would pour down from the eaves in a yellow waterfall, and when it eddied they would swirl up into the air – up and up to twice, three times the height of the roof – then descend in yellow whirlpools onto the road up the slope and into the oak grove.

This always delighted the children. As the wind dropped and the leaves came dancing down, the boys would stretch up their hands to clutch at them, and the girls would catch them in their outspread aprons. Then they would total the numbers of leaves they had caught. 'One-for-me, two-for-me, gingko yellow,' they would chant, throwing away a leaf at a time – that made four leaves. 'Flittery, slippery, gingko fellow' – that made another four. Over and over again they would sing the same refrain, until only one child had any leaves left, and he became the winner.[15]

The author recalls his playmates in a long autobiographical essay called "A Collection of Things of Small Value, Yet Too Precious To Throw Away"(*Keirokushû*), written in 1936. Their names and faces have not faded in the least, although thirty years have gone by. There are some painful memories as well – one of the little girls went hunting for fireflies to the river, and as she was leaning from the bridge, trying to reach a firefly underneath it, she lost her balance and fell into the

[15] *Black Rain*, p. 74.

fast current. All her mother ever found was the firefly broom lying on the boards, and later on her *geta,* floating in a whirlpool downriver and "describing a circle." Although Ibuse reports this tragedy in an offhand, almost journalistic style, the memory must have rankled for a long time. It emerges as a recurrent, urgent motif in several important works, most notably "The River" (*Kawa*), a major story written in 1932.

Which of the two rivers that meet south of the hamlet took the little girl's life is hard to tell; they are both fast mountain streams, cascading over rocks and boulders and creating many shallow rapids and some deep 'holes' beneath them. Shallow and barely trickling in the dry months of late summer, but raging torrents after heavy rainfall or during the spring thaw, one bears the same name as the village, Kamo, and the other one, its tributary, is called the Shigawa. Although their confluence is within a short walk from the Ibuse house and both must have been clear streams in those days, it seems it was rather the mid-stream of the Shigawa that was famous for its trout and sweetfish (*ayu*). In one of Ibuse's best known fishing stories, "White Hair" (*Shiraga*, 1948), we find a detailed description of a 'mountain stream' that can only be the Shigawa with its rows of fruit trees lining the banks:

> On both banks of the stream, at the edge of the paved embankment, all kinds of fruit trees were growing: plum and persimmon trees, fig trees and loquats; but I never heard that fruit trees would be planted along a mountain stream to reinforce its banks. ...Right ahead of us besides a broad plum tree we could see the Dobashi bridge. There, under its right bank is my reserved fishing domain.

The river forms three ideal kinds of water for fishing here – shallows, current and depth. The fish usually stay in the current and wait for bait, that comes floating from the shallows, but since the current is very fast here, the fish hover on the edge of still water and the rushing current. When you don't cast right, or make a noise with your foot, the fish will disappear in the deep.[16]

To get to Ibuse's old fishing hole portrayed in "White Hair" one has to walk from Kamo along the left bank of the Shigawa for about 2.5 kilometers, until reaching a village of the same name: Shigawa. Nowadays, it is a part of Kamo township, together with the neighbouring hamlet of Imobara, another familiar name from the early stories. On the right bank of the river, above a slope held by a long, high stone wall, sits a rambling old farmhouse, or rather a country mansion with a wide-roofed gate, a spacious yard, luxurious garden and many outbuildings, most probably storehouses and toolsheds. Crossing the bridge a little upstream – perhaps the earthen bridge of the story – one must stop for a while at the sprawling white 'mansion on the hill', the residence of the Tange family.

The Tanges go back a long, long time in this area: the landlord I met in 1974, Tange Saishirô belongs to their 29th generation, while the founding patriarch of the clan came here in the Muromachi period, around the beginning of the 16th century. Although obviously the wealthiest landholders in the village as well as one of the oldest families in the entire region, the Tanges are used to visitors and show their house graciously. The old house itself is interesting as a fine example of

[16] IM: "Shiraga." *IMZ IV*, pp. 221–222.

Southern architecture, and since most of the twenty-nine generations of its owners added something to its possessions – be it a piece of handcrafted furniture, a work of pottery, a hanging scroll with a calligraphy by Master Sazan[17] or a musical instrument – it is almost like visiting a museum of local customs, folk crafts and arts.

But the real reason this house became a kind of historical monument is a slim story called *Tange-shi-tei,* or "Life at Mr. Tange's" in its English translation. Ibuse wrote the sixteen-page story in 1931, at a time when the foster father of the present landlord, Tange Ryôichi was the head of the household. Japanese readers like to go on 'literary excursions' (*bungaku no tabi*), looking for real models behind a fictional landscape, somewhat like the English do when tracing the Brontë sisters through the moors of Yorkshire or Wordsworth through the Lake District. Often they look not only for familiar landmarks, but for people who may have been the models of fictional characters. Thus Tange Ryôichi, the mayor of three mountain villages (Shigawa, Himetani and Imobara) and member of the county assembly in the thirties, is commonly believed to have been the model of the story's Mr. Tange (Ryôtarô), a somewhat eccentric country squire and, incidentally, 'mayor and tax collector' of the same three villages. The story portrays a couple of colourful rustics, Master Tange and his servant, yet it is by no means a harsh caricature of country bumpkins:

[17] Kan, Sazan (1748–1827), Confucian scholar and poet in the Chinese song-style of the late Edo period. He founded the famous private school (*juku*) in Kannabe, neighbouring town of Kamo.

Mr. Tange chastised his manservant. (Mr. Tange is sixty-seven, and his manservant fifty-seven.) The decrepit old man was forever taking naps in the middle of the day, and it was necessary, so Mr. Tange said, to have him turn over a new leaf. I have never seen Mr. Tange so angry before…

'Lie down on these mats!' he commanded the manservant.

The servant clung tightly to the trunk of the persimmon, foaming slightly at the mouth from nervousness. A chastisement, even in a remote rural spot like this, is taken very seriously. Mr. Tange pulled out the tobacco pouch tucked in the manservant's sash, and placed in on the mat. Then he said in a grave voice:

'You will lie down here on your back and smoke your pipe while we watch. That's what you always do, isn't it – you put your left heel up on the knot of the persimmon tree, and you lie back, and you rest your right heel on the shin of your left leg, and you go on smoking quite happily until it begins to get dark…'[18]

Although there are some traits in the protagonist's character that his son recognizes as his father's – especially the methodical patience and a reluctance to express his will in too straightforward a manner[19] – they amount only to a few strokes in the rich composite portrayal. The author himself discounts such a direct modelling of real people, saying that both the characters and the story-line are pure

[18] IM: "Life at Mr. Tange's." In: *Salamander and Other Stories*. Trans. Bester, John. Tokyo, New York and San Francisco, Kôdansha International 1981, p. 97.
[19] Iwasaki, Fumito: "IM to sono kyôdo." In: *Kindai bungaku shiron 10*. Hiroshima, Hiroshima daigaku kindai bungaku kenkyûkai 1972, p. 14.

fiction.[20] The characters of the story may be fictional, but the truth is somewhere in between, for the general layout of the house and its outbuildings, as well as its natural environment, correspond to the action of the story point by point. The large tree in the middle of the courtyard, beneath which Mr. Tange punished his servant, is not a persimmon, but a pear tree, but one can indeed observe this 'place of punishment' around the corner of the bathroom, from where the narrator of the story is peering out. The reason the narrator gives for coming to this remote countryside from Tokyo is to try to excavate whatever remains of the Himetani kiln, one of the most ancient pottery work-shops in Japan. And indeed, the road winding up along the Shigawa does lead to the village of Hime-tani and the site of an old kiln. It is located about four to five kilometers northwest from the Tange house. As we walk along the rushing river, pressed on both sides by the lush vegetation of the valley, a passage from another Ibuse story comes to mind:

> Walking through a deep valley on a moonlit night can be a very pleasant thing. The road had been widened for construction and was etched with deep ruts made by the trucks. The thick branches of the pine trees cast their speckled shadows onto the illuminated road. I stopped several times to gaze at the distorted reflection of the moon in the waters of a deep pool and to knock the flowers of a vine with my walking stick. However, my pleasant stroll was unexpectedly short, abruptly ended by a stone wall as long as that around a castle. It had been

[20] Ban, Toshihiko: "Ibuse san kara kiita koto 2." In: *IMZ III, Geppô* 4, p. 1.

erected to bridge the gap between the two mountains forming the valley. This was the dam.[21]

The road we are walking is the same that the young protagonist of "Kuchisuke's Valley" (*Kuchisuke no iru tanima*, 1929) walked more than half a century ago. The dam is about halfway between the Tange house and the Himetani kiln; by now the forest has had enough time to absorb the concrete into its deep verdure and the lake gives a softer impression than that of a 'demon pond' (*mamono no ike*) as it had appeared to young Ibuse. He wrote the story – the first of his successful cycle of village stories – in 1929, publishing it in the same month when the Otani dam was completed. By modern standards it is a tiny dam, but one can clearly imagine the writer's irritation and pain when the work crews invaded 'his valley' and shattered its peace with dynamite and pneumatic drills. The story's title, its plot and its theme all reflect this irritation: first of all, we notice it is called *Kuchisuke no iru tanima*, literally 'The valley where Kuchisuke is', and we might add 'where Kuchisuke is planted'. Old Kuchisuke, the protagonist of this story, and a former *komori* (child guardian, male nurse) of the narrator, has the bad luck to live in a house standing right on the bottom of the future lake. Being as stubborn as he is inarticulate about his plight, he adopts the typical peasant stance: if my house goes, I go with it. It takes the concerted effort of his granddaughter and his young friend to get the old man out of the flooding house, if not to convince him he could live elsewhere. A western reader, especially a

[21] IM: "Kuchisuke's Valley." In: *The Shôwa Anthology*. Trans. Treat, John. Tokyo, New York and San Franscisco, Kôdansha International 1985, pp. 6–7.

North American used to constant mobility, might say: well then, the theme of the story is a romantic protest against modernization; surely such a theme would be obsolete, even naive in today's dynamic, modern Japan where rapid change and adaptation is the order of the day.

I thought so myself before spending a year (1980–81) in Midorii (Green Well), a pretty village near Hiroshima, and watching people's reactions to a major highway project cutting through their community. On the surface, most of them seemed resigned to the inevitable change, yet they did and said things which would surprise any Westerner. Our neighbour, a granny of seventy-two or -three, once pointed to her house, which would be cut in half by the four-lane highway and said: "This is where my husband lived and where he died and now they say I must move... Well, I suppose Japan also must have a constitution".

It was not clear what the constitution had to do with it, but then it dawned on me that government officials must have descended on the old lady, waving papers and maps and explaining to her how important this project is, how much money she will get in compensation, and how all her rights and privileges are protected by the Japanese constitution. The old woman kept her own counsel and came up with a unique solution. Using the substantial compensation from the government, she hired a team of skilled builders and a Shinto priest. The builders painstakingly dismantled her old house, roof-tile by fragile roof-tile, plank by moldy plank, numbering the beams so they could assemble them again on the new site. This process is of course much more expensive than building a brand new pre-fabricated house. The priest then placated the spirits of the ground on which the house had been standing and the move began. Still painful and lamented, but bearable. I understood that what Ibuse talks about in a story written more than half a century ago is not just the familiar romantic lament against 'progress' despoiling tradition and environment, but a profound insight – presented in a light-handed and humorous way – into the basic nature of his people. A house and the plot it stands on are not just so many *tsubo* and so many lengths of board and beam, but a dwelling place of the ancestors' spirits, a sacred receptacle into which generations of people have breathed their souls. Moving then means leaving behind a good part of one's own soul and identity.

Perhaps the sons and the grandsons of these old women will get used to a more nomadic mentality, but then theirs will be an identity that has little to do with the world of "Kuchisuke's Valley" and the particular sensibility it expresses:

> The steep deforested hillsides were ashen in contrast to the red clay of the gentle incline that would become the bottom of the lake. Through the centre flowed the river. At this point the land possessed almost none of the charm associated with a lake. It seemed more like someone's eye wide open in anger. At the waterless bottom of this menacing lake Kuchisuke's house still stood intact. Together we walked down from the dam and toured the area that would be deepest underwater. Kuchisuke stopped on a particular patch of ground and sighed as he stared at it:

'Maybe this is where the monster will rise up,' he murmured.[22]

When I visited this site in 1974, the oldest local residents did remember a house that was claimed by the dam's lake, but the owner's name was not Tanimoto Kuchisuke. Passing the lake called Ôtani and leaving behind Waterfall Mountain, we have to follow the stream for another half hour to arrive in the village of Himetani, a poetic name, meaning Maiden Valley. Reading its description in a 1929 story, called "Valley" (*Tanima*), I realized that the village itself and the site of the old kiln have changed very little, even if Ibuse places it deeper in the mountains than it really is:

> In chapter 14 of the *History of Japanese Ceramics* it says: 'Himetani ware: belongs to the kilns of the Bizen type, and seems to have ceased to exist around the Kansei Era (1789–1801). Its teajars and large plates are valued fairly highly.'
>
> So I set out from Tokyo with a plan to excavate the remains of this Himetani kiln. My scheme was simple: 'I'll unearth some tea-jars and plates and make a lot of money'... All that remained of the kiln turned into a round plateau of reddish clay, but I could see many fragments of pottery where the soil had been washed away by the rains...[23]

On my first visit to Himetani I found everything more or less as described in the story "Valley", including the fragments of pottery, strewn on the red plateau. I doubted that these fragments could be remnants of real Himetani pottery, given the tourist traffic in Japan.

[22] "Kuchisuke's Valley," p. 18.
[23] IM: "Tanima." In: *IMZ I*. Tokyo, Chikuma shobô 1996, p. 275.

It seems more likely that a skillfull local enterpreneur realized the value of mysterious traces of ancient history and spread broken pots and cups from time to time here. As late as 1977 an expert archeological excavation mapped out the size, type and general location of the kiln and filled in the missing information. Yet it was precisely the fact that so little was known about this mysterious kiln that made it attractive to young Masuji. One can imagine the feeling of wonder and anticipation he must have felt when he first came here at the age of nine or ten:

> I was in second or third grade of elementary school when grandfather took me to Himetani, to excavate the ruins of the old kiln... We carried special bamboo hoes, shaped like *kumade* and a large weeding basket full of *senbei* crackers and *o-bentô* (box-lunches)... When we reached the flat plateau above the steep rise of the hill, a wide vista opened up in front of us – we could see the islands, the whole Inland Sea in the distance...[24]

Grandpa told the owner of the site that his grandson is an ardent collector of antiques, an innocent lie Ibuse recalls with a smile in several essays. In fact he never became a collector of pottery or any other antiques. I recall how we once drank tea from precious old Bizen cups in his Ogikubo study and I asked if I am worthy of them. Ibuse said: "Things must serve men, not the other way round. Collecting is a passion that may destroy you." In an essay called "The First Half of My Life" (*Hanseiki*, 1970) he recalls the prestige that Himetani pottery enjoyed in his village with a touch of criticism:

[24] IM: „Hanseiki." In: *IMZ XIII*, pp. 384–385.

Any family that possessed one of these painted plates, was held in the highest esteem by my village. This became especially clear when it came to marriage negotiations: 'They say that in that house there's a piece of brocade-patterned porcelain. And imagine – they also seem to have a hanging scroll by Master Sazan and another one by Master Shorin! It must be a decent family! A family like that – they can have my daughter any time!'[25]

Yet in a sense, Grandpa Tamizaemon was not exaggerating at all. The sensitive boy did collect a store of precious impressions and memories that came in very handy later. He trained his eye to the detail of beautiful handmade artifacts from the distant past, which would figure as authentic objects in the precise texture of his stories or provide a motive for his protagonists to embark on a prolonged trip to unknown places. Even in the late period of his writing career he would return to this theme, most interestingly in a collection of essays called *From Ocean's Depths* (*Umiagari*, 1981). Underlying this practical interest is a fascination with the secrets of the past and a sophisticated awareness of the rich, multilayered repository of Japanese history, as it emerges from the living soil of a definite locale rather than from the musty pages of an encyclopedia.

It was Grandpa Tamizaemon himself who was the passionate collector. As a fairly wealthy landowner he had enough free time to attend various auctions and visit antique shops. On his trips through the district he foraged for scrolls, paintings, pots, plates, cups, tea ceremony utensils, old weights and measures and all manner of odds and ends which the rest of the

[25] Ibid., 383.

family summarily called 'Grandpa's rubbish'. The old man had no one to display them to, so when a team of government officials arrived in the village to check the accuracy of weights and measures in current use, he added his treasures to the utensils currently used in the house and presented them to the officials. They were ancient weights with silver inscriptions in Dutch in a beautiful polished wooden box. Far from the appreciation he was hoping for, one of the officials slapped the face of the errand boy who brought the weights, ordering him to fetch the 'person responsible' for such brazen ridicule of government officials. While solicitous neighbours were arriving with well meant hints of how to bribe the officials, Grandpa was holding his head and murmuring to himself: "What a disgrace I brought on the family name!"[26] It took the concerted effort of half the village acting as character witnesses for the old man, and his grandson composing a written explanation, before the young official agreed to drop the matter.

Ibuse described this unpleasant incident in an essay called "The Calamity of Old Curios" (*Shoga kottô no sainan*), published in 1933. He mentions that his grandfather never displayed his antiques again, growing despondent and withdrawn, until he lost his appetite and died of old age in 1927. And yet after the death of Masuji's father it was undoubtedly Grandpa Tamizaemon who became the most influential male personality in the boy's life and managed to pass his own taste and hobbies to his favourite grandson. Though Ibuse lovingly says that Grandpa had a talent

[26] IM: "Shoga kottô no sainan." In: *Bamen no kôka*, p. 21.

for discovering imitations and forgeries, how many exciting trips to old castles and mansions, antique shops and places that promissed a glimpse of the past, they must have made together! In those days feudal relics like samurai armour, helmets, swords, matchlock guns, saddles, war-fans and bows and arrows were sold *en masse* for ridiculous prices. Ibuse recalls one of these excursions to the Fukuyama castle in *Hanseiki*,[27] remembering that Grandpa examined the whole display of antiques on the three floors of its watchtower, and selected an ancient wick pistol (*tanzutsu*) and a horse whip for himself; for the boy he bought arrowheads of the open work (*sukashibori*) type with carved small cherry blossoms adorning their blades. A passage from Ibuse's best novella, *Waves: A War Diary* (*Sazanami gunki*, 1930) shows how well the six-year-old boy had stored these early memories:

> Our smith was already forging my arrowheads under the rock shelter down at the beach. With help from the two bow-makers, he made his hammer ring from morning to night with his blacksmith's work. The sketch he made showed my special arrows to be basically the carved cherry-blossom type, only with heads filed to a slightly longer, spear-like shape...[28]

These trips into the past did not always require the authentic setting of a ruined kiln or a feudal castle. When they stayed at home, the children only had to beg either Grandpa or Grandma to reach into their rich lore of fairytales and legends for an old story, recited

---

[27] "Hanseiki," pp. 385–386.
[28] IM: "Waves: A War Diary." In: *Waves*. Trans. Aylward, David and Liman, Anthony. Tokyo, New York and San Francisco, Kôdansha International 1986, p. 63.

in the rhythmical *katari* style. Grandpa's repertoire included two types of tales, both cast in a firmly ritual-ized narrative pattern. One opened with:

> *Mukashi mukashi, sono mukashi, aru tokoro ni...* (*Once* upon a time, and a long time ago it was, in a certain place...) and closed on the happy note of... *medetashi, medetashi.*[29]

The other cycle ended with *"kore de yakkora hito-mukashi,"* which Ibuse freely translates as "and thus the story ends."[30] "Rabbit's Revenge" (*Kachi-kachi yama*) and "Tongue-cut Sparrow" (*Shitakiri suzume*) ended with *"medetashi,"* while *Shuten dôji*[31] and *Ushiwakamaru* were concluded with *"kore de yakkora hitomukashi."*

Grandma's tales were on an entirely different note. Resting by the foot warmer (*kotatsu*) in the mellow light of a paper-covered lamp called an *andon,* she would take her grandson on her lap and recite lengthy, slow-paced tales, as if singing a song:

> They were long narratives, but Grandma always dwelt on one real episode, about how terribly the people of nearby villages had suffered during a famine. When I think about it now, I wonder if her narrative wasn't some kind of a traditional local ballad.
>
> '*Gonbô ya, gonbô ya, gonbô wa iran ka nâ.* Burdock for sale, burdock for sale, anyone for burdock?'
>
> '*Yamaimo ya, yamaimo, yamaimo wa iran ka nâ.* Wild pota-toes for sale, wild potatoes, anyone for wild potatoes?
>
> *Chikagoro sappari, sono koe kikanu. Gonbô, yamaimo, hitotsu mo gozaranu. Awatsubu, kometsubu, hitotsu mo gozaranu.* These days,

[29] "Hanseiki," pp. 376–377.
[30] IM: "Mukashibanashi." In: *IMZ XI,* p. 196.
[31] *Shuten dôji* is a well-known story about a legendary bandit who plagued the city of Kyoto until slain by one of the Minamotos.

such voices are heard no more. Burdock, wild potatoes, not one is left. Millet, rice, not one grain is left.'[32]

The ballad was actually an account of the great famine during the Tenpô Era (1830), when forced contributions were collected from peasants and many in the nearby villages died of starvation. When the guardian of Fukuyama Castle in the Lord's absence, a certain Benzô, issued an order that peasants must double their contributions, they truly reached the end of their tether. People of many villages formed a coalition and camped out for two to three weeks in the dry river-bed downstream from Kamo. Having assembled many more comrades in arms by ringing the bell of the Hôseiji, they fell *en masse* on Fukuyama Castle:

*Ushiro hachimaki, takeyari ni, tatetaru hata wa*
Head bands knotted behind, their flag a piece of
*mushirobata. Ei, ei, ô, ô, kuridashite, dotto bakari*
straw mat on bamboo spears. Ei, ei, oh, oh, here they come,
*ni semeyoseru...*
like a mighty torrent rushing into attack...

Though some of the lines have faded, others I remember well:

*Shiro de wa ôzutsu, uchihanatsu. Kesshi wo chikaishi ikki tote, ôzutsu nanzo kowaku nai...*
From the castle, the great guns are booming. But the rebels are sworn and ready to die – who's afraid of popping cannon?[33]

Not only is this magic rhythm one of the fountain-heads of Ibuse's own rhythmic style, but one feels

[32] "Hanseiki," p. 377.
[33] Ibid., p. 378.

45

that his characteristic, unflagging sympathy with the peasant underdog must have its emotional roots here. Although he never joined any leftist movement, and hardly ever indulged in the educated landholder's nostalgia for a 'return to the common people' (so typical of many 19th century Russian writers), Ibuse's writing is marked by a consistent view of things from 'below'. Just as in the country manors where Pushkin and Turgenev were born, the children of the Japanese *jinushi* were often brought up by nannies and guardians of peasant origin. Next to the prestigious *haute culture* to which the patriarchs of the house aspired – French in the Russian manors, Chinese or 'Kyôto' in a house like Ibuse's – there was the more down-to-earth everyday world of the nurse-maids, the manservants and the next-door neighbours with whom the children lived in fairly close company.

The Japanese village of Ibuse's youth was by no means a rustic idyll. Perhaps the most tragic event of his childhood was the suicide of his nurse Okichi and her brothers Ijû and Jôzaemon. Okichi got married and moved to her husband's village, but something went wrong and she was 'sent back' to her parents. This custom was called *demodori* and did not require a formal divorce. While there was talk of a new liaison, Okichi became mentally unbalanced and began roaming the surrounding mountains, avoiding people:

> Okichi took to roaming the hills and when people followed her, she fled like a flying arrow. She'd slide down with ease from dangerous cliffs, stand on a craggy peak one moment, then suddenly appear on top of the opposite peak. She moved around, swift as a banshee, light as

46

the wind, appearing and vanishing with utter freedom. But in the end, Okichi threw herself into Kisaka pond and drowned. I didn't go to see her, but people said she was found floating by the watergate…

They say that the spirits of people who drown in a pond will always call for a mate. So everyone was careful not to go near Kisaka pond. Except Okichi's younger brother Ijû; he died the same way his sister had. Jôzaemon went mad. He began to roam the village with a defense pole nearly four metres long. Sporting a moustache and wearing a striped silk kimono, he would buttonhole people at random, present his calling card and start arguing. And boast: he was a person of great importance who has used his old name to deceive the world; now his real name, Ôemonden Jôzaemon can be seen on the cards… One day his pole turned into a five-metre long affair… and he began threatening passersby… It took twenty coolies to restrain him before he was taken away, tied to a cart. He did calm down at the police station, but shortly after being released hung himself in the forest owned by millionaire Sera.[34]

This was a terrible tragedy for a small Japanese village at the beginning of the 20th century. To the six-year old boy, who knew all three suicides intimately, it gave a traumatic memory for the rest of his life. He never fully grasped the reasons behind it, yet he returns to the painful experience in many short stories and novellas, for example in "The River":

They found the girl's body floating on the surface of the pool, looking as if about two days had passed since her death. Her arms and legs were spread out as if she had

[34] "Keirokushû," pp. 248–249.

no more worries and intended to float there forever, but the whirlpools circling the water from times immemorial would not allow her a moment's rest. The large whirlpool made the rigid body spin, now with its head, now with its buttocks as the pivot. When her head was at the centre, the water tried to pull her down into the depths, but when the large whirlpool changed into three small ones, the force of the spinning water released her and pulled down only her hair and loose clothing. In no time the three eddies joined together again and entrusted her to the large one...[35]

A year later Ibuse wrote an essay, called "Summer Foxes" (*Natsu no kitsune*, 1933), in which he returns again to poor Okichi's fate, this time in a lighter style:

The other day I sent a letter to the folks in my birthplace inquiring whether young maidens still get bewitched by foxes in the country.

I do remember how when summer came, a maiden soon to become a bride might begin to roam the hills and everyone would go out to chase her. As a child, I saw such a young bride possessed by a fox with my own eyes. A girl bewitched by a fox can escape with great ease, ascending steep slopes and sliding down sheer cliffs with utter calm; that's why pursuing her is futile and the matter must be left to its natural course... I remember this usually happened in midsummer – do maidens in your parts still get bewitched by foxes these days?[36]

Naturally the 'folks at home' reply that such weird things do not happen now, nor did they ever happen in the past and must be a figment of the writer's wild

[35] IM: "*Kawa.*" In: *IMZ I*, p. 195.
[36] IM: "Natsu no kitsune." In: *Bamen no kôka*, p. 23.

imagination. Yet Ibuse closes the brief little essay with four categorical, almost harsh lines, quite different in tone from the somewhat playful rest of the text:

> I clearly remember the wild look of a girl possessed by a fox. When Okichi from the mountain hamlet of Kuchi-tani was bewitched by a fox, I was among the crowd chasing her, a child sitting on the shoulders of Yamane Shichirô, a man in the prime of his years.[37]

Although he doesn't observe it from an ideological viewpoint, Ibuse realizes the frequent cruelty of the patriarchal village and in several stories tries to guess the underlying economic reasons for the triple suicide. It is possible that the local millionaire tricked Okichi's older brother Jôzaemon out of his fields and drove him into deep debt, something that could cause great shame in a traditional village community. The sister lost face when her husband shamed her by sending her home and the younger brother who obviously loved Okichi, followed her in a kind of double suicide (*shinjû*). The eldest brother Jôzaemon then despaired not only over his own seemingly shameful situation, but over the cruel fate of his siblings.

Nowadays it is hard to imagine that a child from a well-to-do landowner's family first saw the Inland Sea – less than twenty kilometres away from Kamo – only when he reached seven. And even then it wasn't for fun, but for good medical reasons. The second summer after Masuji's father Ikuta died of a disease, diagnosed as pleurisy (1903), whose cause was most probably tuberculosis, his older brother Fumio was taken down with the same disease, and grandfather Tamizaemon,

[37] Ibid., p. 25.

deciding that the children's health came first, took all three of them – Fumio, older sister Matsuko and young Masuji – to Tomonotsu on the Inland Sea. An old harbour town on the outskirts of Fukuyama City, Tomonotsu was then a combination of a pleasantly rundown seaside resort and natural port-of-call for maritime traffic. Next to a pleasure quarter, it had many inns and temples, and a long street of traditional blacksmiths' shops where they forged huge anchors. In an essay called "A View Of Tomonotsu – The Black-smiths' Street" (*Tomonotsu shoken – kajiya no machi*, 1931), Ibuse recalls that the whole street was black, including the mud on the road, the *shôji* and the beams of the old houses, even the little urchins who blew the bellows. And when it rained, it was like "black ink pouring down the eaves."[38] So the town itself left something to be desired as a modern recreation centre, but Grandpa found a pleasant *ryokan* on a small island about five minutes off the coast by boat, called Sensuijima. Cross-ing over, the ferry rounded another, even smaller island lying right in the harbour's mouth – the Bentenjima, with a two-tiered lacquered pagoda dedicated to the goddess of music and eloquence.

The water was a dark, transparent blue, and white orchids grew on the pine trees of the islands. To a seven -year-old, who had so far never left his mountain hamlet, it must have looked like a true oceanic para-dise. And had he been able to compare, he would have realized that he had come to one of the most genuinely beautiful scenic spots in the world. In today's Tomo, Ibuse once sighed, "the kites have to wash their feet

[38] IM: "Tomonotsu shoken." In: *IMZ IX,* p. 23.

after diving for fish in the harbour's water."[39] But in his youth you could see underwater for nearly ten metres. Yet even half a century of concentrated pollution by the many shipbuilding factories have not robbed the Inland Sea of its natural beauty. The special charm of this ocean scenery lies in the fact that it is in fact more like a large lake, combining placid weather with warm, clear water and sandy beaches, spared of the wild storms and hurricanes of the tropical seas. Even nowadays the fishing is relatively good, but in the old days it was very abundant: there was the local seabream or *tai*, one of the best Japanese fish, about which the proverb says: "Even when it smells, it's a *tai*" (*kusatte mo tai*), the devilish, puffy *fugu*, which can be lethally poisonous, if not properly prepared and the spiny *okoze* (*Pellor japonicum*).

Some of these fish can be found only here, for example *chinu* (black bream) and *gizami* (*Halichoeres poecilopter*). In the ocean, thousands of hilly volcanic islands and islets are scattered, some inhabited, others wild. Those with their own water supply have been farmed for centuries and they look like cultivated gardens with terraced fields and groves of *mikan* oranges that cover the hills; higher up there is a growth of cedar, cypress, pine, oak, wild camelia and azalea. At the foot of the terraces are vegetable patches and little fields of wild chrysanthemums, called *jochûgiku*, used for repelling mosquitoes. From afar it looks like a colourful chessboard.

In the sheltered bays of the more remote islands, huddled together into a natural horseshoe shape, one

[39] In an interview at his home in Ogikubo in 1975.

sees the weatherbeaten, dark wooden houses of the islanders, a barge with the typical high prow moored in front of most. Between the islands there are many lagoons and the stretch of the ocean is seldom monotonous.

"They live with their backs to the ocean, their eyes on the mountain; though they live by the sea, they cling to their land," Ibuse once wrote,[40] meaning that their livelihood had always been divided half and half: the harvest of fish used to be good, but never good enough to be depended on entirely and the fields not rich and plentiful enough to sustain full-time farming. *Mikan* orchards require a lot of watering, and one can imagine what a backbreaking toil it must have been to irrigate this steep, hilly terrain before the advent of the hydraulic pump and electricity, and the light, plastic piping that now crisscrosses the hills.

Even so, when I travelled through the Inland Sea in 1974, there was not one young face to be seen on some of its islands. At first glance it looked like a haven of senior citizens, but then I saw how hard these old people must work – some of their children and most of their grandchildren had left the islands, looking for an easier and more urbanized way of life in the plants and offices of Kôbe, Osaka or Hiroshima. In 1960 Ibuse wrote an essay called "The Seto Inland Sea" (*Seto naikai*), which reads in part:

> As far as I know, the people on Seto islands and the coast fishermen call their area "Setouchi". It's an ocean clear as a lake and there are no disasters like storms and huge

[40] IM: "Kieta ochoro-bune." In: *Hito to hitokage*. Tokyo, Mainichi shinbunsha 1972, p. 309.

waves. But there are too many people and many poor islands where life is hard… According to the theory of a certain ethnologist, if one wants to know the original customs and the character of the people of the Japanese insular culture it is best to explore the local conditions of various islands, extracting and summarizing what they have in common. For better or worse, the essence of the Japanese can still be found there… Strangely enough, it is perhaps on such remote islands, that ancient Japanese tradition survives.[41]

Nowadays a huge bridge with a six lane highway cuts through the Seto Inland Sea and I doubt that much of the traditional lore has been preserved. Ibuse loved this area and placed his highly acclaimed novella (and his own favourite), *Waves: A War Diary*, into its setting. It is a story of a young nobleman from the Taira (Heike) family, who retreats with a small band of faithful warriors from the Capital, occupied by the victorious Minamoto (Genji). They want to reach Dazaifu, the bastion of their clan in Kyûshû. This great political drama is acted out under the blue sky and against the background of picturesque islands, customs and rituals of the local people. The author skilfully uses his intimate knowledge of local topography, as well as its fauna and flora. Thus a young beauty is called Chinu and her maidservant Okoze. Without much explanation, the Japanese reader knows how both women look: *chinu*, or black bream is an elegant, sleak fish while *okoze* is spiny and whiskery, in short not very pretty. And so Ibuse not only paraphrases a well-known heroic tale, he pays his debt to the beloved landscape of his

[41] IM: "Seto naikai." In: *IMZ Bekkan I*. Tokyo, Chikuma shobô 1999, p. 477.

youth. This is also made evident by the fact that he placed the romantic tryst of two young people, young Taira no Tomoakira and the local beauty Chinu in a small town called Tomonotsu where he himself spent unforgettable moments as a child of seven.

Ibuse never forgot the debt he owed to the common people of his native area (be it the Kamo valley or the Seto islands) as a writer. When his close friend Kawamori Yoshizô asked him in an interview how his birthplace influenced his writing, the author replied:

> It had a strong influence on my style. What I'd call the traces of my native dialect in my writing style. It's not Tokyo-like, nor is it a foreign-inspired style. Style is a naturally acquired thing, like the way every person walks, and I can't avoid the feeling that my style is rooted in the rhythm of country speech.[42]

A hundred years ago a remote southern hamlet – two days away by train from Tokyo – was almost a different planet and had its distinct identity, as well as its own language. Although Ibuse exaggerates some of the local speech patterns to make them more amusing for his urban reader, the 'samples' sound authentic enough:

> The people who were my present age (seventy two) had been born in the Bunsei Era (1818–1830). They must have really soaked up the rural customs of the Edo period, and of course their manner of speaking corresponded to those customs.
>
> On a day it rained after a dry spell, the grannies would greet people with: '*Konnichâ, ê uruoi de gozaryansu de*

[42] IM: "Kawamori Yoshizô taidan: Sanshôuo made." In: *Hito to hitokage,* p. 313.

*gozaryansu nâ...*' ('Good day, what a nice drop o' rain we're having...')

Ours is an old farming village and the greetings were all related to rice and field work.[43]

Ibuse often emphasized the musicality of his native dialect, and in one essay he recalls how when two middle-aged farmwives met in the village square to deliver their ceremonious addresses, it sounded like 'the slow, rhythmical chirping of a roller-canary':

*'Ohayô gozaryansu de gozaryansu. Yunbê wa uchi no kodomo ni kekkô na mono wo tsukâsaryanshite kudasaryanshite, honma ni arigatô gozaryansu de gozaryanshita...'*

('Good morning, my dear. Yesterday, you kindly gave something very nice to my child. Many, many thanks.')

Common greetings follow old customs. That's why in my birthplace people must have greeted each other with such rhythmic invocations during the Edo period as well. But even those middle aged housewives never used the doubled verbs '*de gozaryansu de gozaryansu*' except for their ceremonious greetings.[44]

Linguists have defined a complex system of social differentiation by honorific expressions in many premodern languages; the Bingo dialect of Ibuse's childhood obviously preserved such ancient traits. In a witty story with the somewhat awkward title "How Tsu'tsa and Kurô-tsan Quarreled and I Worried about Problems of Diction" (*Tsu' tsa to Kurô-tsan wa kenka shite, watakushi wa yôgo ni tsuite hanmon suru koto*, 1938) Ibuse describes how minute nuances of diction defined people's social standing, and how class distinctions

[43] "Hanseiki," p. 375.
[44] IM: "Zaisho kotoba." In: *IMZ XI*, p. 80.

are reflected even in the way children addressed their parents at home:

> When I was a child, I didn't call my parents *otôsan* (father) and *okâsan* (mother). Although it's truly archaic language, I used the words *totosan* and *kakasan*. I don't think there are many people in my generation – even those who were raised in very rustic parts – who'd use such outdated words...
>
> I don't know who taught me to use them... but as I grew more self-conscious, I began to feel ashamed if I were to utter something like *totosan* and *kakasan* in front of other people. They are antiquated expressions, better suited for *gidayû* ballad recitals...[45]

In *Hanseiki* Ibuse lays the responsibility squarely on Grandpa's shoulders – he was born in the Tenpô era and spoke accordingly:

> Leaving aside obsolete words like *totosan* and *kakasan,* used in our family, the appellations differed from household to household, according to the individual sense of worth of its head. Children from landholders' (*jinushi*) families used *ottosan* and *okkasan*. Children whose parents were members of the village assembly or headmen would use *oto'tsan* and *okakan*. Those from yeomen's families called their parents *otôyan* and *okâyan*. Small tenant farmers' kids used *oto'tsa* and *okaka*.
>
> Crazy as it may sound, this is a fact. Let's presume for a while that a tenant farmer makes a pile of money, buys his own fields and expands his house. Would his children at this point suddenly stop calling him *oto'tsa* and his wife *okaka* and switch to *otôyan* and *okâyan*..?

In my village, class distinctions were also affixed to

---

[45] IM: "Tsu'tsa to Kurô-tsan wa kenka shite, watakushi wa yôgo ni hanmon suru koto." In: *IM shû. Shinchô nihon bungaku* 17. Tokyo, Shinchôsha 1970, p. 299.

people's names. Children did not call each other by the egalitarian so and so *chan* as in Tokyo. Those from the so-called 'best houses' were so and so *san*, the next in line were *tsan*, third in rank were *yan*, fourth *tsa* and last *sa*.[46]

It sounds almost incredible to us that children could honour these minute distinctions at the height of excitement during their games, yet the Japanese village at the turn of the century was a truly different world. Ibuse makes it quite explicit in *Hanseiki*:

These names were like soldiers' ranks in the army... Troublesome as they were, the slightest deviation was resented...

It was even more complicated among adults. When adults formally addressed each other, they'd use the other party's 'shop name' or 'household name' (*yago*), but the interjection preceding this name was charged with the emotional mood of the moment:

*'Oy, Hirataya'* or *'Korya, odorea, odore, Hashimotoya...'* or *'Ano nâ, chotto, Uedaya.'*

(Hey there, Hirata), (Well, as for you, Hashimoto...), (Listen for a minute, Ueda).

When they were intimate and in a lighthearted mood, they'd call each other by the old discriminative affixes of childhood...[47]

These things were all deeply saturated with feudal customs. Customs expressing fear of poverty were especially tenacious. Perhaps it's a local characteristic, but there was a fear that if you were impoverished, your very human personality might be denied.[48]

[46] Ibid., pp. 299–300.
[47] "Hanseiki," p. 389.
[48] Ibid.

But human nature is similar anywhere and even in Kamo, where feudal customs survived for so long, some residents were not content with the community's ranking of their social standing (*mibun*). The serious quarrel between the village headman Kurô-tsan and one of the villagers, called Tsu'tsa according to the local custom, issued from just such an ambition. Although it is fictional, I think the story reflects the actual situation quite accurately.

At one of the village assembly meetings, the headman – who much prefers to be called *sonchô-san* (Mr. Mayor) instead of Kurô-tsan himself – calls Mr. Tsuchi by his plain name of Tsu'tsa. Since it is on a formal, public occasion and not during a casual meeting of the two men in the village square, Tsuchi takes it as an insult. He feels he might have for once been afforded a higher rank, perhaps even a *san*. The headman feels that a simple apology to Tsu'tsa would settle the affair. But since he can't resist closing his apology by asking "and what was wrong with calling you Tsu'tsa anyway," he further complicates the matter and it goes to court. Before the affair gets settled, both families start to raise the ante by introducing fancy appelations: the Tsuchis change to calling father *ottosan* (which previously belonged to Mr. Kurô), the headman escalates to the fancy urban *otôsan*. Ibuse's grandfather commented that introducing these formal Tokyo words to Kamo might be historically premature.

Still the Tsuchis didn't give up. The whole family started using fragments of the most refined city language they could think of, *sato no kotoba* or Kyôto dialect: *okoshiyasu; soya soya, ôki ni* or *akimahen, nô*. People in

58

Kamo were awed, since most of them never heard such fancy phrases. The headman had no other choice but to reach for the dialect of the capital and intersperse as many narrowly pronounced *nê-s* as possible in his ordinary speech.

Masuji's actual encounter with the Tokyo dialect was much less humorous. One evening, when he was about twelve, with no other people in the rambling old house than his grandfather, mother and older sister, someone banged on the shutters (*amado*) and grunted in a low voice: "Open up, open the door!" (*"Akero, doa wo akero!"*). When Grandfather inquired "Who are you and what do you want in the deep of the night…" the man hissed again: "Won't you shut up and open the door? And do it now!" (*"Kora, monku wo iwanêde, hayaku akenê ka? Sassa to akero!"*)[49] Mother locked the children into the dark *itanoma*, ordered them to stay quiet no matter what happens and started calling for help from its latticed window. Then she loudly reported to grandfather: "It's all right. Neighbours at the Mandêya heard me and they are calling for help from the lower guardhouse!"[50] The robber fled, leaving behind five or six footprints in the smooth white sand beneath the veranda – enough for the local policeman to conclude that he must have been a miner from the nearby copper-mine of Hirose, where all sorts of riff-raff worked. Even this episode was used to good advantage in the previous story about the headman's quarrel with Mr. Tsuchi: when Tsu'tsa hears that a villain speaking 'a pure Tokyo dialect' had attacked the Ibuses, he starts

[49] Ibid., p. 394.
[50] Ibid., p. 396.

spreading the rumour that the robber could have been none other than his archfoe, the headman!

No wonder then that a man who grew up in a community with such an acute awareness of linguistic nuances would develop a most sophisticated sensibility towards language. Since he spent the first twenty years of his life in a linguistic milieu that differs so much from standard Japanese, Ibuse gained a distance from the future tools of his trade that is so typical for all great humorists. From the safe backwater of his native dialect he can first look at the terrifying 'foreign language' of Tokyo, and after he has made the great leap into literary Japanese, he can selectively return to his native dialect. No matter how much at home the fish feels in water, it must jump above its element to be able to see it and become aware of it. To be able to transcend the rigid tracks of habitual language, to bend and twist the 'sacred' magic of traditional emotional expressions, to create neologisms with a satirical bite, one needs a vantage point outside of the too close, too unconscious identity of a native tongue.

That Ibuse was keenly aware of such a double existence and the emotional toll it exacts, is suggested in several essays, most clearly in "My Old Lady" (*Ofukuro*), written in 1960:

Every two or three years, whenever an opportunity presents itself, I do my best to pay a visit at my old home in the country. To put it this way may give you the wrong impression, but since my mother's small talk gets on my nerves, I rarely feel a special urge to go down there. Whenever I come home, my mother starts asking questions that are bound to put one in a gloomy mood. There is an almost prescribed pattern to them: 'Masuji, when you write those stories of yours in Tokyo, what do you follow for inspiration?'

Without much hesitation, I answer: 'Well, what you call following for inspiration simply means to observe all kinds of landscapes, rivers and mountains, remember stories I've read in books of history, listen to other people's tales, think up a few things myself and witness others as they happen in this world; those are the things I write about.'

'But don't you need some kind of a model to follow?'

'You might say the more books one reads, the more wisdom one gains.'

'You have to use a dictionary as well. It won't do if you make mistakes in your spelling. To misspell your characters won't do at all...'[51]

In a poem from 1938 called "Thinking of My Mother on A Cold Night" (*Kanya haha o omou*), Ibuse expresses the relationship with his mother even more directly:

Says mother in her letter:
Your stoic endurance serves nobody
What good does it do to write novels
Come back to the country, she says
My mother was always a loudmouth
Now she says I'm a wayward son
I should love the mountains more than ever
I should love my native soil more than ever
I should worship all my ancestors
My mother was always a skinflint
Now she says I should have a savings account

[51] IM: "Ofukuro." In: *IMZ XII*, pp. 56–57.

And worship the Great Founder Nichiren
My poor old mother [52]

As in the English countryside, there was a custom among wealthy farmers in Japan that a family without male heirs would adopt a son-in-law whose own inheritance was insufficient to buy a decent measure of farmland. Ibuse's mother Miya was the heiress and the bearer of the family name (*ietsuki musume*) and at the recommendation of her father married a man called Oyama Ikuta from the neighbouring prefecture of Okayama. He was a second-born son from a modest farming household and didn't have much of a future at home. His son sums it up:

> Since father was what they called 'adopted husband' and mother the 'heiress of the house', he'd be constrained by the demands of his father-in-law in everything he did. In those days a *muko* felt very small in a place like Kamo. As the wise old proverb has it: 'Don't go out as *muko* as long as there's a pint of rice-bran left in your house…'[53]

Mother Miya was widowed at the age of twenty-eight with three children to raise and her situation was not easy. When she saw how father pampers the children, she had no other choice but to play the role of severe mother. Ibuse realizes all this and his satirical view of mother is always gentle and loving:

> Several months after I returned to Tokyo, the film adaptation of one of my old novels, *Money Collecting Journey* (*Shûkin ryokô*), was playing at a movie theatre in Fukuyama. The village youths borrowed this relic from the theatre and, planning to use the income from admission

[52] IM: "Kanya haha wo omou." In: *IMZ IX*, pp. 335–336.
[53] "Hanseiki," p. 387.

tickets towards financing construction work on the river, showed it at the village primary school. My sister-in-law reported as much in a letter to my wife. Her message went as follows:

'On the day *Shûkin ryokô* was to be screened at the local primary school, the young men of Kamo broadcast a loud megaphone announcement throughout the village': 'Tonight at six o'clock, a Technicolor film, *Shûkin ryokô*, based on the original novel by our native writer, Ibuse Masuji, will be presented at the local primary school!' The voice reached Grandma's (my mother's) ears as well, but she just said: 'So Masuji has joined a freak-show,' and retired into a back room. Needless to say, she didn't go to see the film, yet as people from the neighbourhood dropped by for a chat, she learned its basic plot. When they were talking about the film, she sat in silence, as if saying: 'What a useless story to make into a film!' Yet when people departed without mentioning the film at all, she would ask: 'Didn't these people see the film?'[54]

Father Ikuta died when Masuji was five, so he barely remembered him. In *Keirokushû* he says about him:

Father had suffered from pleura trouble for some time and stayed in several coastal resorts like Tomonotsu and Sarayama. He came back home shortly before Keizô died and had a two-floor retreat built near our house on a large cliff with a good view. A lush grove of *mikan* trees was planted around the pavilion and he kept some *mejiro* (white eye) to distract him. When he rang his bell, mother would rush over to ask what he needed. But he was reading books most of the time, lying on his bed. The cause of his disease was iron dumb-bells. They were sent to him

[54] "Ofukuro," pp. 60–61.

by a friend from Tokyo; though he followed instructions, the exercise may have contributed to the deterioration of his health. In those days, lifting dumb-bells must have been a real craze in Tokyo. It seems father worshipped everything that was popular in the metropolis: when he saw an article in the paper or in a magazine that it was fashionable to eat apples in Tokyo, he'd immediately send out a mail order to a Tokyo store specializing in apples. I still remember the wooden crate in which they arrived – this was the first time in my life I ate the fruit called 'apples'. Upon reading that plants like *Rhodea Japonica,* or some species of exotic cacti were in vogue in Tokyo, he'd order them on the spot...[55]

From the several essays that Ibuse devoted to his father one gathers the impression of a shy, fragile man with a pronounced interest in art and culture. To exert his will in a house governed by strong, not to say eccentric, personalities like grandfather Tamizaemon was nearly impossible. In an essay called "Country Chronicle" (*Den'enki*, 1933), Ibuse recalls how he once rummaged in the attic, looking for old boxes with father's books and writings. Knowing that his father's hobby was literature, he hoped to discover some early editions of Goethe and perhaps Shakespeare, but all he found were obscure writers of the Meiji period and his father's diaries that didn't look too interesting. But the last box he opened did yield something precious: a pile of Japanese composition notebooks with translations of Chinese poems into homely, colloquial Japanese. It was not clear who did the translations, but Ibuse thought it may have been his father. He says:

[55] "Keirokushû," pp. 247–248.

These translations would be nothing much to someone well-versed in Chinese poetry… their tone is a bit rough in places and still needs touching up, but they are pleasant enough to hum to oneself when riding in a rickshaw.[56]

He did touch up the translations and copied most of them in the essay *Den'enki*. By now we know that the translations were not the work of father Ikuta, but a haiku poet by the name of Nakajima Gyobô (1725–1793). Here is Tu Fu's well-known quatrain, the third of "Twenty Poems on Sadness":

*Doko mo kashiko mo ikusa no sakari*

With battles raging back and forth

*ore ga zaisho wa ima dôja yara*

What's become of my old home?

*mukashi kaetta toki ni sae*

Even when I went back long ago

*zuibun najimi ga utareta sô na*

Too many of my mates were struck down.[57]

Or Li Po's nostalgic "Quiet Night Thoughts" (*Sei-yashi*, 1936) whose last two lines later became Ibuse's favourite dedication poem that he often inscribed into his books or on the edge of Japanese fans:

*Nokiba no tsuki wo miru ni tsuke*

Seeing the moon over the eaves

*zaisho no koto ga ki ni kakaru*

Memories of home weigh on my heart.[58]

In any case the Chinese poems created a kind of bridge between father and son and perhaps took the

---

[56] IM: "Den'enki." In: *Bamen no kôka*, pp. 13–17.

[57] Ibid., p. 16.

[58] IM: "Seiyashi." In: *IMZ IX*, p. 210.

edge off the harsh tone of Ikuta's last will, written in formal *kanbun*:

> 'It is a solemn wish of mine that my children be strictly prevented from following the path of literature; they must be given an honest calling.'[59]

Father Ikuta wouldn't have dreamed that his second-born son will one day become a great Japanese author, live a respectable life equal to the great scholars or politicians, and be awarded the highest honours of the country. He was not declared a "living national treasure" only because this honour is traditionally not awarded to writers. Yet I walked with Ibuse through his district of Ogikubo, visited the kabuki theatre and travelled with him in the country and I felt that in the hearts of his people he earned this position.

When he reached fourteen, Masuji was sent to the prestigious high school in nearby Fukuyama, called *Seishikan* (Institute of Truth and Sincerity). This famous school was founded by illustrious men like Mito Nariaki, a member of the Tokugawa family and Abe Masahiro, a leading politician and the shogun's adviser. A great emphasis was put on classical Chinese learning – a long tradition in Ibuse's native area. In the nearby town of Kannabe (about eight kilometers from Kamo) the poet Kan Sazan founded his well-known private school (*juku*) whose poetic name was *Yellow leaves, Setting sun, Rustic dwelling*. As old Mr. Tange used to proudly observe when showing Sazan's letter and calligraphic scroll called *Wax Plum and the Seven Word Poem* to respected visitors, his own garden's atmosphere resembled the hills behind Master Sazan's

---

[59] "Den'enki," p. 11.

school, though his mansion could hardly be called a rustic dwelling.

Perhaps it was because of the authentic aura of Chinese learning in the novels and stories of Mori Ôgai (1862–1922) that he became Ibuse's favourite author. Yet when Masuji and his friends read Ôgai's lengthy biography of Izawa Ranken in Osaka's *Mainichi Shinbun*, they felt that the great author paid too much attention to a rustic healer. They knew Ranken's story well, since he came from their native area and so Masuji's friends suggested that he write directly to Ôgai. Adopting the pen-name Kuchiki Sansuke and pretending that he is an old-timer of the area, Masuji concocted a sensational announcement, which he wrote out in a dense, ornate *kanbun* style; later he described this incident in a short story called "Prank" (*Akugi*, 1931):

> Pressed by the complicated situation in foreign affairs after the advent of American envoys, the Lord of Ise, Abe Masahiro had no other choice in his unfortunate predicament, but to conclude treaties with these foreign powers, though his true intent had always been the expulsion of barbarians. But to the Chief Councillor of the Bakufu, Ii Naosuke, who had favoured the opening of the country for some time, the lengthy manoeuvres of His Lordship were highly irritating. Using the services of the daimyo's court physician, Izawa Ryôan, he had Lord Abe dispatched by poison. Both Ryôan's father Jian (Ranken) and his younger brother Banan were sworn into the secret; after the deed Izawa Ranken sent both his sons into hiding in Hikone, under the tacit protection of Naosuke's family.[60]

[60] IM: "Akugi." In: *IMZ IX*, p. 20.

Ôgai's answer to these sensational revelations was brief and to the point: he expressed his thanks for the important information, but regretted to say that the old doctor (Ranken) had passed away eighteen years prior to Lord Abe's demise and Izawa Ryôan, his son, died five years before his Lordship. Not one of the three Izawas had ever lived in Hikone. He concluded:

> I was very surprised when I read this [the letter of Kuchiki Sansuke]. I suspected it's either the fabrication of a madman, or perhaps someone's idea of a practical joke. But the handwriting did look like that of an old man, and the style showed touches of genuine sincerity.[61]

Some fifteen years later Ibuse wryly sums it up in "Prank":

> Saying that my style showed touches of genuine sincerity may have been Ôgai's way of adding weight to his reference material. But in actual fact he was the first man of letters who was kind enough to offer a critique of my style. Yet come to think of it, he rewrote my *sôrôbun* [formal epistolary style] so thoroughly that it wasn't really my style he was praising – it was his own![62]

Naive as this student's prank may have been, it also contains a more serious meaning. The young reader had followed the protagonist through three hundred instalments of a dry account of a rather pedestrian life and he was probably longing for a bit of excitement, a touch of dramatic action to enliven the lengthy narrative. The budding writer was asking a serious question: what is the right balance between fact and fiction in historical prose? Ôgai made a great effort to

[61] Ibid., p. 22.
[62] Ibid.

solve this problem, coining two phrases for it: "history as it is" (*rekishi sono mama*) and "distanced from history" (*rekishi banare*). In his later years he dismissed one of his best stories, "Sanshô the Bailiff" (*Sanshô dayu*), as too romantic, too remote from real history. As he grew older, Ibuse's solution of this question began to weigh more and more in Ôgai's favour, yet we shall see that there is a subtle difference in both men's treatment of historical and fictional material. While Ôgai's solemn style serves a rendering of history that is as serious as possible, Ibuse's always aims at a poetic and playful quality.

Before he really decided on a writer's career, Ibuse was attracted by painting. As a high school student he had already sketched and painted in water colours, so when he graduated from Fukuyama's *Seishikan*, he ordered a set of painting supplies from Tokyo. At a Fukuyama oculist he bought a new pair of tinted sunglasses and towards the end of May he set out on a painting expedition (*shasei ryokô*) along the Inland Sea coast. After staying at various islands where he spent more time fishing than painting, he payed a visit to Mt. Kôya and Nara, finally arriving in Kyôto, the Mecca of aspiring painters at that time. Ibuse found an old-fashioned *ryokan* in the Maruta district and during a few months produced over twenty water colour paintings. His landlady happened to know a disciple of Hashimoto Kansetsu (1883–1945), the master-painter of Kyôto, and Ibuse's portfolio was delivered to the master. Given the fact that it's hard to find a view of Kyôto that hasn't been painted before, his work couldn't have been too original. What was worse, he realized a little too late that the three basic colours on his palette were almost used up, while the rest had hardly been touched. The monotonous selection of colours was caused by the sepia tint of his cheep sunglasses, and so Masuji was not too surprised when a curt rejection finally came from Hashimoto.

I often saw Ibuse's water colours and his ink sketches and own some of his beautiful calligraphy. Several times I watched his hand when he tried to illustrate on paper something he was explaining and it's clear to me that he had a considerable artistic talent. Yet every time I walk the Imadegawa street in Kyôto that leads to the Silver Pavillion past the museum of Hashimoto Kansetsu, I quietly offer my thanks to the painter for rejecting his young applicant. Instead of Ibuse Masuji we may have had one of the mediocre painters who go to study in Paris and call themselves Henri Ibuse. Besides, Ibuse loathed the snobbish atmosphere of the refined painting circles of Kyôto as much as he disliked the tea ceremony. When I consulted him once where to travel in Japan, he said: "Take a map, find all the places that pride themselves on tea ceremony and then avoid those like the plague!"

In front of Hashimoto's museum there is a stone pillar with a carving: "Those who indulge in drinking, should not enter this place!" To order Ibuse that he mustn't drink would be like telling Dylan Thomas that he must not enter a pub. The *sakaba* and its blarney play too important a role in his writing.

An urgent question, precisely formulated by Yasuoka Shôtarô, offers itself: "Why did Ibuse leave his elegant and dignified home in the country and go to

Tokyo?"[63] Why did he trade the security and dignity of a rooted existence on his native farm for the ragged life of a bohemian outcast in far away Tokyo? Several possible reasons come to mind: in 1963 he wrote a short story, called "This Is a Little Abrupt" (*Tsukanu koto*), which is a caricature of an adopted husband's life, a fate that might have befallen Ibuse himself. The sad lot of poor 'fox-possessed' Okichi and the role the superstitious village played in it may also have weighed on his heart.

After Kansetsu's abrupt rejection it was clear to him that the road to a painting career was forever closed and that there was only one place left to go if he wanted to be an artist: the foreign planet of Tokyo, the city where people speak that awful robbers' dialect, the very language that will have to become the future writer's tool. Yet when he finally left his birthplace, Masuji travelled to the City – as Yasuoka once so aptly put it[64] – like Father Noah: in the ark of his imagination every tree, every bird, every unique character of his native valley and his beloved islands was carefully stored. The task that lay ahead of him was to express the soul of the valley and thus find his own.

---

[63] Yasuoka, Shôtarô: "IM den." In: *IM. Gendai nihon bungakkan 29.* Tokyo, Bungei shunjû 1968, p. 25.
[64] In a lecture given at the University of Toronto in the spring of 1973.

"SALAMANDER," "CARP"

*I arrived in Tokyo towards the end of August in the sixth year of*
*Taishô (1917). I'd heard many a tale in my native place about the*
*various temptations of the city, but in those days I thought all that*
*'temptation' meant was to become intimate with a woman;*
*I was unable to distinguish other forms of temptation.*
*Thinking it would be good to get it over with as fast as possible,*
*I lingered over an hour at a streetcar stop, but no one was kind enough*
*to seduce me. Although human traffic in Tokyo streets was overwhelming,*
*I couldn't find a single familiar face in the vast crowd. I thought:*
*what a lonely feeling this place gives one!*[1]

Ibuse Masuji

Ibuse wrote this memoir when he was thirty-eight, a
time when he could afford a humorous look back at the
timid country boy's first steps in the vast city. But when
he stepped off the train at Tokyo station that sultry
summer afternoon, he couldn't have felt too amused
about his situation. Back at home he resolved to speak
standard Tokyo Japanese, but the very first discussion
with the station rickshaw man made him realize that it
would take a long time before the pronounced diction
of his native dialect was washed away. I came to know

[1] IM: "Jôkyô chokugo." In: *Bamen no kôka*. Tokyo, Daiwa shobô 1966, p. 66.

72

him when he was sixty-eight and even then the soft consonants of the Hiroshima dialect were still traceable in his speech.

As for any country boy who arrives in the city, Masuji's main concern was to find suitable lodging. He visited a few boarding houses in the university neighbourhood and finally settled in a four-and-a-half mat room at a place called the *Seinankan* opposite Waseda's main gate. This is the smallest space in a Japanese house and must have felt rather claustrophobic after the high-ceilinged, airy rooms of his native mansion. In Europe the first world war was nearing its end and Japan was enjoying a modest boom. So prices weren't too high and the small room would cost less than ten yen a month and include three meals a day as well as most of the services needed by a young boy living without his mother's care for the first time. The streets were unpaved and after a rainfall one had to wade through mud, yet the neighbourhood offered rows of second-hand bookstores, private tutors of anything from foreign languages to *shamisen* ballads, pawnshops, bohemian cafés, Japanese noodle shops and even a high-class European restaurant where young Masuji ate *tonkatsu* (pork cutlets), using knife and fork, for the first time in his life. The cafés were called *kôhiya* and in one of them, the *Kaiyôken,* Masuji had his first taste of another exotic drink – coffee.

Masuji's first trip to school – to attend the entrance exams for Waseda's two-year prep course – was far from pleasant. At the main gate a robust student who looked like a *jûdô* champion grabbed him by his kimono collar and growled: "Hey, students are not allowed to enter the campus!" But his comrade noticed Masuji's civilian dress and said: "You're just a candidate, not a regular student, aren't you? You are lucky, otherwise we'd beat the hell out of you!"[2] Only then did Masuji notice the broken windows in the university building and realized that Waseda was in the midst of a major riot. Compared to other leading institutions, especially Tokyo University, Waseda's atmosphere was fairly liberal and attracted students with artistic inclinations. Most of the schoolmates who joined Ibuse in the first year of the prep course were aspiring playwrights or writers. "A few too many to make it," as he later commented wryly.[3] Out of the more than two hundred students in the prep course, only one rose to fame in the literary world – Ibuse himself, although he would have been genuinely surprised if someone had predicted it then.

It wasn't until he joined the Department of Literature as a full-time student that Masuji began meeting schoolmates like Yokomitsu Riichi (1898–1947), Nakayama Gishû (1900–1969), Tsuboi Shigeji (1897–1975) and Wada Tsutô (1900–1985). Of course Yokomitsu was such a rare visitor to morning classes that for a long time Ibuse had him mixed up with the poet Tsuboi, whom he slightly resembled. Moreover, those who looked most promising in their second or third year of university were not necessarily the ones whose fame would last. For example Wada, who was the 'hope of the class' as Ibuse recalls, publishing as many as three instalments a year of a novel in the prestigious *Waseda*

---

[2] Ibid., p. 68.

[3] IM, Kawamori Yoshizô: "Taidan: Sanshôuo made." In: *Hito to hitokage*. Tokyo, Mainichi shinbunsha 1972, p. 324.

*bungaku* (*Waseda Literature*), became a minor 'rural writer' (*nômin sakka*) and is practically forgotten today. Though in his modest way Ibuse was already more serious about an artistic career than some of the other literary adepts (*bungaku seinen*), he was still receptive to stylish outside prescriptions as to what an artist should or shouldn't do:

> In a book I was browsing through in one of the second-hand bookstores of Tsurumaki-machi, it said that a novelist who hasn't passed under the shop-curtain of a pawnshop couldn't write about real life. Although I had a feeling that the author was just trying to justify his own bankruptcy, I chose to interpret his advice as: 'Try to understand human nature and the world' and pawned my watch without really needing the money. Yet when I did pass under the shop-curtain and saw the clean-swept earthen floor, and the elegant lattice work of the counter, my impression was rather that of a holy place far from the madding crowd.[4]

In *Keirokushû* he puts it even more ironically:

> When I first came to Tokyo, I dreamt about becoming a poverty-stricken author who frequents pawnshops; what a beautiful existence it must be, I thought, to live from hand to mouth while turning out one novel after another.[5]

Many years later, in the summer of 1980, I sat with Ibuse in his favourite *sushiya* in Ogikubo as he recalled those early days. "You know," he said wistfully, "poverty was the artist's trademark then – we made a great show of it."

[4] IM: "Hanseiki." In: *IMZ XIII*, p. 424.
[5] IM: "Keirokushû." In: *IMZ IX*, p. 281.

In a short story written in 1930, Ibuse vividly evokes the atmosphere of the Waseda classroom in mid-Taishô. It is aptly called "Rest Period" (*Kyûkeijikan*) and it is one of the very few stories inspired by his student experience retained in the collected works:

Classroom number seven in the Department of Literature is the oldest one at this University, and the dirtiest. On a rainy day, a steady trickle of raindrops seeps through the cracks in the windows, wetting the windowsills and the wall below. A gloomy twilight reigns inside the room most of the time, and the writing on the blackboard is hard to read. On a sunny day a thick layer of dust can be seen collecting on the desks and the benches. Whenever the students want to sit at their desks, they must wipe the filth off with their hats or their handkerchiefs.

But the students like nothing better than listening to lectures in this classroom. No doubt this is because the room itself brings to mind many a nostalgic episode. If what the students say is true, this historical room should perhaps be called 'The memorial hall of Japanese Literature'. As student legend has it, this is the room where the great Doctor of Literature, Tsubouchi Shôyô, gave his Shakespeare lectures. Tsubouchi-*sensei* was still in perfect health then, the very personification of a passionate literary pioneer; how his words about Romeo and Juliet's love or Ophelia's pure heart must have stirred the emotion of his students! They say this is the very room where Professor Shimamura Hôgetsu gave the lecture on his new literary theory. One can almost see Hôgetsu's frowning face, standing on the room's lectern and announcing that solemn manifesto of Naturalism, now carved on his oval tombstone at the Zôshigaya cemetery, to his students:

'Follow reality as it is, and contemplate the real meaning of existence. That is true life devoted to one's true liking. Such a state of mind is what we call art.'[6]

Although Ibuse arrived too late for Tsubouchi's famous Shakespeare lectures, given in the late 1890's when the great scholar was in his prime, he still had the opportunity to attend the professor's special weekly lecture on *A Midsummer Night's Dream*. Tsubouchi (1859–1935) not only knew the whole play by heart, he had considerable acting talent and recited its passages with the proper intonation. He loved theatre and wrote a play about the Buddhist sage Nichiren which he personally recited in the big auditorium of Waseda University. The huge hall was packed and among the audience were famous writers and playwrights, well-known kabuki and *shingeki* actors, *rakugo* storytellers and even the former premier, Marquis Ôkuma Shigenobu, who founded the university. Ibuse recalls that Tsubouchi's performance was as good as Danjûrô's from the ninth generation, or Kikugorô's from the fifth. He could shed tears on cue and when he recited Nichiren's famous street sermons (*tsuji seppô*), his voice sounded like "the thunderous roar of a giant", only to be followed by the squeeky voice of a little girl. When one reads Tsubouchi's major work, *The Essence of the Novel* (*Shôsetsu shinzui*) today, there isn't much that has withstood the test of time. Perhaps his real contribution was in these majestic performances that influenced several generations of Japanese intellectuals.

Since Ibuse later joined the Department of French Literature and often mentions his youthful fascination

[6] IM: "Kyûkei jikan." In: *IMZ I*, pp. 80–81.

with French and Russian 19th century writers, critics tend to forget how well acquainted he was with the Anglo-Saxon literary tradition. Not only did he read Shakespeare's major plays, benefitting greatly from Tsubouchi's unusual rapport with their poetic spirit, but he was also influenced by the then prevailing symbolist mood which cut across the conventional Anglo-French cultural barrier. One of the first lectures he came to attend during his first week at Waseda was Professor Yoshida Genjirô's inspired reading of Arthur Symons' *The Town of Arles*. Besides Symons, author of the influential *The Symbolist Movement in Literature* (1899), Yoshida taught Blake, Burns and Yeats, preferring them to the orthodox selection of classics. This made him very popular with his students. Yoshida was a man of many interests and a best-selling popular author in his time. His lectures were enlivened by spirited 'asides':

> In between his lectures, Professor Yoshida would express his feelings about such things as Love, Bashô, Shinran's thought in *Lamentation of Divergencies (Tannishô)*, Marcus Aurelius, Eternity and Jesus Christ, putting our young hearts in a state of utter rapture with his passionate eloquence. I can still hear his melodious voice, as he stood there, rubbing the skin of his forehead between the eyebrows and orating with pathos:
>
> 'There can be no doubt that the Christ who annointed Mary of Magdala with the fragrant oil of nard was a lovable youth, nay, a lovable child of Nature. To him there was no difference whatever between the courtesan, the tax-collector and the pauper. All people were brothers and sisters...'

As I listened in ecstasy to the professor's words, I could see in my mind's eye the clear, blue sky of Galilee, and imagine the mustard flowers, blooming on a cliff in the wilderness. When he talked about Bashô, I could almost touch the lonely, desolate roads of the Northern provinces. I was more than happy.[7]

Although these enchanted memories of a thirty-eight-year old Ibuse do contain a touch of irony, the critical distance is more obvious in his rendering of the same material some twenty-five years later, when he was sixty-three. In a short story, called "Supplication Letters" (*Mushinjô*, 1961) the fond recollections of youth are more stylized and the sceptical irony is already vintage Ibuse:

Soon after entering Waseda, I came to worship Professor Yoshida. We were fascinated by the occasional poetic interludes that marked his lectures. Their topic changed from occasion to occasion: from Jesus Christ to Isaiah of the Old Testament, from Tolstoy to Michelangelo, from Pascal to Matsuo Bashô, Ryôkan, Love, Shinran and similar topics, each lasting about thirty minutes or so...

Although I was deeply impressed by Professor Yoshida's oratory, I lacked the will to follow the path of these venerable sages. To put it bluntly, I was always short of pocket money, and had to ask for special contributions from home. I sent letters of supplication to my brother, beseeching him to forward extra funds; my excuses were not outright lies, but they weren't the truth either.[8]

---

[7] "Keirokushû," pp. 273–274. *Tannishô* is a Buddhist text compiled several decades after Shinran's death by his disciple Yui-en. It is a record of the sage's proverbs, his sayings and thought in 18 sections.

[8] IM: "Mushinjô." In: *IMZ VIII*, p. 383. There was another outstanding English professor at Waseda, Masuda Tônosuke, fondly remembered not only by Ibuse

Years later, when Kawamori Yoshizô asked Ibuse in an interview if he felt there was any influence of Christian teaching in his work, he replied: "No, I don't feel any such thing." The sentimental ravings of his favourite teacher obviously did not leave a mark in his soul. In the autumn of 1918, roughly one year after he had arrived in Tokyo, Masuji summoned his courage and asked a fellow student, who came from his native region, to introduce him to Iwano Hômei. Hômei came from an old family of hereditary samurai on the island of Awaji, located in the Inland Sea on the west side of Ôsaka Bay, not too far from Ibuse's and his friend's birthplace. The reason why I suspect a sentimental connection comes from a feeling of genuine puzzlement: why, of all people did young Ibuse choose Iwano Hômei, the scandalous *enfant terrible* and the typical self-destructive bohemian of the Taishô literary circle to be his first literary mentor? Perhaps it was Hômei's reckless life-style, one scandalous affair after another, that made him the ideal romantic idol bound to impress any young man, let alone an aspiring artist. He squandered a great deal of his explosive creative energy on fancy artistic theories such as mystical animalism – one can't help thinking that such theories were often nothing but highflown public justifications of Iwano's own sexual scandals – or on his theory of monistic description (*ichigen byôsha*). In an essay called "The First Man of Letters I Ever Met" (*Hajimete atta bunshi*), written in 1935, Ibuse recalls his first visit with the artist:

but by Hirotsu Kazuo who majored in English, graduating from the university about four years before Ibuse's arrival. Ibuse admired Masuda's light translations of Eliot and studied the English poet with him.

The first man of letters I met was Mr. Iwano Hômei. It was just at the time when Master Iwano really got going in the polemic about his theory of monistic description, and so when I first came to see him, he told me…:

'An artist may know about empathy, but if he doesn't understand my theory of monistic description, he's a lost man. The artist who introduced monistic portrayal into painting was Cézanne. In poetry, it was Baudelaire. The first playwright to use it was Gorki. In the art of the novel, it is Japan's Iwano Hômei.'

But aren't there artists in Europe – say Chekhov and Maupassant – who are using such a technique by giving a distinct focus to their description? Perhaps they are not consciously applying the 'monistic description', but it is still positively manifested in their work. So I said to Mr. Iwano: 'Isn't Maupassant also writing in a monistic style?' He gave his big laugh and replied:

'What are you talking about? Sit down and read one of Maupassant's novels and my Osei stories – then you'll understand what monistic description is all about. The one who introduced it into French style is none other than Baudelaire.'

Master Iwano pronounced Baudelaire's name as Bodler, and Verlaine's as Verlen… Although the stylistic handiwork of Iwano's trilogy and some of his other works strikes one as being fairly rough-hewn, he was fond of making extremely assertive statements about style in front of an audience…[9]

[9] IM: "Hajimete atta bunshi." In: *IMZ IX,* pp. 148–149. For a detailed study of Hômei's literary theory, see Nagashima, Yoichi: *Objective Descriptions of Self: A Study of Iwano Hômei's Literary Theory.* Aarhus, Aarhus University Press 1997, pp. 179–180 and passim.

A brief glance at one of Iwano's representative works called *The Woman Who Drank Poison* (*Dokuyaku wo nomu onna*) will show a typical work of Japanese naturalism, striving for a unity of authentic dialogue and poetic image with the author's connecting text. If I understand Iwano's ideal of monistic description correctly, then its most perfect example is Flaubert's prose. It is not an accident that Ibuse never took an example from his tutor, but rather from the French master whose technique he considered to represent one of the highest achievements of prose writing. It seems he learned rather from Iwano's mistakes: for example, an editor had to correct the too intellectual diction of his heroine Osei, who was supposed to be illiterate, while the speech of Ibuse's characters is usually authentic, though somewhat stylized.

In April of 1919, Ibuse joined the Department of Literature as a full-time first year student. Not that he had grown more devoted to his studies – on the contrary, as he began to feel comfortable in Waseda's bohemian climate, his school attendance became less and less frequent. On his way to the library he would often stop at the *Kaiyôken* coffee shop, change into the prescribed wooden-soled sandals, and watch a group of his schoolmates rehearse a play of *shingeki* (new theatre). In 1919, they were doing Maeterlinck's *Blue Bird;* the Belgian symbolist poet and playwright remained a craze throughout the Taishô years. An even bigger craze among Waseda's crop of aspiring artists was Tolstoy, especially his philosophy of 'abandoning the world'. Ibuse recalls that some of these Tolstoy fans even walked around in Russian peasant *rubashkas* with a broad belt over them. Among the regulars of the *Kaiyôken* were three classmates with whom Ibuse developed a close friendship, and who were all fascinated by Tolstoy. Not surprisingly, they all came from remote rural areas of Southern Japan.They all hoped to become novelists, and one did stay in Tokyo long enough to graduate from Waseda before going back to the country. The other two had followed Tolstoy's advice even earlier and returned home, one to his native place and the other to a village in Izu, where he started a utopian chicken farm.

It seems appropriate that the schoolmates Masuji chose as intimate friends were all from the South, and of a similar background as himself. Although Tolstoy's popularity was probably as widespread among intellectuals as the Katyusha song[10] was among the Taishô population at large, one detects the added attraction of Tolstoy's rural nostalgia here: these southern boys must have all felt a similar loneliness in the cool impersonal climate of Tokyo, and they instinctively banded together into a natural coalition to cope with it. It was precisely at this point that Masuji met someone completely different in every way imaginable, a friend who was to influence him more and mean more to him than any other human being, teacher or schoolmate, that he met in all his Waseda years: Aoki Nanpachi. Many Ibuse readers mistook this strange-sounding name – Kôno Toshirô calls it a humourous-looking name – for their author's characteristic creation. Even

---

[10] The Katyusha song, composed by Nakayama Shinpei, comes from Tolstoy's play *Resurrection* which was extremely popular in the twenties. It was first put on stage in 1914 and the song was sung by Matsui Sumiko.

83

the faithful editor of his early works, Nagai Tatsuo, believed for some time that Nanpachi was a fictional character. But behind the name was a rather extraordinary person:

> Among my close friends, there was a boy named Aoki Nanpachi who commuted to school from his own home in downtown Tokyo... Although he had the same literary ambitions as the rest of us, he liked studying and attended his classes with the utmost regularity. After school he studied in libraries: on the odd days he worked at Waseda's and on the even days at Ueno Public Library. During the summer holidays he would work on translations at his family's seaside cottage. He was extremely nearsighted, but gave people a cheerful, eager impression.
>
> In the past years I have written frequently about Aoki. Besides essays and semidocumentary pieces I wrote a memoir called "Aoki Nanpachi." In a small work called "Carp" (*Koi*) I even entrusted my feelings towards Nanpachi to a fish. In short, I've already written too much and can't do much more than repeat myself. But it was Nanpachi who stood by me most staunchly throughout my student years and it wouldn't do at all not to mention him in this 'chronicle of my early life' (*Hanseiki*).
>
> It seems Nampachi came from a long line of brilliant people. His older brother Tokuzô was an outstanding expert in numismatics and another older brother, Kusuo, excelled in bridge building... Nampachi himself was considered a genius and, as so often happens in life, the prodigy is drawn to the idiot. Thus the brilliant Nanpachi took excellent care of a nitwit: myself.[11]

[11] Hanseiki," pp. 434–435.

Of course Nanpachi never thought of Ibuse as a nitwit. Since he allowed only three hours of sleep daily to himself, he may have disapproved of the lackadaisical academic habits and late rising hours of his friend. But as long as he saw sheets of writing paper spread by Masuji's pillow when he dropped in between the morning lectures, he was satisfied, believing that his friend had spent the whole night labouring on a new manuscript. Although Ibuse jokingly claims that he would often scatter some discarded manuscript paper around his bed just to get away with a few extra hours of sleep, the truth is that it was around the spring of this year that he started writing really seriously, no doubt thanks to Aoki's prodding and support:

> Nanpachi reminded me every day that constant writing practice is the first duty of an aspiring novelist. Writing, even for practice, was a sacred activity to him. Since he had a poet's soul himself, he was dead serious about it. That's why when he came to wake me up and sometimes found an unfinished manuscript on my desk, he would always seat himself properly and read the whole piece. Even though it could hardly have pleased his demanding critical eye, instead of saying 'It's no good', he'd say 'But it's O.K.', or 'You'll make it, don't worry!'[12]

His background was as different from Masuji's as could be: having spent the first year of his life in Matsue, where he was born, he had travelled from prefecture to prefecture with his father who was a top-ranking bureaucrat working for various prefectural governments. So before he came to Waseda, he had lived in Wakayama, Niigata, Hiroshima, Tokyo, Sap-

[12] Ibid., pp. 435–436.

poro and Tokyo again, a very unusual experience for a Japanese youngster of those days, when, despite all the modernization and its new ways, a 'static' background of someone like Masuji was far more common. Other studious, hardworking types were scoffed at and called derogatory names (e.g. *gainen sensei*)[13] by their fellow students but there was something about Aoki's character that impressed everybody. Perhaps it was the rare combination of a keen, knowing mind with a childlike purity and an easygoing, gentle manner.

So when Masuji returned to Kamo that summer, it was with a new and somewhat surprising awareness: there were human beings in that 'robber's land' of Tokyo who might not have a *furusato,* and who might even speak with that atrocious accent, but they were not only capable of emotional communication, they could serve as mentors and guides into as yet unknown mysteries of art. The young writer spent his summer vacation well. Before the two months were over, Aoki received no fewer than five stories (perhaps sketches in the *shaseibun*[14] manner would be more accurate): "Dragonfly" (*Yanma*), "Antlion" (*Arijigoku*), "Toad" (*Gama*), "Seeing a Jewel Insect" (*Tamamushi wo miru*) and "Giant Salamander" (*Sanshôuo*). It seems they were all inspired by animals and insects common to Masuji's native area. Except for *Sanshôuo,* which would become his debuting work some years later as "Confinement" (*Yûhei*),

[13] Literally master of abstract concepts. "Keirokushû," p. 267.

[14] The concept of *shaseibun* was developped during the Meiji period by the poet Masaoka Shiki, who borrowed it from painting. It means faithful sketching of the real world. For an interesting discussion of the concept, see Karatani, Kôjin: *Origins of Modern Japanese Literature.* Durham, and London, Duke University Press 1993, pp. 179–184.

we don't know how these stories or sketches looked originally, although Ibuse did include a short story called *Tamamushi wo miru* in a collection called *My Precious Reality* (*Natsukashiki genjitsu*) published in 1930, and in 1974 wrote a short story called "Antlion" (*Arijigoku*).

Judging from the extensive textual changes in the successive versions of "Salamander", I'd say that these early attempts had little in common with the later works of the same title. In an interview with Ban Toshihiko,[15] Ibuse recalled that *Yanma*, like all the other stories, had about eight to ten pages, and one gathers that *Tamamushi wo miru* was probably also a light, impressionistic sketch that may have served as a departure point and inspiration for the later story of the same name. The story's fragile, jewel-like insect shows up in a series of unpleasant incidents which, with the exception of the first one, happen in Tokyo to a poor young bohemian. The symbolic design is obvious: the fleeting, jewel-like memory of home, far from offering support to the young artist, only serves to exacerbate his miserable condition by its very beauty that cannot last in the rough Tokyo climate:

> A few days passed. One morning towards dawn, as I was lying in bed, I thought I'd have a look at the *tamamushi* in the sleeve of my kimono. I had been drinking *shôchû* the night before, and no matter how much water I had, I felt thirsty even in my dreams and couldn't sleep properly.
>
> When I found the long-forgotten insect, I discovered that it turned into a speck of ugly dust, so I tossed it out of the window.[16]

[15] Ban, Toshihiko: "Ibuse san kara kiita koto 1." In: *IMZ IX, Geppô 3*, p. 1.
[16] IM: "Tamamushi wo miru." In: **IMZ I**. Tokyo, Chikuma shobô 1996, p. 61.

Ibuse never lost his remarkable sensitivity towards tiny creatures and in his late years liked to return to the milieu of his youth. In the summer of 1975 he invited me to his summer home in Takamori (old province of Shinshû, now Nagano Prefecture) and as we were leaving for a walk one afternoon, a beautiful moth landed on the lapel of my *yûkata*. Ibuse looked at it with interest and remarked: "What a nice accessory for our walk." In the evening I suggested that we bake some potatoes on the open hearth in the earthen-floored central room (*doma*). Ibuse tasted a potato with butter and salt and said: "Not bad, but rice is rice." Under the floor of the bedroom in his beautiful 19th century country house runs a brook from the mountains, which the master called natural climatization. I never slept so well as when a cool stream from the Japanese mountains murmured under my pillow.

Masuji did not spend the next summer of 1920 in Kamo, but instead travelled to Nikkô. His first literary mentor, Iwano Hômei, had died in May of the same year and there was nobody among Masuji's teachers, or the established writers of the *bundan*, to whom he could turn with his literary attempts. But at least he seems to have lost some of his intense shyness during the first three years in Tokyo, for when he came back to the city in the fall, he paid a visit – without any roundabout introductions or family connections – to Tanizaki Seiji, the younger brother of the novelist Jun'ichirô. Although only eight years older than Masuji, Tanizaki was an experienced member of the literary establishment, having graduated from Waseda's prestigious English Department. Unlike his older brother, Seiji was more of a critic and scholar than a bohemian artist. Not only had he supported himself throughout his studies, working night shifts at a power plant, he was one of the few young men of letters to complete his education and later to follow an impressive academic career:

> … Although his judgments about my work weren't as severe as they are nowadays, in a way he was even more serious then… I brought manuscripts of short stories like "Salamander" (*Sanshôuo*) and "Diary of My Blues" (*Maiutsuki*) to our first meeting. He certainly didn't praise them, but then he didn't say they were useless either. I felt that I'd gained a real helping hand in my endeavours.[17]

Under Tanizaki's practised guidance the young writer started working systematically and most days he was able to complete a short story. Towards the weekend he brought them to his mentor, who advised him what to improve in their content, style or grammar, even the choice of characters. When his strict teacher occasionally mumbled: "Don't throw this one out," Masuji felt stimulated to keep working.

It was at this time that an unpleasant conflict with one of his teachers at Waseda began, serious enough to make him leave the university eventually. There was a young Russian scholar by the name of Katagami Noboru at Waseda, whose lectures on Tolstoy were extremely popular with the students. Unfortunately, the professor was unable to differentiate between the love of literature and love of his students – he often invited his favourite boys home, and though Ibuse never spells it out in his essays, it is very likely that Katagami made

[17] "Keirokushû," p. 283.

indecent proposals to them. Masuji suspected this, and so when the professor invited him into the privacy of his home, he took two schoolmates with him. He presumed correctly that with two witnesses present the professor would hardly dare anything:

> It looked like rain that day, so I set out with a new oil-paper umbrella borrowed from my landlady. When we arrived at *sensei's* house, he looked disgusted at first, and just kept staring at the three of us. But when Kôzô [Nose] and Bunsuke [Taguma] started asking him their favourite questions about Tolstoy, his mood improved. Taking out a volume of photographs of the Russian writer, he passed it around cheerfully. Yet all the while he kept sniffing in my direction, and mumbling to himself: 'What's that stink? Must be a woman's lingering body odour. Not a young girl's though, it's the smell of a matron, thirty-five to thirty-six...,' and he sniffed again, repeating disgustedly: 'What a stink!' Kôzô and Bunsuke, mildly interested, willingly sniffed at my head and shoulders, and concluded that the smell must have rubbed off on my hands from the new umbrella's scented oil. *Sensei* dismissed us at this point and we returned home.[18]

The conflict with Katagami got worse so that in October of 1921 Masuji had to leave school.[19] First, he was expected to pay a visit to his family in Kamo. Yet when he arrived there, he couldn't find the courage to explain to these country people exactly what had happened in Tokyo, although his mother questioned him every day and his older brother watched him with

[18] Ibid., pp. 270–271.
[19] He later commented: "I escaped without a word to my classmates." "Keiro-kushû," p. 273.

a disapproving eye. All he managed to say was that he'd like to appologize and get away from the world. He then asked his mother if she'd let him roam Kyûshû for a while, but she retorted that she saw no reason why he should travel to such a faraway place. Brother Fumio decided the matter, saying "Well, why don't you go to one of the islands around here and take it easy for a while."[20]

Through the customary roundabout route of introductions a suitable *geshuku* was found in the small town of Mitsunosho on Innoshima, an island in the Inland Sea of about 34 square kilometers, lying across the bay from the city of Onomichi. The room was on the second floor of the local medical establishment of Dr. Doi Uraji:

> The room faced the south and had an excellent view. Straight ahead you could see the small island of Hyak-kanjima, and in the distance behind it the mountain ranges of Shikoku. Below the window lay the ocean. The rooms on the northern side faced the castle-hill, a mild slope covered with *mikan* groves and vermifuge chrysanthemum fields. They say that in the old days the *wakô*, or Japanese pirates, had built their main fort on this hill… From its crest, one could see the ocean in all four directions through the gaps in the surrounding hills – an ideal location for the headquarters of a pirate navy, indeed.[21]

In his memoirs, essays and interviews Ibuse often dismisses the whole island experience saying that he spent most of his time fishing and drinking sake with the doctor, or learning to play the *shamisen* from a local

[20] Ibid., pp. 271–272.
[21] Ibid., p. 272.

geisha.[22] When time was too heavy on his hands, he'd read a little Tolstoy or Chekhov. Yet the island and the days spent in Dr. Doi's rustic medical establishment offered an important source of inspiration to Ibuse. One of his best-known novellas, *No Consultations Today* (*Honjitsu kyûshin*, 1950), takes place in just such a small doctor's hospital and could not have been written without a detailed, intimate knowledge of its daily traffic. In 1948 Ibuse wrote a humorous story about postwar smugglers, located on the island and entitled *Innoshima*. One of his favourite characters, the lovable old pirate Miyaji Kotarô in *Waves: A War Diary,* comes from Innoshima and speaks its soft dialect. Another experience which stayed with him throughout his writing career was the intimate rapport with his favourite Russian writers gained from long hours of quiet reading. Especially Chekhov, for many aspects of Ibuse's own short-story technique suggest that he read the Russian master in far greater depth than just to kill time during his stay on the island.

In March of 1922, after six peaceful months on Innoshima, Masuji returned directly to Tokyo, although, according to Japanese etiquette, he should have stopped at the family home in Kamo to pay his respects to his older brother and mother. As might be expected, brother Fumio was very upset by this slight. But when he received a brief, formal letter from Professor Katagami two months later saying: "Your honorable younger brother has on this day withdrawn

[22] I heard this story from a midwife at Innoshima, Mrs. Takahashi Chieko, who stressed that the girl was very proper; Ibuse recalls the geisha in an essay called "Shamisen uta." In: *IMZ XI*, p. 443.

from school...," the "cord of his patience," as Ibuse puts it,[23] finally snapped. He had no idea that his younger brother was not really behaving wilfully and actually made an effort to rejoin the university. What really seems to have happened is that Katagami did make a pass at the boy and tried to cover it up by removing the potential witness; he obviously feared that he might be dismissed from the university. From today's perspective, this was a clear case of sexual harassment, usually ignored in those days, or resolved in the professor's favour.[24]

In the same year Masuji's close friend Aoki Nanpachi died of tuberculosis and the young writer did not have much to show for the following year or so. It was not before the July of the next year, 1923, that he joined his first *dôjin zasshi* called *Seiki* (*Century*). Like most of these literary journals, it was short-lived and its members' names sound totally unfamiliar today. In *Ogikubo Chronicles* (*Ogikubo fudoki*)[25] Ibuse recalls that there were about seventeen to eighteen members, mostly classmates from Waseda's Literary Department. They found a rich sponsor from Kyôto who was willing to finance the operation, and a bookstore in Kanda that could do the printing. There was no editor-in-chief, and so the editorial policy was most lenient – every-

[23] "Keirokushû," p. 273.

[24] Katagami Noboru (1884–1928), also known as Katagami Tengen, spent three years in Russia (1915–1918), collecting books for Waseda's newly established Department of Russian. He brought back valuable works by avantgarde artists (Kruchenykh, Chlebnikov), but also supported Japanese naturalists and influenced the theory of proletarian literature.

[25] IM: *Ogikubo fudoki*. Tokyo, Shinchôsha 1982, p. 57. *Fudoki* literally means *Record of Natural Features*, or *History of Cultural Climate*.

body could write whatever he pleased. Yet Ibuse was able to place his debut work, "Confinement" (*Yûhei*), in *Seiki's* first issue. Though Ibuse earned a bit of a bad reputation for changing *dôjin zasshi* too often, the writer himself points out how fruitful his affiliation with this string of literary journals was:

> I first became a member of *Seiki,* then switched to *Jintsû jidai* (*Era of Labour Pains*), *Bungei toshi* (*City of Arts*) and *Sakuhin* (*Oeuvre*). A little later I joined *Bungakkai* (*World of Literature*). I remember that this journal was discontinued during the war while I was evacuated in Kôfu. However, *Bungakkai* was restored after the war, even before I returned to Tokyo, and soon became a regular literary journal, published by the *Bungei shunjû* company... That's why from my early membership in *Seiki* in the summer of 1923 till 1948 or 1949 I always had connections with *dôjin zasshi*... Even when I was conscripted and sent to Malaya during the war, I kept sending manuscripts to Kawakami Tetsutarô's *Bungakkai*. You might call these *dôjin zasshi* faithful companions of my early professional life.[26]

On September 1, 1923, the third issue of *Seiki* was printed and ready for distribution, but it never reached the bookstores. Ibuse was just sitting at his desk in his rented room at Shimototsuka, writing a story about two legendary Chinese monks whose title he borrowed from Mori Ôgai (*Kanzan jittoku*), when the house was rocked by the first wave of the Great Kantô Earthquake. The author remembers:

> September 1, 1923. On that day, a terrible downpour started around dawn. It sounded like a sudden cloudburst and the rattle woke me up. The lines of rain were

[26] "Hanseiki," p. 448.

thick as sticks and I wondered if it wasn't the kind of heavy squall one hears they get in the Southern Seas.

The rain stopped as abruptly as it had begun and the morning sky turned a bright blue after sunrise. In the newspaper and magazine reports of the following days it said that the sky was an almost transparent blue and that the morning was hot and humid, but I think that's not quite true. I have a feeling that the morning after the rain was a cool summer morning, but as it grew hotter, huge thunderhead clouds appeared in the eastern sky at some point. They were strange clouds with delicate curls...

The quake struck at 11:58 A.M. and lasted three minutes. A series of lesser tremors followed, so I dashed out of my room and down the staircase. The moment I jumped off the last stair, the whole staircase lifted into midair and became unusable for the people left in the house...[27]

To read Ibuse's recollections of this, the most frightening experience of his youth – though no doubt somewhat stylized and edited – is interesting in itself. But what is really important for a critical understanding of his major work, *Black Rain*, is to note how the imprint of this shattering experience influenced his imaginative rendering of a far more devastating event – the atomic annihilation of Hiroshima. Its description is characterized by the same kind of modest, unexcited and at times ironic account of the wild rumours that accompany large-scale emergencies in his, and probably any close-knit society. In reality, these dangerous rumours were aimed at Koreans during the Earthquake,

[27] *Ogikubo fudoki*, pp. 28–29.

and some were massacred by the angry populace. Ibuse knows that, and he knows the tension-releasing mechanism of designating a scapegoat equally well. Yet he is not interested in playing it up or even exploring it as a writer. When I discussed the documentary aspect of *Black Rain* with him, he mentioned that when researching the background of the novel, he came across some grisly facts about the massacre of foreigners in Hiroshima, but all he included of it in the novel is the following brief vignette:

> Near its center, the bridge reared in a hump about a yard high, and on what one might have called the crest of the wave a young foreigner with fair hair lay dead with his arms clasped about his head.[28]

In actual fact, Ibuse told me, there was a seminary of resident German priests in Hiroshima at the time of the bombing which was massacred to the last man. They probably came to Japan on a programme of cultural exchange between the Axis powers, but a blond-haired foreigner inevitably attracted the wrath of the angry mob, whether friend or foe. The mob and its hysteria never interested Ibuse, though his novel could have been more 'dramatic' had he included such incidents. He could have dramatized the xenophobic feelings of some of the survivors, condemned the foreign enemy and the like. Yet all we find of such sentiments in the long novel is one abrupt remark by Shigematsu: "It's the act of a vicious bully, if ever there was one."[29]

[28] IM: *Black Rain*. Trans. Bester, John. Tokyo and Palo Alto, Kôdansha International 1969, p. 108.
[29] Ibid., p. 50.

That the disaster occurred at all, and that such human phobias were at its source on both sides is horrible enough. But why make it the driving force of one's narrative? What Ibuse tries to do is to commemorate the quiet courage of decent people, the silent suffering of innocent victims rather than the dramatic gesture of the more outspoken actors, the 'movers' of human history. To put it differently, Ibuse prefers to portray history's underdogs, its passive civilians and peasants, rather than the 'active' people – the warlords, the Buddhist bonzes or the bureaucrats. This is a far more difficult task, for a *daimyô*'s life will usually look more eventful, and therefore more colourful, than the drab existence of his serf. The upper classes are also more articulate or at least in command of a richer vocabulary than the 'mute' peasantry, their mentality nearer to the educated writer's own and thus somewhat easier to portray. One perceives another striking parallel between the two disasters, – one natural and the other man-made – in Ibuse's description of the devastating fires that raged for days after both. This is his account of burning Tokyo after the quake:

> At that point, the cumulo-nimbus clouds spread all over the sky and the entire downtown horizon changed into a sea of flames. The earth-tremors continued all the while. I told my friend Kojima, how when a farmhouse burnt down in our neighbourhood during my childhood, my whole body wouldn't stop shivering for hours on end. We moved over to the third base, from where the conflagration in the downtown area could better be seen.

As the sun went down, the huge clouds turned a bright red, reflecting the sea of flames. Towards dawn they went pitch black and when the sun rose they were back to pure white with fine curls again...[30]

While some of Ibuse's descriptions of the 'sea of flames' (*hi no umi*) or a 'huge column of flame' (*hibashira*) are the same in both instances, as is his attention to the strange relation between the fires on the ground and the ominous clouds in the sky, there are also obvious differences. This, for example is how the atomic cloud is described:

> As I got up from my prone position, the first thing to meet my gaze was a great, an enormous column of cloud. In its texture, it reminded me of cumulo-nimbus clouds I had seen in photographs taken after the great Kanto Earthquake. But this one trailed a single, thick leg beneath it, and reached up high into the heavens. Flattening out at its peak, it swelled out fatter and fatter like an opening mushroom.[31]

Changing his own vivid memory of the clouds that accompanied the Kantô quake into 'photographs' is Ibuse's concession to the accuracy of his character's portrayal. Shigematsu, the protagonist of *Black Rain*, spent his early life in Kobatake village near Hiroshima and was thus not likely to have been in Tokyo on the fateful day. But there is not a categorical difference between the way Shigematsu perceives the horrendous destructive power of the atomic blast and Ibuse's own perception of the quake:

[30] *Ogikubo fudoki*, pp. 33–34.
[31] *Black Rain*, p. 53.

I fully understood the horror of earthquakes. All of a sudden everything is blown to smithereens. Then follows the frightening inferno of the fires...[32]

It is said that in moments of great upheaval, when reality as we know it is nearly destroyed, the human mind tends to preserve its integrity by clinging to meaningless details; when the larger orderly structure falls apart, concrete details provide the remaining links with a new reality. One notices a characteristic attention to such detail both in Ibuse's memoirs of the quake and in the somewhat more stylized descriptions of *Black Rain*. In *Ogikubo Chronicles* he recalls two distinctly different patterns of crumbling plaster on the walls of his dormitory. One of the walls, replastered during the summer, had wide cracks in it, while the other, which had been fixed around the winter holidays, disintegrated totally. Another episode relates the experience of Ibuse's cousin, who looked out of the window when the quake was at its peak and saw the dome of Tokyo Station roll in high waves; yet it showed not a single crack afterwards, perhaps thanks to Frank Loyd Wright's brilliant design. And two or three massive railway ties were lodged in the depth of the square well at Ogikubo Station; nobody could imagine how they got there.[33] It is this kind of 'magic', the unexplained, bizarre behaviour of things during a major upheaval, that fascinates Ibuse in *Black Rain*. Some readers may even feel uncomfortable about such innocent direct interest, unmitigated by moral compassion. And yet

[32] "Hanseiki," p. 441.
[33] *Ogikubo fudoki*, pp. 32–35 and pp. 43–44. Ibuse concludes, rather tentatively, that this may be some kind of magic.

such a factual documentary technique of observation greatly contributes to the narrative's authenticity.

Shigematsu of *Black Rain* can only reach his destination walking along railway tracks amid smoldering rubble and newly erupting fires. Following this last remnant of a communications system allows Shigematsu to accomplish his heroic journey of many miles through the burning city. The nature of the two cataclysmic events that caused the devastation of the two cities – the atomic blast of Hiroshima and the great quake of Kantô – could not be more different, yet the fiery hell that followed in the wake of both was very much the same. Just as in Hiroshima, the fires in Tokyo kept raging for almost four days, with huge columns of flame shooting up even three days after the quake, as department stores like the Shirakiya of Nihonbashi or the Great Hall of the Imperial University erupted in flames. Here too, walking the railway line was the only remaining means of transportation:

> On the fourth day, everything that could burn was gone. The cumulo-nimbus clouds were still hanging in the sky; perhaps they had some connection with the heated atmosphere. The quake itself may have been linked to the phases of the moon somehow. On the night of that fourth day, I pounded the unpolished rice, served again in an empty beer bottle by our landlady, with a pestle, and on the morning of the fifth day I had a bowl of bland *miso* soup for breakfast. Having filled my stomach, I put on my straw-hat, and groping my way through the scorched debris, set out straight along the municipal streetcar line...[34]

[34] Ibid., p. 35.

The accurate, realistic detail of Ibuse's description of Hiroshima's fires is so convincing because it is based on direct personal experience. Many a scene that Shigematsu witnesses during his anabasis through the ravaged city is just like the one that follows:

> The water of the ditch at Takebashi was completely drained, and people's corpses were scattered here and there. A woman's body, clad in her Sunday's best lay right below the stone embankment. She was still clutching her shopping bag with the sign of a famous shop. All the dead women I saw were staring into the sky, while the men were lying with their faces down. These people must have sought refuge in the water while its level was still high, but when the flames lapped it up in one sweep, they were left high and dry. I still remember how dizzy I felt when I glanced at that embankment on the other side of the canal.[35]

When Masuji heard that incoming trains of the Central Line (*Chûôsen*) were running as far as Tachikawa, he decided to walk all the way there along the tracks. From Tachikawa he'd try to catch a train to Nagoya, and from Nagoya the route to Hiroshima lay wide open. So on the seventh day after the disaster, Masuji said goodbye to his landlady and fellow-boarders, put on a straw-boater and a pair of fair-weather clogs, and set out in the direction of Okubo station. Except for minor tremors that shook the telegraph poles lining the tracks from time to time, the long hike went smoothly. More than half a century later, Ibuse wrote in *Ogikubo Chronicles:*

[35] Ibid., p. 36.

On the day I arrived at my birthplace, there was a minor earthquake towards evening. I had gone to bed earlier than the rest of the family, but woke up the very moment the earth shook. Throwing open the shutters, I shot through the verandah and out into the garden. Ours is an old-fashioned country house and the shutters are secured by wooden latches, called *kozaru*. Having lived in Tokyo boarding houses for so many years, there was every reason for me to forget how these carved latches were opened. I couldn't help admiring myself for being able to unlock them instantly in the dark, just by touch. It was dark outside, too. I began washing my feet in the pond nearest the verandah when my mother came out with a candle to give me some light. She laughed and said: 'That quake in Tokyo must have really given you the jitters, if such a tiny tremor makes you run from the house!'[36]

In his native area, major earthquakes are virtually unknown and the massive beams and rafters of the old *minka* so solidly joined together that Masuji really had nothing to fear. And yet even years later, when he was rebuilding his house in Tokyo, he asked the carpenters to use extra strong beams. The fear of earthquakes would remain with Ibuse for the rest of his life, as would a certain fascination with cataclysmic events.

By the end of October, less than two months after the quake, Masuji was back in Tokyo. He would have liked to relax in the peaceful atmosphere of his native place a little longer, but the village was just entering harvest time, and strolling through the countryside during its busiest season is not a popular activity, as

[36] Ibid., p. 49.

Ibuse dryly remarks in *Ogikubo Chronicles*.[37] All *Seiki* members had come through the quake unscathed, although the magazine's entire September issue had been destroyed by the fires. His Waseda friends – Nakayama Gishû, Yokomitsu Riichi, Tominosawa Rintarô and others – who gathered around the *dôjin zasshi* called *Pagoda (Tô)* were all safe and Yokomitsu was even working on a commissioned manuscript.

At this point one of his schoolmates from Shikoku introduced Masuji to another man who thoroughly influenced his writing career: the poet and essayist Tanaka Kôtarô (1880–1941). Tanaka came from a family of hereditary sailors and shipwrights in the Kôchi Bay of Shikoku and had their independent and flamboyant nature. Though he published two literary journals, *Keigetsu* and *Hakurôsa* and wrote several interesting collections of ghost stories (*Kaidan zenshû, Kidan zenshû, Nihon no kaidan*), he was more a capable organizer and a kind of literary mover of his time than an important creative writer. He was extremely sociable and on Masuji's first visit, Tanaka took him to a European restaurant, where he ordered Japanese drinks:

'Let's have a drink. Hey miss, bring us some sake…!' He told me to drink as much as I could, since his credit was good in this restaurant. It didn't take me long to put away a substantial amount of sake and get into a relaxed mood. He too abandoned himself to the drunken mood and said:

'Well, your drinking shows promise. Here, have some more!' I thought it wouldn't do to drink myself into a stupor and collapse on the floor, so I mentioned the

[37] Ibid., p. 55.

precepts of our professor, Mr. Kataguchi, who always stressed restraint in drinking.

'Who cares,' said Tanaka -san, 'such literati are dwarfs.'[38]

When one of the young writers who frequently assembled in Tanaka's sitting room declined a drink, saying formally *'Sensei*, I'd rather abstain today,' Tanaka scolded him, 'A man who doesn't drink sake is no better than a savage.'[39] According to his theory, every man has a heavy load of rocks weighing on his chest that women and children have no way of understanding, and sake is the magic fluid that makes this burden bearable. As in any Japanese art, Tanaka insisted, there is a ritual in drinking that must be observed: 'Remember that the place where you drink is your Hall of Sermons; where sake flows, there is your sanctuary.'[40]

I participated in various drinking parties with Ibuse, either in his house at Ogikubo or in small Tokyo pubs and drinking joints in the country. When we first met in 1966, his drinking habits were already polished like an ancient ceremony. He told me: "You know, I prefer whisky now, since sake is not a fully fermented beverage and gives you a headache." Since then I always brought a bottle of Glenfiddich or Black Label and the same ritual was repeated every time: his wife Setsuyo brought a bowl of pistaccio nuts or green beans, put some ice cubes in a silver container and the sipping of *mizuwari* could start. On another occasion we sat with a larger company in a country *ryokan* in Kôfu (where Ibuse was evacuated during the war) and he arranged

[38] "Keirokushû," p. 288.
[39] IM: "Tanaka Kôtarô sensei no koto." In: *Hito to hitokage,* p. 70.
[40] Ibid.

the seating order himself, saying: "I want to be sure that our drinking has the right kind of rhythm!"

Virtually all of Ibuse's stories and novellas inspired by Shikoku have some connection, direct or indirect, with Tanaka Kôtarô. Even the novella *Tajinko Village* (*Tajinko-mura*, 1939) whose locale is not clearly identified as Shikoku (although Ibuse once mentioned to me that a Shikoku village served as his model) opens with a haiku as its motto: "Rippling waves/ On the ebbtide shore; / Then into the village/ Where the plum's in bloom."[41] We can find this poem in Tanaka's *Collection of Haiku*, even if Ibuse introduces it as "a verse by a certain poet" in the novella. Other directly inspired works are numerous. Next to Ibuse's longer historical works dealing with shipwrecked Tosa sailors like Nakahama Manjirô, later nicknamed John Manjirô during his American adventure, there are the briefer essays and stories in which he relates in more or less fictional form how he researched his background historical material ("Japanese Castaways" or *Nihon hyômin*, "Chôhei from the Desert Island" or *Mujintô Chôhei*, "Chôhei's Grave" or *Chôhei no haka*). There is also the outstanding short story, "Pilgrim's Inn" (*Henrôyado*, 1940) inspired by the traditional pilgrimage to the eighty-eight temples of Shikoku. The route of the pilgrimage ran right by Tanaka's old family house, since its neighbouring building was temple number thirty-two, the *Zenjibuji*.

But even the technical details of seamanship and navigation which create the characteristic documentary accuracy of Ibuse's description in other ocean-going

---

[41] IM: "Tajinko Village." *Lieutenant Lookeast and Other Stories*. Trans. Bester, John. Tokyo, Kôdansha International 1971, p.135.

stories, such as *Usaburô the Drifter* (*Hyômin Usaburô*, 1954) or *Waves: A War Diary* (*Sazanami gunki*) could probably be traced back to Ibuse's long relationship with Tanaka Kôtarô and his native Tosa. The old privateer in *Sazanami gunki*, Miyaji Kotarô, the one literary character whose violent death in the novella Ibuse still regretted years after having written it, resembles Tanaka Kôtarô in more than one way. He is an old-fashioned romantic who cherishes outdated ceremony and the classical antiquity of the East. There is another charming old Kotarô in *Black Rain*, and one wonders if Ibuse, whenever he wanted to present an ideal of "old fashioned humanity" (*mukashi no ningensei*)[42] did not reach for a kind of composite portrayal of his own eccentric grandfather and his older friend Tanaka Kôtarô. Like his namesake in *Sazanami gunki*, Tanaka was an authority on Chinese classics who liked to project the image of a gentleman-poet of old, fond of the moon, pleasant trips in friendly company and sake parties. Yet he knew well that his young protegés couldn't live on sake and moonviewing alone, so he used his numerous connections in literary circles and the publishing business to get them as many part-time jobs, or *arubaito,* as possible. There were few private phone lines then, so when he managed to secure a job, he'd send out a telegram: "Have interesting project, come soon!" (*"Omoshiroi hanashi ari, sugu koi!"*)[43]

Such jobs usually involved a bit of ghost-writing, or a short translation, but sometimes they were fairly

[42] During a trip to the mountains of Shinshû Ibuse asked a cab driver to guess his occupation and the man said: "A money lender? You have an aura of old fashioned humanity..."
[43] "Keirokushû," p. 289.

long, solid research projects such as Tanaka's own dictionary of Chinese compounds and idioms. This project not only provided a year and a half of carefree livelihood for Ibuse, but gave him an opportunity to study Mencius' essays, Confucius' analects and other Chinese classics in depth. His mentor's love and admiration for the great sages and poets of classical China was not lost on the young man and some Japanese critics suggest it is here that we should look for one of the important sources of Ibuse's Eastern identity. Some of these projects took the young writer into the contemporary Western literary world as well. For example, he was asked to do a translation of Hermann Sudermann's naturalistic novel *Katzensteg*, called *Father's Sins* in Japanese.

Tanaka was concerned that Masuji's stories didn't sell, saying: "I know nothing about prose writing and I guess it's time to introduce you to someone who does…!"[44] And so in the fall of 1926 Ibuse met another influential figure of his early career, Satô Haruo. Having made his debut in 1918 with *Rural Melancholy (Den'en no yûutsu)*, a minor classic by now, Satô's position in the literary circle of late Taishô was already firmly established, although he was only six years older than Ibuse. He had a reputation of a refined aesthete and discriminating critic, especially in matters of style. No wonder that Ibuse felt a little intimidated by him and asked a friend, Tomizawa Uio, to accompany him on his first visit to Satô's house.[45] Clutching a clipping from the recently published "Carp" (*Koi*), which would serve as

[44] IM, Kawamori, Yoshizô: „Taidan: sanshôuo made." In: *Hito to hitokage*, p. 329.
[45] Ibid.

his 'calling card' and Tanaka's letter of introduction, Ibuse and his friend arrived at Satô's home. With his *pince-nez* and a pale intellectual's face, Satô – actually a young man of thirty four – already looked like a senior authority. Satô's own son, as rumour has it, put it less reverently when he observed that his father's face resembled a gas-mask. This is how Ibuse recalls him in *Keirokushû*: "When I first met Mr. Satô, I felt he had none of the childish traits of Tanaka-san; there was something forbidding about him..."[46]

Satô used a convenient evaluation technique for other people's writing, not unlike the marking system at school. Very good stories scored around 85 points, and 70–75 corresponded to a 'good B':

When I brought my first manuscript to Mr. Satô and he finished reading it, he said:

'This would get you about 70 points.' I still remember how his wife called him to the phone from the sitting room, just as he had read the first five or six lines; getting up from the chair where he sat in a cross-legged position and stretching his legs, he said: 'This sounds interesting – I'd like to read more.' I was so happy I couldn't sleep when I returned to my boardinghouse that night.[47]

Satô may not have been the easiest man to deal with, but he had the refined literary sensitivity of a first-rate poet and his articulate, lucid criticism made him an extremely valuable tutor to a young writer whose prevailing concern would be the creation of a unique

---

[46] "Keirokushû," p. 290.

[47] Quoted in Nakano, Yoshio: *Gendai no sakka*. Tokyo, Iwanami shoten 1962, p. 136.

personal style: "I learned so much about literature from Mr. Satô. He was the one who taught me the alphabet of style..."[48]

What Ibuse means is that Satô was capable of explaining the finest emotional nuances of a given style in objective, critical terms. Having mastered 'the alphabet of style', Ibuse of course understood that developing his own style would mean a clear realization of the differences between master and pupil. In an interview with Kawamori Yoshizô he points out the difference, while paying homage to his tutor:

> He [Satô] had a remarkably discriminating eye... He could also clearly express in words what he felt... I am unable to express myself in abstract terms, I'd rather use free, living words about such things...[49]

It is not quite true that Ibuse couldn't express himself in abstract terms. Some of his early stories and sketches reveal a remarkable versatility in abstract terms and concepts. What really happened is that Ibuse learned to conceal this aspect of his mind, finding it incompatible with the style and the authorial image he was trying to develop. When Kawamori asked him in the same interview: "Satô's rapport with classical poetry was extraordinary too, wasn't it?"[50]

Ibuse couldn't resist a gentle poke in his revered mentor's rib:

> Yes, but when I came to consult him about a real *affaire de coeur*, I found him a poor mentor in matters other than literature.

[48] Ibid.
[49] Kawamori, Yoshizô: *Sakka no sugao*. Kyôto, Shinshindô 1972, p. 123.
[50] Ibid.

The girl I courted came from a strict household and couldn't be reached either by mail or in person... In my distress, I appealed to Mr. Satô. 'What is the girl like,' he asked. I said 'She is like a pointer, you know, the western dog. Smooth and soft...' 'Well,' replied Satô, 'put a lump of sugar in her mouth and try to kiss her!'[51]

When Ibuse won his first literary award in 1938, the Naoki Prize for *John Manjirô: A Castaway's Chronicle*, Satô was on the committee that voted in favour of his work. He must have believed in his student's talent, although Ibuse later joked about it in a newspaper interview: "I heard that Mr. Satô voted for me, explaining his reason for doing so as: 'Let's give it to Ibuse, he owes money to half the pubs in Tokyo...'"[52]

Seven years prior to the Naoki committee meeting, in the summer of 1931, at a time when not one among the older generation of critics was yet taking Ibuse seriously, Satô Haruo wrote a dense two-page article in *Sakuhin,* called "A Kind of Graceful and Sensitive Mockery" (*Isshû onga naru yûjô kokkei*). A personal letter from a strict but loving teacher rather than an orthodox critique, this short review of Ibuse's collection of short stories (*Shigotobeya*) shows better than anything else Satô's penetrating insight into the nature of Ibuse's artistic endeavour, and his trust in Ibuse's future potential. It may be that Satô's lucid awareness of the categorical difference between art and real life, between aesthetic and political loyalties, helped his pupil to sail safely through the stormy years that en-

[51] Ibid.
[52] Hori, Toshisada: "IM-shi ni kiku: Satô Haruo-shi ni shikararete." In: *Mainichi shinbun.* Nov 10, 1971, p. 5.

sued. As so often happens in Japan, almost overnight the whole *bundan,* or at least its younger members, embarked on a leftist political campaign. It was a time when, as Ibuse recalls, those who did not belong to some leftist group had to "sneak by the roadside like thieves:"[53]

> In 1926, I was invited by former *Seiki* associates and some new members to join a *dôjin zasshi* called *Jintsû jidai.* But the whole group – with the exception of myself – was swayed by a newly arrived militant to join the leftist movement. They even changed the title of our magazine. I was left alone. It was a time when social movements became very popular and the Party of Workers and Peasants was established – and crushed – almost on the same day. In the same year the Japanese Cultural League of the Proletariat was founded, with *Bungei sensen (Cultural Front)* as its central organ. There were some major figures even among the established writers who converted to 'proletarian writing'.
>
> To a nameless young scribbler the whole movement looked rather formidable...[54]

Some of the established writers, most notably Shiga Naoya, could afford to stay aloof from the leftist hysteria and simply stop publishing in the popular *zasshi* for a while. Others, like Tanizaki or Satô, had an instinctive aversion to anything that confused ideology with aesthetic issues. Ibuse may have shared their feelings, but his belated debut and his strained relationship with his family made him very vulnerable to economic pressures. Although he continued to publish in his other

[53] Quoted in Nakano, Yoshio: *Gendai no sakka*, p. 136.
[54] "Hanseiki," pp. 446–447.

*dôjin zasshi, Bungei toshi* which bravely ignored the popular leftism and upheld a high artistic standard, it sold so little that it could hardly have paid any royalties:

> When I became a member of the magazine *Bungei toshi,* published by the Kinokuniya bookstore, the leftist magazine *Senki (Battleflag)* was able to sell about 100 copies a day in their book store. The other leftist organ, *Bungei sensen* sold the same amount in one week. Our *Bungei toshi* which had no leftist orientation, sold barely 15–20 copies a month.[55]

There were of course ample political and economic reasons in post-World War I Japan to give rise to a powerful leftist movement. Postwar inflation had boosted the prices of rice four times higher than they had been before the war, and this in turn caused violent 'rice riots'. Japanese industry had expanded during the war and with increased capital growth, Japanese capitalism in general had become more aggressive not only on the domestic scene, but vis-a-vis foreign markets as well. The epoch-making novelty of the Soviet revolution was not lost on the Japanese intelligentsia, although its attraction reached Japan with the usual delay. Even so, it provided the obvious ready-made model for any kind of effective radical opposition. No wonder that leftism became the 'current of the times' for progressive young intellectuals who found it impossible to ignore the political and economic realities of their time. But why did Ibuse resist the leftist movement so vehemently, even at the cost of severe ostracism by former friends and colleagues?

[55] Ibid.

Was he not sympathetic to the workers' and peasants' cause? How do we reconcile his well-known sympathy for the common people with the stubborn reluctance to support what appeared to be their cause by joining a 'progressive political movement'? First, let's listen to Ibuse himself:

> It wasn't because I was sulking about the current trend that I did not write leftist works. As much as I may have wanted to, there is really no reason why I should have been good at writing ideological stories. I am not only naturally clumsy, I am also fairly lazy, and I know that when you try to integrate a brand new -ism of ordinary life into creative work, you'd have to cast off your old skin as a human being too. And that can't be done without tremendous spiritual courage. Besides, I've never really read *Das Kapital*...[56]

Elsewhere, he attempts to refer to Marx a little more seriously:

> I've tried to read a page or two of Marx's theory of capitalism, but it has little to do with literary theory, don't you think?[57]

The issue is too serious to be discussed in a casual interview, and Ibuse typically prefers to evade it by a light joke. But that does not mean he did not give the conversion to leftism and Marxism itself very serious thought. What he says about shedding one's old skin as a human being brings to mind the eternal dilemma of all revolutions: how to create a 'new human being'. Perhaps it was because he knew the Japanese peasant's mind so well that Ibuse under-

[56] Ibid., 447.
[57] *Hito to hitokage*, p. 330.

stood better than his comrades the basic identity of the common people. He also realized that the urban proletariat in Japan, unlike their counterparts in old industrial countries like France or Britain, consist mostly of people who came to the factories from the countryside. His sympathy for their plight was no less genuine than that of his leftist friends, and yet he was unable to suspend his pragmatic sense of reality and his critical judgment as easily as they did. How deeply, he must have been asking himself, is this imported communist movement and its ideology related to the real existence of the Japanese people? Several stories written in the late twenties reveal how he felt about the leftist movement in greater depth than his memoirs or interviews. In 1930 he published a short story, called "Late Spring" (*Banshun*), which offers a charming critique of ideological rigour. Two striking workers are accused of being strike-breakers, because they climb the fence of the picketed factory to feed dandelions to the rabbits they keep in a shed behind their workshop. In another story from 1930, called "A Letter to Masuji" (*Masuji e no tegami*) he treats the issue even more humorously. The letter of the title was sent to the protagonist by a young relative, a nineteen-year old girl, who is a sophomore at a woman's college. She scolds him for not joining the proletarian literature movement:

'The machines behind the factory window stood still. Only the pale face of a working girl was showing through the glass. She is being exploited, I thought with great fervour, we must rise for her cause, for the cause of her entire class.' (As for Masuji, he thought her turn of phrase was atrocious. She must be scolded when she next shows up.)

'The pale face of the working girl against the gloomy silhouette of the machines in that window! What a theme for a novel by someone like Hayashi Fusao! A writer of his caliber could express my excitement... Why is it that you don't convert to proletarian writing? Only a proletarian writer deserves to be called a true novelist...'[58]

Sure enough, a writer of Hayashi Fusao's caliber did appeal to young people, but as Ibuse correctly recognized, it was the quality of his melodramatic sentiment rather than the impact of his ideology that moved them. His appeal did not diminish in the least when, almost overnight, Fusao the ultra-leftist became Fusao the ultra-nationalist. Ibuse liked the other -ism no more than the first, as his postwar satirical works clearly show. Being aware of the human condition in general and the romantic idealism of youth in particular, Ibuse realized that belonging to a movement– any kind of movement – may have been more important to his fellow Japanese than the proclaimed cause of such a movement. In other words, their motivation may simply have been the search for a lost community rather than the realities of modern political struggle. In *Ogikubo Chronicles,* an eighty-two year old Ibuse looks back at this tendency with mature understanding, saying that people always try to form a group and stick together.

The image of a frolicking group of minnows observed by a lonely salamander from the prison of his dark cave is used in Ibuse's debuting work, "Confinement" (*Yûhei*, 1923). His own self-imposed inner exile

[58] IM: "Masuji e no tegami." In: *IMZ I*. Tokyo, Chikuma shobô 1996, p. 252–253.

must have been lonely, and the continued pressure, not to say harassment of his former friends made it no easier. Time and time again they would come to negotiate, always threatening: this is our last attempt at negotiation. Ibuse even wrote a story in 1928 called "Negotiation" (*Danpan*) and one gathers that these 'negotiations' often resembled a trial of a renegade soldier by a group of Red Brigades rather than a friendly discussion:

> From spring to fall of 1927 I lived on the Hatchô street in Ogikubo, where I rented a room above a sake shop... Four or five of my friends would often come there for 'negotiations'. 'Join the leftist movement, or –', they'd say. I was reading Lao Tzu at that time, but they said: 'Forget about such worm-eaten stuff and become a leftist!' I don't think I really understood Lao Tzu either, but at least he had a soothing effect on my mind. When they ordered me: 'Read Marx,' I pleaded: 'Give me some time to get into the right mood.'[59]

Ibuse had other, more practical things on his mind than the romantic concerns of the proletarian literature movement. In September he moved into his own house in the village of Iogi (present Suginami ward in Ogikubo), a rustic, quiet countryside in those days. In October, his friend and mentor, Tanaka Kôtarô, arranged his marriage with Akimoto Setsuyo, who was to be Ibuse's lifetime companion.

He was nearly thirty years old now, an age when many other writers had written their major works, and a time in an artist's life to take stock of what he had

[59] Quoted in Kumagai, Takashi: *IM. Kôen to taidan*. Tokyo, Hato no mori shobô 1978, p. 203.

116

done so far. Ibuse had written a dozen short stories, several poems, some essays and a few translations, done mostly to earn a living. Less than half a dozen of these stories, e.g. "Plum Blossoms at Night" (*Yofuke to ume no hana,* 1925), "Carp" (*Koi,* 1926) and "Salamander" (*Sanshôuo,* 1929) were later included in Ibuse's collected works. The last two still deserve our critical attention, "Salamander" because it is Ibuse's debuting work and his artistic manifesto which employs a very unusual allegorical technique, "Carp" because it still stands out as the most carefully crafted and the most accomplished piece of writing among his early stories.

### "SALAMANDER"

No other work by Ibuse has received as much critical attention as his debut story "Salamander." For some reason, a brief tale of mere five or six pages has intrigued nearly every Japanese critic, and even many a fellow writer to make a statement about it. For several decades it had been included in high school native literature readers, so that when you mention Ibuse, every Japanese will automatically respond: "Ah, Salamander!" No other Ibuse stories – even the better ones – have been translated into English four times. When the author revised the story's finale in his last *Selected Works* (*Jisen zenshû*), published in 1985–1986, he started a lively public polemic. His readers found it hard to accept the sceptical, even pessimistic tone on which the story now ends. Apart from the obvious importance that every debuting work has in a writer's *oeuvre,* what is the special quality that has made this story so attractive to critics, and indeed to the entire literary audience? First of all, it employs a highly unusual allegorical technique:

The salamander felt sad.

He had tried to leave the cave that was his home, but his head stuck in the entrance and prevented him from doing so. The cave that was now his eternal home had, as this will suggest, an extremely small entrance. It was gloomy, too. When he tried to force his way out, his head only succeeded in blocking the entrance like a cork, a fact which, though an undoubted testimony to the way his body had grown over a period of two years, was enough to plunge him into alarm and despondency.

'What a fool I have been!' he exclaimed.[60]

In Japanese literature and painting, both classical and modern, the technique of personified allegory is extremely rare. Apart from the well-known 12th century scroll called "A Caricature of Birds and Beasts" (*Chôjû giga*) which presents a satirical portrayal of human foibles acted out by monkeys, rabbits and frogs, there is virtually nothing that would correspond to Aesop's fables, or Swift's satirical allegories. The few modern works in this genre, Sôseki's *I am a Cat*, Ibuse's "Salamander" or Akutagawa's *Kappa* are rather an exception to this rule. Perhaps they were conceived by their authors as a conscious reaction to the absence of this genre from their native literature and thus represent an adaptation to Western techniques. But why did Japanese writers and painters in the past avoid allegory? To put it very simply, it was because they felt that every

---

[60] IM: "Salamander." In: *Lieutenant Lookeast*, Trans. Bester, John. Tokyo, New York and San Francisco, Kôdansha International 1971, p. 59.

creature has an authentic existence of its own: humans are humans, animals are animals.

The Japanese have never entertained an anthropocentric view of the cosmos, in which man would be the sole and the ultimate measure of all things. Animals may be useful to humans, yet they have their distinct identity. Older aesthetics, such as Bashô's haiku rules,[61] emphasized that a poet should carefully listen to what flowers and birds have 'to say' about their own life, not impose his will upon them. In older oral literature, such as folk tales and fairy tales, animals do speak in human voices, but this is a genre apart from the tradition of *haute littérature* and could hardly be called allegorical. But even here we can see that not only is the onomatopoeic vocabulary used to approximate animal voices more varied than in most western languages, but many tiny creatures such as insects are given their own stylized voice. In serious classical literature human and animal existence touch upon each other at times, most notably when a man or woman is possessed by a fox or badger. But this is rather the opposite of what we understand as allegory in the West: an animal spirit enters the human frame without giving up any of its bestial characteristics. On the contrary, it is the non-human, the natural spirit that comes to dominate the human mind. So the kind of Aesopian allegory Ibuse employs in this story is very unusual in the context of Japanese 'pure literature'. Why did he reach for this particular technique? First, we might consider what the author himself has to say about the background of the story which first came out under the title "Confinement" (*Yûhei*):

[61] *Matsu no koto wa matsu ni narae, take no koto wa take ni narae.*

119

"Salamander" is the first work among my surviving early attempts. When I was in the second year of Waseda's prep-course, at the age of twenty one, I wrote about seven short pieces ("Dragonfly," "Antlion" etc.) during my summer vacation and sent them to Aoki Nanpachi. They were all about animals and "Salamander" was one of them. In fact, I borrowed its theme from a short story I read at the time, called "The Bet." It was by Anton Chekhov and it impressed me a great deal. I wanted to describe how a human being goes from despair to *satori*, but when I tried to pursue the process of enlightenment, I realized I had nothing to back it up with and the story would result in a didactic explanation. So I gave it up.[62]

Although Chekhov's "The Bet" does not contain a single trace of allegory, it is built on the same central theme of confinement as Ibuse's story. It is an interesting story, though not the most typical for the Russian master's output. Here is its outline: a company of people in the salon of a rich banker discuss whether capital punishment is justified or not. Many are for it and some against, but one young student especially condemns capital punishment in most passionate terms, saying that long term imprisonment, though equally immoral, at least lets you stay alive. The banker teases him: "Would you be willing to prove your conviction by deed and be imprisoned for five years?" "Even fifteen, if it had to be," replies the student and bets two million roubles that he'll spend the next fifteen years in the banker's garden pavillion. He won't be allowed to communicate with a living soul, but he'll have ac-

[62] IM, quoted in Nakano, Yoshio: *Gendai no sakka*, p. 131.

cess to the whole cultural heritage of mankind. The after-dinner joke becomes gruesome reality: the student does spend the next fifteen years in the pavillion, learns to read and write in six languages, reads all the great philosophers of the world and gets acquainted with all the great religious traditions. While reading famous novels, he experiences in his fantasy life great adventures of love. And yet, when the time comes to pocket his money and rejoin the world, where he'll meet real people and love women of flesh and blood, he sits down to his desk and writes the banker a letter in which he gives it all up. When the banker, who in the meantime lost all his money and worries how to pay the huge debt, comes to the cabin, he finds a haggard old man sleeping peacefully on his pallet. He sighs with relief, hides the letter in his pocket and goes to live on his usual unenlightened life.

In the twenties Chekhov was one of the most popular writers in Japan, although most intellectuals read him through the English translations of Constance Garnett. "The Bet" was first translated in 1910, then again in 1920 and last in 1922. Chekhov's plays were also very popular in the New Theatre (*Shingeki*). Another indirect influence may have been an Aesopian fable by the Russian satirist Saltykov-Shchedrin about a newt. Yet even if the Russian stories did provide a degree of literary stimulation, or perhaps a kind of prestigious bouncing board for trying out Ibuse's own variation on the theme, there is the native background and the raw material of his story to be considered. The animal protagonist in the English version of Ibuse's story may look outlandish, and even a little unreal like the mythical unicorn,[63] but in southern Japan there occur as many as fifteen different varieties of salamander (*sanshôuo* or *hanzaki*). The giant salamander of the story, a somewhat grotesque-looking creature that may grow to over one metre, with tiny gold-rimmed eyes in a large head and little paws on a tubular body, used to be a common inhabitant of the marshes, swamps and mountain streams of Ibuse's native area. Nowadays it is an endangered species, though some innkeepers in the fishing lodges of the Chûgoku range keep them in pools or live-wells around the house to increase the attraction of their place. When young Masuji attended the *Seishikan* high school in Fukuyama, one of his teachers kept two of these salamanders in a shallow pond of the school yard, and the boys often fed frogs to them. In *Hanseiki*, Ibuse recalls in considerable detail how he and one of his schoolmates once quarrelled about the salamander's eating habits. The other boy, an expert fisherman and naturalist, later wrote a book about this and other experiences of their youth:

> In 1968 Miyahara published a collection of his essays about fishing, called *Ashida River*. In a chapter, entitled "Salamander" (*Hanzaki*) he writes about the pond of the school garden beside our penmanship room, where the salamanders were kept. He also describes how we fed

---

[63] In the Western literary tradition, the salamander is often associated with fire, e.g. in the *Autobiography of Benvenuto Cellini* we read: "Happening to look into the fire, he spied in the middle of those most burning flames a little creature like a lizard, which was sporting in the intensest coals... that lizard which you see in the fire is a salamander, a creature which has never been seen before by any one of whom we have credible information." Trans. Symonds, John A. New York, Garden City Publishing 1932, pp. 7–8. There is also Karel Čapek's famous political allegory called *War with the Newts*, written in 1936. In this novel the newts or salamanders are far more humanized than in Ibuse's story.

'earth-frogs' to them. Once I came there, he says (using different characters, Ibuki, to give my name a fictional slant) and claimed that when a salamander gets hold of something, he won't let go even if thunder should strike. And so started our quarrel: will he or won't he let go?[64]

It is interesting to note that not only does this youthful experience contain the various natural characteristics of the principal character of the later story, but also those of his prey, the frog. It is personified in the story as the salamander's 'prisoner' – of which he wouldn't let go no matter what – and finally his companion. Furthermore, there is an interesting co-incidence between the student's bet in the Russian story, and the bet-like quarrel between the two Japanese students. According to his classmate, Miyahara, Masuji lost the argument. When the boys tested the salamander's tenaciousness by offering him a frog on a sturdy fishing line during a severe thunderstorm, they found that indeed he wouldn't let go no matter what happened around him. Yet when they examined the animal's 'peach-coloured mouth' closely, they realized that the reason why it wouldn't let go of its prey was mainly because its jaws were lined with row after row of sharp, indented teeth. Rather than being tenacious, it was naturally unable to release its catch. In any case, Ibuse mentions in *Hanseiki* how this experience influenced his debuting work:

> Later, during my learning years at the Waseda Litera-
> ture Department, I wrote a short piece of fiction on this
> subject. I wrote it being constantly aware of the body
> structure of the salamander to which we used to feed

[64] "Hanseiki," pp. 413–414.

frogs with Miyahara, and its comical, laggard features. This animal, sometimes called a living fossil, can stay alive without eating anything for one or two years. Leeches are like that, too. But a salamander, when he gets too starved, may endure by eating his own fingers. This too I kept in mind when I was writing the story.[65]

But on examining the story's last published version, we find surprisingly little naturalistic detail in the salamander's description. A careful comparison of "Confinement" (*Yûhei*, 1923) with "Salamander" (*Sanshôuo*, 1929) further reveals that the earlier text did contain such information, e.g. "During the two and a half years he [the salamander] only ate two frogs and five killifish. One frog a year was more than enough for him."[66] In "Confinement," such straightforward descriptive passages are followed by sentences of abstract contemplation that abound with standard intellectual vocabulary. Instead of saying 'meet with disaster' (*osoroshii me ni au*) Ibuse used the Sino-Japanese compound *osoroshii me ni sôgû suru* or 'encounter disaster'. In the same sentence, words like *kannen* (idea), *kyôkun* (precept) are used, providing contrast between the precisely observed naturalistic detail of the story's setting and the tortuous, ironic expression of an intellectual consciousness. What Ibuse attempts to do in this story is to detach himself from all prescribed models of 'good writing'. Like every beginning artist, he had to work in a certain context, absorbing some stylistic techniques of the past and at the same time trying to transcend them and create his own style. The

[65] Ibid., pp. 415–416.
[66] IM: "Yûhei." *IMZ I*. Tokyo, Chikuma shobô 1996, pp. 5–10.

prestigious models of writing Ibuse had to cope with were the authentic and highly expressive, if fairly private and sentimental, narrative style of the I-novelists (many of whom were ardent believers in Naturalism as well), the finely observed natural detail of a style called *shaseibun* (nature-sketching) and the overall dictates of 'elegant prose' or *bibun,* a tradition that favoured hazy melancholy over modern satire and the resigned, genteel sigh over the bold intellectual caricature that is so characteristic of these early stories by Ibuse.

Ibuse once remarked, half in jest, that literature is a skillful telling of lies. No doubt he was reacting to the naturalists' obsession with 'Truth' and their neglect of stylistic refinement. Although not a romantic himself, Ibuse would have wholeheartedly agreed with Izumi Kyôka's critique of the naturalists' style:

> The naturalists, who say that stylistic technique is unnecessary if only one portrays the 'Truth', are like an archer who attempts to strike the bull's-eye, not by notching the arrow and taking aim with the bow, but by clutching the arrow in his hand and crawling to the target and thrusting it in...[67]

Like most young artists of his generation, Ibuse had experienced a fair share of misery and youthful torment. But his disillusionment with the leftist movement and with the fickleness of his literary friends, even his despair about human affairs in general, was never allowed to take the conventional form of the sentimental lament so typical for the *watakushi shôsetsu* school. Rather than an I-novelist's lament Ibuse presents an

---

[67] Izumi, Kyôka: "Romanchikku to shizenshugi." In: *Izumi Kyôka zenshû XXVIII.* Tokyo, Iwanami shoten 1989, p. 686.

ironic self-portrait. We know that he had described himself as "naturally clumsy, and fairly lazy." As a young man he may have felt a little more plump than he should have been to cut a stylish image, and so in a way the salamander became a caricaturized expression of the artist's basic self-perception. Yet just as the salamander – plump, awkward and ponderous as he may look to the outsider – the young writer felt himself part of the Southern scenery. He did not realize it yet, but in time he would become a landmark of his birthplace no less unique than the salamander. We do recognize, of course, more than one satirical poke at his former friends in the story's imagery. Japanese critics often point it out, usually quoting the following passage:

Large numbers of killifish (*medaka*) seemed to enjoy swimming in and out between the stalks of the duckweed, for there was a shoal of them in the forest of stalks, all trying their hardest not to be carried away by the current. The whole shoal would veer to the right, then to the left. Whenever one of them veered to the left by mistake, the majority, of one accord, also veered to the left for fear of being left behind. Should one of them be forced by a stalk to veer to the right, all the other little fish without exception veered to the right in his wake. It was therefore extremely difficult for any of them to make off by himself and leave.

Watching the little fish, the salamander could not help sneering at them.

'What a lot of excessively hidebound fellows,' he thought.[68]

[68] "Salamander," pp. 60–61.

What is important to realize here, is that the original has: *"Nan to iu fujiyû senban na yatsura de arô!"* This means literally "what a lot of extremely (or excessively) *unfree* fellows." Of course *fujiyû* could be translated as: 1. inconvenient; 2. wanting, being in need; 3. being disabled. But I don't think that, in the given context, it means any of the three. 'Hidebound', as John Bester renders it has a connotation of narrowminded, unyielding in opinion; and this undoubtedly fits the leftists' description. Yet one wonders if Ibuse is not trying to say, above all, that the salamander laughs at these group-oriented creatures because they lack freedom. The salamander is physically even less free than the minnows, his only freedom being that of the mind. Less pessimistic than Sartre's 'no exit' situation and his basic understanding of human relationships as *"L'enfer ce sont les autres,"* Ibuse's symbolic representation of the human condition in this story seems to suggest that ideal freedom – perhaps even the Western existentialist's 'freedom of choice' – is an illusion. One is either trapped within a social group and its limited consciousness, or in the cave of individual loneliness.[69] The only way out is a resigned acceptance of the given situation, and perhaps the possibility of capturing a companion to share one's misery. Modern and unusual as the story may look in terms of style and treatment, its sceptical conclusion points to several cultural constants, such as the Buddhist philosophy of mellow resignation (*akirame*), the 'retreat within' and the

[69] A Western reader will associate the story's cave-outside reality conflict with the well-known episode from Plato's *Republic,* where a man trapped in a cave sees shadowy reflections of the real world on its walls.

generally sceptical Oriental view of romantic, idealized relationships.

The progressive development of the story from "Confinement" to "Salamander" suggests a kind of intensifying dialogue between Ibuse the sentimentalist and Ibuse the sceptic. The two points of view are still expressed in "Salamander," though in a stylized and carefully controlled form. The salamander's viewpoint is a more direct and personal one (although he is described in third person), while the narrator's constantly objectifies his experience. We might add that a third point of view is implicitly present, though not expressed, namely the author's. It manipulates the two viewpoints and carefully controls the story's different stylistic devices:

1. The style of literal translation (*chokuyaku buntai*):
When a western work of literature is closely translated into Japanese, the natural flow of the native sentence stiffens and a somewhat forceful relationship between the subject and the object of the sentence must be hammered out by using personal pronouns more often than they'd be used in a 'Japanese' sentence, e.g. *kare wa kare no sumika de aru...* Also, the various parts of a sentence are forced into a more logical syntactic order by a series of conjunctions.

It is precisely the most ponderous-sounding sentences in the story's English version that have originally been conceived as a deliberate caricature of the 'translation style':

When he tried to force his way out, his head only succeeded in blocking the entrance like a cork, a fact which, though an undoubtable testimony to the way his body had grown over a period of two years, was enough to plunge him in alarm and despondency.[70]

> *Sore wa maru ninen no aida ni kare no karada ga hatsuiku shita shôko ni kosowanatta ga, kare wo rôbai sase katsu kanashimaseru ni wa jûbun de atta no da.*

While in the original the deliberate clumsiness of this style conveys to the reader an almost physical feeling of the salamander's ponderous, laggard movements, one wonders if any of this effect communicates through the English text. Furthermore, the comic, and sometimes nearly grotesque exaggeration of diction ensures that the story will not slip into the stereotyped wailing tone of the *watakushi shôsetsu*:

> *Nan taru shissaku de aru koto ka!*

*Nan taru* is an archaic way of saying 'what a' and *shissaku* is an unusual, bookish variation of *shippai* (failure). So rather than "What a fool I have been!" as John Bester renders it,[71] trying to make sense of the original's idioyncrasies, the original Japanese sounds more like "T'is a most unfortunate predicament..."

## 2. Scientific terminology:

Some passages in the story sound like descriptions from a botanical encyclopedia:

> ...the hair moss had dainty flowers on the ends of its very slender, scarlet carpophores. The dainty flowers formed dainty fruit which, in accordance with the law of propagation among cryptogams, shortly began to scatter pollen.[72]

[70] "Salamander," p. 59.
[71] Ibid.
[72] Ibid., p. 60.

Although we still find a touch of lyricism here – "the dainty flowers formed dainty fruit" – or in Japanese *"karen na hana wa karen na mi wo musubi,"* the overall tone is dry, precise, even 'scientific'. Comparing the text of "Confinement" with that of "Salamander," it soon becomes obvious that the first is more of a 'felt description', while the second is closer to an 'observed description'. Consequently, a passage in "Salamander" is introduced with the verb *nagameru* (to observe, look intensely) and whereas "Confinement" simply has *"hana o motagete iru"* or 'raising blossoms', the "Salamander" passage ends with the visual emphasis of *"hana o nozokasete iru"* or, literally "displaying blossoms, making them peep out."

"Confinement" still abounds with conventional devices of lyrical description, e.g. the hazy magic of "in the depths of the stream," the poetic repetition of adjectives (slender, slender), the sentimental simile of children's kitestrings on New Year's day, the combination of *yukkuri to nobite*, etc. In "Salamander," the "stream's depths" simply becomes "bottom of the water" (*suitei*), the adjective slender (*hosoi*) is not repeated, the simile is dropped altogether, and "stretching leisurely" (*yukkuri to nobite*) becomes "stretching in a straight line" (*itchokusen ni nobite*). Saying *yukkuri to nobite* of course amounts to projecting the observer's human affection onto a 'neutral' natural object, just as comparing it to a man-made, emotionally charged thing, such as "the children's kitestrings on New Year's day" transfers a part of that emotional aura onto it. The writer really has no way of knowing if the duckweed stalks stretch leisurely (*yukkuri*) or otherwise. Similarly, as his imaginative eye looks up from the riverbed, out of the vast number of other possible similes, the ready-made tool of the "kitestrings" simile offers itself to convey the cool world of the underwater flora with a certain affective warmth. There is only one somewhat emotionally tinged word in the entire "Salamander" passage, namely the adjective *hogarakana*, or cheerful, as Bester renders it, but it modifies a fairly literary and abstract sounding Chinese compound, *hatsuiku* (growth) which absorbs its implied 'warmth'.

So it seems the young artist resented any cultural programming, rejecting a mechanical acceptance of his literary heritage, as much as his modern European counterpart would. Though not exactly reaching what Barthes calls 'writing degree zero', or Robe–Grillet's detached visual coldness, Ibuse did achieve by this stylistic shift a certain cooling of the observed objective world and detached it from the traditional affective fallacy of the lyrical eye. The many scientific terms he uses, such as *carpophores* and *cryptogamia* are not only well suited to convey such an effect, they also give the reader a sense of stylistic novelty, for no other Japanese writer had used them for natural description before Ibuse.

3. The surprising usage of Chinese compounds (*kanjukugo*):
Japanese critics generally divide their literature into two large stylistic mainstreams: the masculine and the feminine tradition of writing. The first is characterized by dry, terse 'Chinese' diction and syntax, relies more on Chinese character and phrase, and was practised by

men ranging from the classical *zuihitsu* writers like Yo-shida Kenkô and Kamo no Chômei to modern authors such as Mori Ôgai and Shiga Naoya. The feminine tradition, established primarily by the Heian court ladies in their diaries and *monogatari,* relied on the mellifluous sound of long *yamatokotoba* (native Japanese polysyllabic words), a rather hazy syntax and a lyrical blend of the inner and the outer landscape. Although this style has its outstanding modern followers among male writers, most notably Kawabata Yasunari, Ibuse has from the very beginning of his writing career adhered to the former school. But whereas Mori Ôgai will use Chinese characters in a fairly straightforward, serious way, his major concern being an exact expression of his ideas and his view of the hard objective world, one feels that in Ibuse's early stories the difficult *kanji* compounds do not always fit their context. While retaining their usual weight and terse precision, these Chinese compounds are often placed in such a way that they are given a slight twist, or a little shift in meaning. To feel the subtle nuance of such a shift is difficult, if not impossible for a non-native reader:

> He [Ibuse] will unexpectedly use a Chinese compound that does not quite fit into the normal flow of the sentence, and the resulting feeling of a break gives the passage a strange sense of reality... None of these phrases is particularly hard to understand by itself, and yet they do not fit into the given context. In each case there is a slight divergence of the Chinese word's usual weight from its context... When the reader focusses his eye on the Chinese compounds, a fairly 'heavy' world emerges. But when he shifts his eye to the [images] they convey,

he finds himself in a light, personified world. And so by alternating the light-heavy effect these expressions give the text an unusual appeal.[73]

We could liken the ironic effect of using such high-flown literary words in an ordinary situation to saying in English abscond himself or evacuate the premises instead of simply "make off by himself and leave" as Bester translates *"tonsô shite iku."* The comical effect of stilted or bureaucratic language often comes from just such a pompous use of words. But in Japanese, there is the added impact of the Chinese character as a visual icon. Thus the particular Sino-Japanese word will not only sound unusual in the given context, it will *look* unusual as well.

As a young artist's manifesto, the story codified Ibuse's rejection of the Romantic mode. It helped to assert his own sceptical view of life and establish a detached narrative voice. The cool third-person narration, focussed on a grotesque, animal other not only allowed a radical caricature of self, but enabled a bold stylistic experimentation with existing norms of nature description and current modes of expressing the self.

### "CARP"

In 1931, Kobayashi Hideo wrote a brief essay on Ibuse's short stories, singling out "Carp" (*Koi*, 1926) as one of the author's best stories:

> In *Plum Blossom by Night* (*Yofuke to ume no hana*) there is a little story, called "Carp." I think it is one of his masterpieces. This short work of a few pages, written in one flowing

---

[73] Makibayashi, Kôji: "Sanshôuo." In: *IM kenkyû*. Isogai, Hideo Ed. Hiroshima, Keisuisha 1984, p. 240.

sweep of the brush, is so tightly constructed that not a single character is wasted; if I were to sum up here what it is about or point to this or that episode in it, I would have to quote the whole story.[74]

These were the first words of genuine praise for Ibuse by an influential Japanese critic. As usual, Kobayashi's instinct was right. It is an important story, one that offers a key to the dense symbolism of Ibuse's later works. His craft was still in the making and the seams and stitches that will be skillfully concealed in mature stories can be detected here by a careful eye. Western readers usually perceive the story as a 'charming little tale' or as a young writer's naive *esquisse*. The colloquial simplicity of Ibuse's language encourages such a casual reading, especially in the English translation, where many delicate nuances and subtle tensions between words blur or disappear altogether. The story opens with the flowing sentence "For more than a dozen years past, I have been troubled by a carp." (*"Sude ni jûikunen mae kara watakushi wa ippiki no koi ni nayamasarete kita"*), followed by "The carp was given to me in my student days by a friend, Nanpachi Aoki (deceased some years ago)" (*"Gakusei jidai ni yûjin Aoki Nampachi – sennen shikyo – ga… watakushi ni kore wo kureta"*)[75] The alternation of smooth, colloquial Japanese with the terse, staccato brevity of Chinese compounds is a characteristic device of Ibuse's, and there is little the translator can do about it. But he must watch for the

[74] Kobayashi, Hideo: "IM no sakuhin ni tsuite." In: Kawamori, Yoshizô: *Ibuse san no yokogao.* Tokyo, Yayoi shobô 1993, pp. 121–122. Also in *Kobayashi Hideo zenshû IV.* Tokyo, Shinchôsha 1967, p. 33.

[75] IM: "Koi." In: *IMZ I.,* p. 12.

emotional nuances of words, e.g., "troubled by a carp" for *"ippiki no koi ni nayamasarete kita"* might better have been rendered as "haunted by a carp." Neither does "far away in a pond in the country near his home" for *"yohodo tôi zaisho no ike"* do justice to the poetic intensity of the word *zaisho*. It is one of Ibuse's favourite words and his readers know his celebrated translation[76] of Li Po's poem built around the emotional appeal of this word. It combines the flavour of *inaka, furusato, kokyô,* and yet is simpler and lighter than any of them. Perhaps the peculiar aura of words like *zaisho* must remain in the original. But when the translator does: *"watakushi wa hakurankai no Taiwankan de, daishô nijûyonko no hana wo tsuketa shaboten o katte…"*[77] ("I bought a cactus with twenty-four blossoms, large and small, in the Taiwan pavilion at the exhibition"), as "I decided I would buy a cactus in the Formosan pavilion at the exhibition…,"[78] he is withholding crucial aesthetic information. It even makes a difference when Ibuse spells cactus as *shaboten* instead of *saboten*[79] and of course a plant that flowers sparsely having twenty-four blossoms makes it as rare a present as the white carp and certainly more exotic. Similarly inadequate is the translation of *oshiruko-iro no bôshi* as "brown student's cap." Not only does it misinform western readers unaware

[76] *Nokiba no tsuki wo miru ni tsuke zaisho no koto ga ki ni kakaru.*
[77] "Koi," p. 14.
[78] IM: "Carp." In: *Lieutenant Lookeast.* Trans. Bester, John. Tokyo and Palo Alto, Kôdansha International 1971, p. 92.
[79] *Saboten* is the standard approximation of the original Spanish *sapoten* (cactus). *Shaboten* is the colloquial southern (mainly Okinawa) pronunciation. Using it gives the word a homey flavour, 'warming' it up and reminding the reader of the plant's native place.

that Japanese students' caps are *black* when new, it also diminishes the aesthetic value of the image: we will see later the importance of the contrast between the fading, reddish cloth of Aoki's cap and the white-wood coffin on which it rests.

The story is 'slight', and the author himself admits that it was written in one sleepless night;[80] rather than a short story, it is a prose-poem, a text of poetic rather than prosaic intensity. And this is precisely what makes the critic's job so difficult: with a heavier, more obviously dramatic story, one might discuss themes and conflicts, symbolic meanings and chains of imagery even in their translated form. Not with "Carp". One soon finds that in English even the story's title becomes too pale a reflection of the original "Koi" (carp) which has a significant *double entendre* of *koi*, love. Just as the two meanings blend inseparably in the auditory aspect of the title-word, the story's theme is not love alone. The carp is so clearly focussed and has so much presence throughout the story that it is more than a prosaic image. One is tempted to call it a theme in itself. But how do the two themes relate? Do they exist in the story to make each other possible? If so, what kind of symbolic relationship do they have?

Approaching the carp as a cultural and literary symbol, one soon gathers the obvious data: there is the Boys' Festival (*tango no sekku*) with *koinobori*, the paper-cloth streamers hoisted for each son in the family and symbolizing will, strength, health, and long life. The story itself is about boys, and the carp's robust health stands in sharp contrast with Aoki's fragility and short

[80] Ban, Toshihiko: "Ibuse san kara kiita koto." In: *Geppô 3, IMZ IX*, p. 2.

life, suggesting a kind of animistic exchange. Rather than a mere symbol of the boys' friendship, the carp almost becomes Aoki and the protagonist refuses to share this living embodiment of his dead friend with anybody, least of all with Aoki's girlfriend.

As a literary symbol, the carp appears in earlier works, such as the Chinese-inspired "The Carp that Came to My Dream" (*Muô no rigyo*) by Ueda Akinari, and in several modern works. In such stories, the fish often becomes the abode of the human soul, acquiring spiritual connotations similar to the early Christian symbolism of fish as spirit, or as the cryptic signature of the 'Fisher of Men' himself.

Yet this kind of first-level symbolic analogy stands out so clearly from the smooth texture of the story "Carp" that one wonders: was it not deliberately placed there to discourage the reader from precisely that kind of 'symbolic reading' and lead him on to subtler levels? Ibuse is a clever writer, and his *naïveté* is a skillful illusion, rather than spontaneous simplicity. Far from being a naive youthful sketch, the story is a subtle polemic tackling of some technical problems in symbolism which confronted Ibuse as a young artist. Needless to add, it is an artist's polemic – not a critic's – and as such may be partially unconscious.

That he considered different symbolic modes and gave some thought to the then fashionable symbolist movement is apparent from Ibuse's own reflections on the genesis of this story:

> I wonder what kind of influence made me write so many animal stories? It must have been the symbolism then in vogue both in poetry and painting. I just wanted to try

my hand at it. When I look at my attempts today, I think they were too serious and all failures.[81]

As we saw, Ibuse's unpublished early stories were all about animals or insects (e.g., *Tamamushi wo miru, Arijigoku, Yanma*) and so is his well-known debut story "Salamander,"[82] conceived some time before "Carp". The last of this 'animal series', that kept his interest for about ten years, is "Sawan on the Roof" (*Yane no ue no Sawan*) written in 1929. From the early sketches that were probably exercises in *shaseibun*, Ibuse's interest moves briefly towards allegory in "Salamander" and then towards an effective compromise between Western and native symbolic modes in "Carp" and "Sawan on the Roof."

At first glance, the imagery of these two stories recalls the symbolist poets' favourite trappings: death, exotic flowers, water-birds, fish and water, 'the mirror of the soul' itself. Both in Ibuse's remarks on "Carp" and in the story proper, we find conscious and unconscious reactions to French art, or more precisely the influence of the mood of French symbolism. Again, Ibuse's likes and dislikes are obviously not systematic, and he refers to artists like Cézanne and Flaubert, who had little to do with this symbolist mood. Edmund Wilson calls Flaubert's novels "masterpieces of this second period of modern classicism,"[83] and the same description could be applied to Cézanne at his best. It is both men's struggle to "hear, see and feel with the

---

[81] Ibid.

[82] The actual debut was "Confinement" (*Yûhei*, 1923) but for convenience's sake, I am referring to the later revised title.

[83] Wilson, Edmund: *Axel's Castle*. New York, Charles Scribner's Sons 1969, p. 8.

delicate senses of Romanticism... [while] disciplining and criticizing the Romantic temperament,"[84] that must have appealed to young Ibuse. He describes in great detail the place he wrote the story, and reveals the inspiration of a number of its images:

> When you passed the gate of that temple [*Seikanji*], you came to a house for rent by a bluff, cut out of the ground when the old cemetery was cleared. That's where I wrote "Carp". From the bluff you could see the pool at Waseda, and the skulls that kept coming out of the ground. I wrote it through one sleepless night... After adding the final scene on the diving board, I published the story in *Mita bungaku*. The swallows that skim the surface of the pool – that's straight fact. The scene by the pool, with the big compound leaf tree, is like the one in Cézanne's picture [*The Bathers*]. I was writing it with that picture in my mind. The opening line – 'For more than a dozen years past' – is a distortion. In fact, I wrote the story just one year after Aoki's death. My fascination with Flaubert shows in the passage about hanging handkerchiefs to dry on the railing outside the windows of the boarding-house, when Aoki brought the carp. At that time I worked in a publishing house called Shuhôkaku and felt very low for some reason. Yet this is the one line I'd like to change...[85]

Not surprisingly for someone who almost graduated from the Department of French literature at Waseda, Ibuse's awareness of French writing as well as French painting is quite pronounced. His remark about the skulls suggests an interesting coincidence

[84] Ibid., p. 11.
[85] Ban, p. 2.

– in their explorations of Death, the early symbolist poets fell in love with one particular image: Hamlet contemplates the skull of his dead friend Yorick. Of course, the image soon became a cliche; perhaps in the whiteness of the carp, we can glimpse a double suggestion: a direct one of the skulls at the *Seikanji* that coloured Ibuse's perception of the Waseda pool, as well as an indirect, ironic one of the poetic convention itself. The remark about Flaubert's influence on the handkerchief scene indicates how much Ibuse admired the French master's precision in selecting the one telling, concrete detail.[86] Yet aiming at a similar effect does not necessarily bring similar results, and Ibuse's later displeasure with this line would suggest that he realized how little is needed to shift a story's mood from a stylized and detached account of self into the restrictive, self-centred Romantic mode, or in other words, back into the context of the *watakushi shôsetsu*.

These seemingly casual reflections about how the story was made reveal the care and attention that went into its every line. Particularly interesting is the connection between the pool-scene at Waseda and Cézanne's *Bathers*. Ibuse calls the picture *suiyoku* (bathing) which makes its identification a bit difficult: bathing men and women was a life-long subject of Cézanne's and he painted many variations on it. Some of these tableaux are called *Baigneurs* (men bathers), others *Baigneuses*, such as his largest and best known *Women Bathers*, painted between 1898 and 1905. One is tempted to draw a

---

[86] A male student, especially before the war, would not have washed most of his linen. Yet hanging out a towel or handkerchief to dry on the railing is a kind of first personal touch to a new *ryokan* or boarding-house.

direct parallel between the softly stylized bodies of Cézanne's *Bathers* and Ibuse's young swimmers at the Waseda pool. But at closer examination, we find that there is no "big compound leaf tree" in the tableaux depicting male bathers. By contrast, the triangular, more formal composition of the painting of women bathers is always closed off by inclined trees. According to Meyer Schapiro, the different composition is significant:

> … these two conceptions originate in different feelings about the subjects. The male nudes go back to an important part of Cézanne's boyhood to which he often returned in memory: the enchanted days spent with Zola and other friends on the bank of the river, swimming, playing, talking and reciting verses – verses in which women were the objects of romantic fantasy.[87]

Cézanne tried to free himself from a certain anxiety about women by transposing his early erotic themes onto less disturbing 'classic' objects, constrained and enclosed by very formal composition. And yet, "something of the original anxiety is reflected in the arbitrariness and intensity of the means of control."[88]

Ibuse might have had *Women Bathers* in mind when he wrote "Carp"; it might also have been an earlier painting called *Baigneurs et Baigneuses* (1892) which is also closed-off by inclined trees. Although it is called "men and women bathing," the bodies of the bathers – male and female – are very much alike, almost androgynous as their bluish liquid contours softly merge with the blue-green background of water and

[87] Schapiro, Meyer: *Paul Cézanne. The Library of Great Painters*. New York, Harry N. Abrams, 1962, p. 116.
[88] Ibid.

leaves. So there is more to this than an interesting coincidence. Ibuse must have been attracted to Cézanne because something basic in the Frenchman's temperament struck a deep chord within him: we can detect a similar tone of anxiety about women in many an Ibuse story. The innocent love between the two boys in "Carp" is of the same light fabric as those 'enchanted' days spent by Cezanne with his friends by the river. Aoki's girlfriend – not a romantic fantasy anymore – brings a disquieting note into this relationship. Just like Cézanne, Ibuse feels the mysterious connection between water and woman's erotic attraction and, like the French painter, he employs a similar 'classic' restraint and formal stylistic means to control these forces. In this, he departs from the romantic to go beyond the symbolist mode. An awareness of symbolism is always there, but his concrete imagery has a tendency to give it an ironic slant. Thus, to the orthodox symbolist poet, water would have been the ideal mirror of his soul and fish messengers connecting two realms – the visible world of things and the unseen world of the soul. We might even think of the symbolist perception of reality as "a literature in which the visible world is no longer a reality, and the unseen world no longer a dream"[89] as being reflected in the spatial structure of this story. After all, the carp does connect reality and dream.

We might stretch the interpretation of the story's poetic space and the carp's travel through it a bit further yet and find that the carp is a very fitting symbol

[89] Symons, Arthur: *The Symbolist Movement in Literature.* New York, E. P. Dutton and Co. 1958, pp. 2–3.

of the symbolic mode itself as Carlyle defines it: "In a symbol, there is concealment and yet revelation: hence therefore, by Silence and by Speech acting together, comes a double significance."[90]

Whenever the carp comes up into the visible world, it makes communication between the characters possible – it becomes *speech* in the most essential sense of the word. And when it sinks into depth, there is *silence*.

But rather than abstract 'water', we will note that Ibuse deals with different kinds of water as the carp moves from country to town, from garden pond to university pool. One might say that the carp's moves represent the story's emotional 'movements', its shifting moods:

1. *Zaisho no ike:* serious, lyrical
   (pond in the country house)
2. *hyôtan no katachi wo shita ike:* dirtiness of city existence
   (the gourd-shaped pond)
3. *koibito no ie no sensui:* dramatic conflict
   (the pond in the girlfriend's garden)
4. *Waseda daigaku no pûru:* lonely, sad, scherzo, lively
   (the pool at Waseda).

There is a suggestion of an even more essential difference between the murky water of the ponds and the clean, transparent water of the metallic washbasin where the carp is kept during its brief visits to the airy world: "The carp sank deep into the pool, together with the water from my basin." This brief line gives one the feeling of two 'realities' touching each other,

[90] Ibid., p. 2.

or of common, profane time being absorbed by the inner space of 'sacred time'. In this respect, the parallel between Ibuse's waters and the inner, unseen world of the symbolists would seem to hold: these various water surfaces do 'mirror the heart' but there is a substantial distance between water and heart, unlike their lyrical union in Verlaine's famous verse, *"Il pleut dans mon coeur."* The carp is swimming not only in the protagonist's heart, it has also a separate existence in its own element: each of the four ponds reflects a more complicated condition than that of *'mon coeur'*. At each point, the water rather seems to reflect the total mood of all involved while the carp becomes the visible focus of their relationship as it emerges from the water. Using a musical metaphor, we might say the carp is the *leitmotif* with which the various 'instruments' of the piece call and touch each other.

Yet the carp is also very much itself, for the author carefully circumscribes his narrative viewpoint by the dividing line between water and air. He does not follow the carp into the water's depth where it is on its own, out of the author's reach. Deep down, it 'means' something different to itself and its fellow creatures – perhaps there it is a king swimming at the head of a procession of smaller fish. It is free and yet it is not – there is a man sitting by the pond who tries to catch it again. Note that it takes eight days and a very special kind of bait – a silkworm grub – to hook the carp.

Fishing for a fitting *correspondance*[91] or 'objective correlative' would probably require less patience. What

---

[91] *Correspondances*, originally the title of Baudelaire's poem; later used as critical term for subtle parallels between the soul and the objective world.

makes the analogy really interesting is Ibuse's respect for the reality of things, e.g., his care in selecting the only kind of bait – *harugo no sanagimushi* – that the carp will take at this time of the year. Or perhaps I should say his respect for the reality of relationships between things, because neither separate, isolated objects nor the subject-object dualism constitute reality to Ibuse. Everything is connected and yet separate at the same time, free to follow its own will and yet always dependent on other wills.

And so we are back to the fundamentals of the Japanese mind. Why then go through the whole tortuous argument? Why not stay with the native animism which would expect Aoki's *tama* (soul) to enter the carp and would regard the carp's fetish-like importance to the protagonist as the most natural thing in the world? And if we must discuss symbols, why not apply Konishi's theory of 'tenorless' or Zen symbolism?

> The image in Zen creates a spiritual focus by means of which the self is united to the object of the image. For instance, in the typically terse phrase "willows: green, flowers: red" there is no attempt to explicate the meaning of the images. They are simply set forth, evoking the deeply felt greenness of the willows and the redness of the flowers – and the spiritual experience of being one with these things.[92]

Could not the whole story be summed up in two words – *carp: white*? The answer to all three questions is yes and no. First, just as his intelligence prefers a cer-

---

[92] Konishi, Jin'ichi: "Japanese Literary Studies in Japan." Mimeographed paper presented at the Conference on the Status of Studies in Japanese Literature. New York, American Council of Learned Societies, SSRC 1969. p. 4.

tain distance from murky waters, Ibuse's mind seldom plunges blindly into ancient animistic feelings. He is aware of them, but more often than not in a gently ironic way: "I made up my mind to write a letter to Aoki's girl. (I reproduce it here in full, lest Aoki's spirit should misinterpret my motives.)"[93] Second, even if we managed to discard Ibuse's ideas about symbolism and Western artists as the self-conscious statement that is more common in bohemian bars than in the writer's study, there are too many images in the story itself pointing to various conventions of western art. Take the following passage:

> The carp was still as white as ever, and no thinner. But there were transparent parasites lodged on the tip of its fins. Carefully I removed them, then filled a metal basin with cold water and put the carp in it. I covered it with a fig leaf... many times I took the fig-leaf in my fingers and tentatively lifted it. Each time, the carp was opening and closing its mouth, breathing easily and peacefully.[94]

There is something soft and tender, almost 'naked' about the carp as it breathes peacefully in its basin, covered by a fig-leaf. But the function of the fig-leaf as a 'cover of nudity' is a purely Western convention – Japanese painting does not know it at all. Rather than a coincidence, I would say this is a playful reflection of the Western convention.

Or consider the twenty-four blossomed cactus – it is so very exotic that one wonders: was this desert flower of dryness not created partly as a reaction to all the water-lilies and moist orchids of the symbolists as well

[93] "Carp," p. 93.
[94] Ibid., p. 92.

as the obvious poetic contrast to the water/carp image within the story?

Let us also recall the affinity – temperamental, thematic, even stylistic – between Cézanne and the author; it goes too deep to be dismissed as a marginal coincidence. In short, a modern Japanese artist cannot and most often does not return to his cultural roots in a direct line. Whether he likes it or not, Japanese literature has recognized – and perhaps overestimated – the authority of Western writing. In the search for his own style, the Japanese artist has to digest current conventions of style and technique, arriving at a compromise between foreign and native modes that will be uniquely his own. "Carp" reflects such a search for compromise.

And third, *carp: white* unquestionably sums up the essence of the story. Yet since the author used more space to make this point than a Zen poem, we must examine how it was made. The first thing that strikes one about the colour-scheme of the story[95] is the tremendous emphasis on the carp's *whiteness*: the word *white* or *pure white* is repeated no less than four times on the first page alone, each time with a slight variation: *masshiroi iro o shite ita* – *masshiroi ippiki no ôki na koi* – *hakushoku no koi* – *koi wa masshiro no mama*. This is the kind of repetition we know from fairy tales – it establishes a strong awareness of pure whiteness in the reader's mind, especially when conveyed by the original *kanji*. It is a primal, innocent whiteness – the magic whiteness of fairy tale – that

---

[95] Many writers in Japan are painters *manqués*. As pointed out in Chapter I, Ibuse seriously prepared himself for a painting career and had a considerable talent for it.

has the potential of both the frightening white of the legendary snow-woman (*yuki no onna*) and the sacred whiteness of *yamabushi* garments. Yet it is an almost overwhelming whiteness which makes us wonder: where have all the other colours gone? And, indeed, compared to this frequency of *masshiroi*, *hakushoku*, and *masshiro*, repeated throughout the story, other colours are mentioned only twice in the entire text; there is the faded, reddish brown of Aoki's cap as it stands on his coffin, and the ripe yellow of the *biwa* fruit in the girl's garden. One realizes the design: when the white sinks deep into the reader's mind, changing it into an open, receptive canvas, the other two colours – Aoki's faded, *reddish brown* and the girl's *ripe yellow* – begin to glow with an almost unbearable intensity against it. Moreover, the tendency of the carp's white to overwhelm weaker colours, or at least cast a whitish reflection on things that come into contact with it, is perhaps expressed through another chain of 'silent', reflected whiteness: (white) handkerchiefs – (white) silkworm grub – (white) transparent parasites – (white) pinewood coffin – (white) snow.

This is why it is so important that Aoki's cap be of a fading, 'vanishing' colour. As it rests on the coffin, one has a feeling that the little remaining vestige of Aoki's frail life-force is being sucked in by the white of the coffin. All bright, 'full' colours will eventually change into white, as all life will join death. Yet fading into white will also prepare the canvas for a new painting. If all the other images in this chain of 'reflected' white suggest a corrupted form of the carp's clean whiteness, the last image of the white frozen pool dramatically inverts the whole picture: while through most of the story the carp was canvas and people and things its colours or lines, now the snow *above* the frozen pool is the canvas and the carp the line. The mysterious realm *under* water is closed off by ice and the protagonist's imagination is ready to recreate it *above* the water, in the thin snow that covers the ice. *'Koi'* – the carp and the love that have been eluding him in so many ways for so long (to the girl, into the water, and into death) – has been brought up from the depths for the last time.

But this time the white 'death'[96] into which it materializes is of a more esoteric nature. The young man who has "suffered for a dozen years past" finally discovers more sublime ways of catching a carp – or Love – and of escaping death. The man who says "I was utterly content" is not the same young man, of course. For better or worse, he has accepted the coldness – and the freedom – of yet another symbolic remove. He has grasped the 'inner space' and expressed it. In other words, he has accepted the artist's lot.

---

[96] Readers of classical Japanese literature and some works by Kawabata Yasunari (e.g., *Snow Country*) will recall that snow often has the traditional symbolic connotation of 'seasonal death', ie., death as the peaceful, deep sleep of nature in winter, devoid of the oppressive, 'raw' aspects of a narrowly defined human death.

III. RETURN TO THE COUNTRY

## "KUCHISUKE'S VALLEY," "LIFE AT MR. TANGE'S"

*By this time it seems likely that the art that speaks most clearly, most explicitly, directly and passionately from its place of origin will remain the longest understood. It is through Place that we put down roots, wherever and whenever birth, chance, fate or our travelling selves may set us down; but where these roots reach toward is the deep and running vein of the human understanding.*[1]

Eudora Welty

In an age of globalization Welty's words sound almost prophetic. The sense of local identity of which she speaks so fondly is gradually getting lost and with it a spicy and original spoken language. At the outset of his writing career, Ibuse was not quite sure where to look for the sources of inspiration either. To absorb all the different moods prevailing in the literary circle of the mid-20's was not easy for a young artist. Out of a great variety of available artistic techniques and modes – both imported and domestic – the aspiring writer had to select the ones that would best suit his artistic temperament and the expression of his experience. Although even his early animal stories like "Salaman-

[1] Eudora, Welty: "Place in Fiction." In: *Three Papers on Fiction*. Northampton, Smith College 1962, p. 15.

der" and "Carp" owe their original inspiration to the native valley, the extreme allegorical technique in one and the search for symbolic expression in the other place them rather into the intellectual context of the city *bohème*.

Glancing at a list of Ibuse's early works published in the eight or nine learning years between his debut with *Yûhei* in 1923 and the first accomplished masterpieces such as "Life at Mr. Tange's" (*Tange-shi-tei*, 1931) and "The River" (*Kawa*, 1932), one notices that his thematic interest fluctuates between the two familiar settings of the city and the country. From the student environment of Waseda it shifts to the rustic setting of small, remote islands and mountain hamlets, and back again to the favourite haunts of contemporary bohemians – the artists' cafés, the dingy bars, the *oden* stalls and the pawnshops. Although the style used to express these settings does not differ as much as their ambience, the ratio of failure is much higher in the city stories. It is the stories with a deep sense of Place – above all "Life at Mr. Tange's" – that are the most original, and strike the reader as lasting Ibuse masterpieces even seventy five years after having been written. The writer with deep roots in such a place, unlike his colleague in the city, can build on a well established and ritualized, if somewhat inbred, linguistic culture, taking it a step or two further towards his own unique, stylized expression. Compared to this fine linguistic sensibility, the feeling for the subtle nuances of an 'in-language' in modern cosmopolitan cities is almost nonexistent, except perhaps in some urban subcultures. Yet one of the current conceits of the modern urbanite is his belief that he is more sophisticated verbally – he'd say more articulate – than the taciturn rustic. More fancy words and a greater number of words he may generally be using, but the question is: can he use the simple old words effectively? Can he give them the inimitable eccentric twist, that charming mark of linguistic originality so characteristic of rural speakers? Yet to be an intrinsic part of such a linguistic community is one thing and to communicate its rich inner experience to the city reader quite another. For the serious rural writer – or simply a writer who uses rural themes and characters in his work – addresses himself primarily to the urban reader and faces the danger of being looked down on as an 'uneducated' rustic.

There are many pitfalls lying in the writer's path as he sets out to portray country people, whose behaviour he knows well enough, but from whose thinking and speech he is somewhat alienated by the burden of his education. The best among the writers of rural experience do not pretend to possess a knowledge of the inner world of a too-wide variety of rural characters. The ones they portray most convincingly are usually the domestics they knew intimately as children and to whom they are still attached emotionally; no wonder that Ibuse admired the loving portrayals of servants in Russian 19th century novels. One thinks of Pushkin's folksy nannies and particularly of his old servant Savelyich in *Captain's Daughter*, Ibuse's favourite Russian novel. He may have been the literary influence on one of Ibuse's most vivid rural characters, old Kuchisuke, while the real life model was perhaps the author's own *komori* (male nurse). It has been said about George

Eliot that she presents her peasants as landscape and a leading Japanese critic makes a similar observation about Ibuse: "Most of his protagonists are ordinary people, or rather the progagonists are the landscape, the setting itself."[2]

The English novel closest to the Japanese feeling for landscape and the decisive influence it exerts on character is Brontë's *Wuthering Heights*. As in many Japanese novels, Brontë's scenery never serves as a mere backdrop for the human drama – it is an active participant in the novel's plot and in the life of its characters. Perhaps it is even the real protagonist of the novel and its only eternal character, always the same and yet constantly changing with the seasons. Man's chance to play a role in the life of this great presence is to mingle his own feelings with the flow of its moods; Brontë's landscape is more alive and her rapport with its spirits more intense than Eliot's or Hardy's. One recognizes the passionate animistic participation in the spiritual ambience of her place, so typical for Japanese poetry and the Japanese lyrical novel.

To present emotion and speech so distinctly original it must strike the city reader as nearly quaint, the skillful local writer will often use a narrative convention of the visitor, someone like Lockwood in *Wuthering Heights*, who can mediate the unfamiliar emotions of the place to the urban reader. Ibuse uses the same device in his early village stories and the young man who assumes this role usually has many of the characteristics of the author's own background: he

[2] Isogai, Hideo: "IM no ichi." In: *IM kenkyû*. Isogai, Hideo Ed. Hiroshima, Keisuisha 1984, p. 11.

may be a student on vacation, or a publisher's employee visiting his old home, or simply an amateur art collector from Tokyo who comes to Bingo to search for the highly valued dishes and jars of Himetani pottery. Like Brontë's Lockwood, this perceptive visitor serves as narrator of the stories. Like Hardy's Clym who is entranced by the 'microscopic world' of plants and insects upon returning to the countryside, Ibuse's narrator 'sees small'. His viewpoint is based in the borderland between customary folkways and urban education, between an attachment to his place and an awareness of impending change. Although the author knows the local dialect, his narrator does not use it himself. He speaks a polite, if colloquial version of standard Japanese and his rendering of the local speech patterns is very selective. Discussing dialect in Hardy,[3] Raymond Williams points out that Hardy faced and in his own way succesfully solved the basic dilemma of the rural writer: how to blend in one narrative form the indispensable voice of the storyteller, compounded of his linking narration and his conscious inquiry – always including some abstract vocabulary – with the customary speech patterns of the local characters. Ibuse also decided against a too-faithful recording of dialect by means of careful orthographic simulation, for it implies two dangers: it tends to reduce personalities to types and it may put too much distance between the narrator – and consequently the reader who identifies with him – and the local personalities.

[3] Williams, Raymond: *The Country and the City.* London, Chatto and Windus 1973, pp. 197–214.

It may be safer to present peasants in their collectivity and let them speak in a kind of balladic chorus than to portray them as unique individuals; the writer will avoid projecting externally conceived thoughts and attitudes into their heads. Yet Ibuse's old men particularly stand out as individuals, if not for the originality of their ideas, then for their eccentric behaviour and language. Instead of transcribing the many local varieties of pronunciation, Ibuse selects only those with a pleasantly distinctive ring – a touch of archaic flavour here, a rhythmic, sonorous sound or repetitive sing-song pattern there; in short, elements of dialect that create character without much authorial intrusion. These elements he blends into a personal 'aesthetic dialect', a kind of *patois* with humorous overtones that often sounds more authentic than the real dialect itself, as Professor Fujiwara Yoichi, the great connoisseur of Southern dialects, once observed admiringly.[4]

Animating his country people with such personal, poetic dialect, Ibuse can share his consciousness with the ones for whom he feels most, avoiding not only the patronizing attitude of many rural novelists, but also the contrived picturesqueness which often results from a less stylized rendering of customary language. Furthermore, the eccentricities of speech and action of his old men draw attention to problems of consciousness without really going into lengthy descriptions of individual psychology. Although Ibuse would probably deny a deeper knowledge of previous important writers of the rural experience, during his Waseda years he was an avid reader of European novelists. He read

[4] During my interview with him at Hiroshima University in 1975.

155

them mostly through Japanese or English translation, such as Constance Garnett's Chekhov. His reading knowledge of English seems to have been good enough to aquaint himself with at least the major works of Austen, Eliot and Hardy. As a student he translated and edited a major novel of German naturalism, Hermann Sudermann's *Katzensteg,* located in the remote countryside of East Prussia. It abounds in colourful portrayals of rustics and provided a useful model for Ibuse. He is also quite skillful in sidestepping some of the pitfalls which the earlier writers occasionally fell into. Even George Eliot sometimes slips into the patronizing posture of looking at her rustics as the honest-living, quaint-talking country folks. One of the achievements of Ibuse's rural stories is the delicate balance he maintains. Precisely at the moment when one feels his sympathetic portrayal of a rustic might slip into sentimentality, it is tempered by a touch of satire or gentle caricature.

## "KUCHISUKES' VALLEY"

Ibuse's student pen-name, Kuchiki Sansuke, translates in a revealing way. Kuchiki not only means 'decayed wood', but also 'old man', 'aged person'. Sansuke is a common given name, but it also means 'bath attendant' and thus has connotations of a lowly servant who performs menial tasks. As Ôgai observed,[5] Ibuse's style had a certain patina of age even as a young student and the pseudonym was obviously well chosen. Whether young Masuji deliberately used antiquated language, or whether his voice had a natural tinge of age is less

[5] IM: "Akugi." In *IMZ IX,* p. 22.

important than seeing that the persona of an old – or just an elderly man – would become Ibuse's favourite literary character, and would best express his innermost thoughts and emotions. The first memorable *rôjin* figure in this long gallery of old men is Tanimoto Kuchisuke of "Kuchisuke's Valley". His given name is a contraction of young Masuji's pen-name *Kuchi(ki) (San)suke*, and his family name, although fictional, is an interesting creative 'translation' of a real person's name, Yamane Shichirô.

Yamane was a next door neighbour to the Ibuses and used to look after little Masuji as a *komori* when he lost Ijû of the unfortunate Satô family. Kuchisuke is a fictional character to be sure, but some of his traits seem to have been modelled on Yamane. The name consists of two Chinese characters, *yama* (mountain) and *ne* (root, base, core). The fictional name, Tanimoto (meaning valley and base, core, fount) echoes the essence of the other name, suggesting that these old men's existence is tied with the very soul of the mountains and the valley. It is this fine crafting of detail, a careful attention to every nuance of the text that Ibuse readers appreciate.

The story's outline is simple: Ibuse's narrator once again returns to his native valley, but this time he comes as a visitor from Tokyo, a young man who "leads the unfortunate life of a literary apprentice." He has rushed back because a major catastrophe threatens his old guardian Kuchisuke: a dam is being built in the valley and is about to swallow the old man's cottage. Ibuse's childhood memories are introduced into the story, but they are organically built into its *sujet* and absorbed by it. Old Kuchisuke is introduced in an interesting way:

> Seventy-seven year old Taniki Kuchisuke is especially fond of me. Each year when fall arrives and one's breath turns white in the air, he sends me a gift of rare pine mushrooms even if I am far from home on a trip. He lines an old noodle box with moss, fills it with the dried morsels, and addresses its cover with the salutation 'Happy Autumn.'
>
> Kuchisuke is the caretaker of the mountain, where these mushrooms grow. Although we sold this mountain to another family back in my grandfather's time, Kuchisuke stubbornly continues to do things as he did in the old days.[6]

The story's first two pages define the setting and its people. From the very outset we feel that we are being introduced to a very unusual, not to say eccentric old man. Though he obviously belongs to the valley, the scope of his experience reaches far beyond it. In his younger days, we are told, Kuchisuke emigrated to Hawaii[7] and worked there for some years. This not only qualifies him as the boy's first tutor of English, it also spices his colourful language with occasional English words, usually distorted enough to make them sound funny. These are clearly fictional touches, others are

[6] IM: "Kuchisuke's Valley." In: *Shôwa Anthology*. Trans. Treat, John. Tokyo, New York and San Francisco, Kôdansha International 1985, p. 2.
In this translation Kuchisuke's family name is given as Taniki (following the 1964 *IMZ*), but in the first published version of the story and then again in the last authoritative **IMZ** of 1996 it is Tanimoto. Hereafter, bracketed numbers after quotes refer to the page numbers of this edition.

[7] Around 1885 massive Japanese emigration to Hawai began from the poorer agricultural areas. In the same year, the U.S. and Japanese governments concluded the Immigration Convention.

not. In *Keirokushû*[8] Ibuse reminisces how when he came home to Kamo for his grandfather's funeral, old man Yamane dropped by and asked him for a drawing of a rat. Since he was born in the year of the rat, he explains, and his ward is now a painter, he'd like to have his zodiac animal's portrait. The old peasant has no clue what the young man might be doing in far-off Tokyo, but he saw him sketching in the valley and concludes he must be a painter. In the story, this episode is developed into full-scale caricature:

> I have yet to respond candidly to Kuchisuke's inquiries about my choice of career, since I am sure literature would please him the least.
>
> Every time I visit my family in the country, he comes over and immediately interrogates me about my work. I avoid a direct reply and have allowed him to form the false impression that I am a dentist, or at other times, an engineer. On his way home he stops in at the neighbors' and boasts that I am a Tokyo dentist, or engineer, as if it were all his own doing. (4)

By placing the story's main action some twenty years after the brief introductory 'journal of recollections', Ibuse distances the emotion-filled memories of his childhood and achieves a more balanced, smooth fictional integration of character. When he introduces the third major character of the story, a young foreign maiden by the name of Taeto, whose portrayal is completely fictional, she blends naturally with the other two:

> 'I must tell you something about myself. My name is Taeto and I came to my grandfather's place two years ago

[8] IM: "Keirokushû." In: *IMZ IX*, pp. 298–299.

from Hawaii. My grandparents were both Japanese, but my mother married an American. Some years ago Father left mother and me without warning and returned to the mainland. I may look like an American, but in fact I am Japanese … Mother, who passed as a Japanese, managed to save a little money and soon found herself a new husband. Only two months later, however, she died. Perhaps the change in climate was too much for her. But she raised me as a Japanese, and I came here with her willingly. Japan is a better place than Hawaii. Japan is the land of my ancestors. I act and feel like a Japanese, and am very content now to live in this valley.'(6)

The girl's name, Taeto, is not ordinary either. It does not sound like a Hawaian name, nor is it a common Japanese woman's name. The ending -*to* sometimes forms the last syllable of a man's name, such as Masato or Fumito. Of the three possible semantic meanings of the phoneme *tae* (*taeru:* endure, *taeru:* to end, *tae-naru:* exquisite, delicate, charming) the third sounds most appropriate in the given context. Although Ibuse spells the girl's name in *katakana,* the last *tae* is written with a character, usually read as "myô"(妙), which also means 'miraculous', 'wonderful', 'strange'. A thing of exquisite beauty is often perceived as being rare, even strange. An expatriate girl, returning home to a small mountain hamlet from a land far across the ocean, would have appeared as strange and 'rare' in those days as the mysterious yearly visitors of myth, called *marebito* (literally 'rare people').[9] Like those ancestral spirits of old, the young Japanese American returns

[9] See Orikuchi, Shinobu: „Kyaku to marebito to." In: *Kodai kenkyû. Orikuchi Shinobu zenshû II.* Tokyo, Chûôkôronsha 1975, p. 3.

to her forefathers' home when it is in dire need of outside help. Her last remaining kin, grandfather Kuchisuke, is so much part of his surroundings that we might even say he has 'grown into' his habitat and is therefore physically unable to detach himself from the situation. (This is suggested in the original title of the story, *Kuchisuke no iru tanima*, literally "The Valley where Kuchisuke Is)". His reactions are typically unreasonable and would even appear masochistic to the outside observer. He throws himself into his daily chores with increased vigour, overdoing some so much that they become a kind of inverted torture and punishment at the same time:

> The sound of logs splitting stopped, and then branches were being violently shaken. It was like leaves rustling in the wind. Soon I heard great numbers of apricots tumbling to the ground. I got out of bed and shouted:
>
> 'Kuchisuke! All the unripe fruit will fall, too!'
>
> 'I don't care. I'm going to try and drop a few more.'
>
> He began shaking the branches again. When I looked out the window I saw that he had climbed the apricot tree and, striding a limb, was shifting his own weight to and fro. He rocked the tree so much that it looked as if it were in pain. (7–8)

The old man is hurting himself as much as the tree, as he calls out the only lament he knows. What emerges from these lines is a portrayal of a rugged yet vulnerable individual, who knows the rules of his Place well enough, but cannot cope with the pressures of the modern world outside. By contemporary standards, his displacement is negligible: he will be moved to a new house built by the dam authority on the banks of the artificial lake and will even receive a regular salary as its watchman. But to dismiss the old man's loss by pointing to the tragic, large scale dislocations of whole populations in our time does not amount to much. To see old people returning to the radioactive no-man's land of Chernobyl only makes one realize how much was lost in the last seventy years and how inhuman, by old Kuchisuke's standards, our world has become. They were not foolish standards, although Ibuse skilfully presents the old man as a bit of a fool:

> 'Consider which is tastier, thrushes or shrikes. Shrikes are better, I'd say. But pheasant is better still. What I mean is, a pheasant has some meat on its bones. After pheasants come shrikes, then thrushes, in that order, I suppose. Oh well, this rainy valley is about to become a rainy lake. They say it's going to be more than five miles around, but if a mallard or a heron were to fly high enough overhead, it might go right by and never realize there was a lake directly below. They say you'll be able to fish for carp in it. Twenty years from now the carp'll be two feet long. If I live till then, I'll go looking for them. What a sight it would be to see two-foot-long carp leaping up out of the lake in the evenings just before it rains.' (13)

So the old man keeps mumbling to himself in a charming monologue filled with solid first-hand experience of his place and its creatures, his dreams and fears, and what we'd call superstitions. Ibuse does not have to add any authorial comment, or provide more introspection into Kuchisuke's character. The man reveals his inner world to the reader most convincingly by the way he speaks. The original sentence is of course highly idiosyncratic and reveals a whole array of stylistic skills:

> *Megane wo nuginasaru to anta wa naosara ni agurî*
> When you don't have your glasses on, you look even more
> *desu ga nâ. Hayô megane wo kaketorinasai to iutara.*
> ugly than usual. Hurry up and put them back on.
> *Shitaredomo watakushi wa kore wo kakete mitarô.*[10]
> Wait, let me have them first.

The expression with which the sentence begins is deliberately faulty and therefore sounds droll in Japanese. Correctly it would be *"megane wo hazusu,"* "to take off your glasses." The word *agurî* is a mutilated transcription of the English word 'ugly' and again provides graphic and aural novelty, as well as comic effect. Like Kuchisuke himself, the story is rooted in local soil, and yet keeps reaching out. The comic English gives the theme a touch of universality, linking it with the outside world. In a typical Ibusean roundabout or inverted way, it also expresses the old man's intimacy with his younger friend and a fondness he'd never state in sentimental terms.

The sentence-ending *desu ga nâ* comes from the old Bingo dialect and is practically extinct by now. Similarly, the conjunction *shitaredomo* – roughly equivalent to *shikashi* (but, nevertherless) in modern Japanese – is straight archaic language, belonging to classical Japanese. Remote dialects sometimes do preserve archaic words that have long fallen out of usage in the standard language, but not in this case. It is Ibuse's stylistic device to make the old man sound a little eccentric and perhaps even a relic of bygone time. The

[10] IM: "Kuchisuke no iru tanima." In: *IMZ I*, p. 47.

following *watakushi* (*I*) on the other hand, is standard Japanese and would be rather *washira* in the colloquial diction of the Bingo dialect, as it is elsewhere in the story. By the same token, the standard verbal form *-te iru* is usually contracted into *-toru*, e.g. *shite iru (oru)* becomes *sh'toru*. The very frequent dialect sentence ending of *-ke* is not employed at all, for its sound is not pleasing to the standard speaker's ear. Ibuse also avoids the frequent dialectic corruption of words by a phonemic assimilation, such as *nani to iu* becoming *nanchû, obi wo* changing into *obyû* and the like. We see the author carefully filtering out those sounds and forms from his native dialect that he needs as style-forming ingredients and completely ignoring others that do not suit his purpose. Like a subtle tuning device, Ibuse can turn the dialect on and off, modulating the speaker's emotional volume. Accordingly, when Kuchisuke mumbles to himself before falling asleep, the flow of dialect thickens. The standard sentence ending *desu* becomes *degasu, watakushi* changes into *washira,* etc.

Although old Kuchisuke's portrayal is partly a projection of Ibuse's own innermost persona and perhaps his way of saying goodbye to the vanishing world of his childhood, it is the young narrator of the story who was obviously closer to the thirty-one year old writer. Like the protagonist of other early Ibuse stories, he still displays some of the traits of a city intellectual which are expressed in the mannerisms of his diction and his choice of metaphor. This is often functional and sets the two types of perception, the Country's and the City's dramatically apart:

Kuchisuke stood in one corner of the house and listened to the clamor with close attention. He remarked that the highest pitched sounds came from three axes chopping away at one huge, dead oak tree. Then there was one sound that reverberated more solidly than the others: this was undoubtedly from the single tree that stood off by itself. It had the measured tone of a cello at the heart of a symphony. Kuchisuke recognized this muted sound as that of cherry wood being chopped. (16–17)

Elsewhere, a closing device in the dam's lock-pipe is likened to the thick drop-curtain of kabuki, called *donchô,* which provides the same effect. But it seems that describing the charms of a young country maiden offered the greatest challenge to Ibuse's pen. While in later stories, such as "Life at Mr. Tange's" the narrating 'I' will withdraw from the foreground, becoming merely an observing 'eye', the young protagonist of this story tells us about his likes and dislikes and thus is more emotionally involved than later Ibuse narrators:

I know. We see a lot of it. It seems that those girls in the big city dance-halls, the ones who are always ahead of the fashion, find a look like Taeto's interesting. They apparently think it sophisticated to sport a jacket both one size too big and a bit too worn. But none of the green, high-collared jackets you might see at the dance halls would ever be as grimy or ill-fitting as Taeto's. (10)

Ibuse did write several stories about women and one novella which is narrated by an elderly geisha (*Oshima no zonnengaki* or *A Geisha Remembers,* 1952), but female figures do no get as much attention in his work as they do in Tanizaki's. In other words, he managed to ignore the dictum of popular modern literature which owes a good deal of its popularity to the love story. It does not mean that Ibuse's mature works are dry and lack erotic appeal, but his Eros is more diffused and 'polymorphous', as Freud would say. In an early version of the story, the young woman's erotic charm is still expressed in a direct and somewhat naive way:

> The bright afternoon sun cast green shadows on her naked body. It looked as if this greenish light was gliding and flowing down her skin. The roundness of her shoulders and breasts… I averted my eyes and looked again at the swarm of caterpillars on the tree.
>
> I know, when facing a naked woman, one can't think that life is sad…[11]

I'd say that the author's voice comes across best when it is impersonal and makes its points in a roundabout, low-keyed way. Addressing the city reader directly, the narrator draws too much attention to himself, and perhaps even reveals the anxious author behind his shoulder, trying to get through to his peers in the city's intellectual community. So an earlier story called "Crooked Design" (*Ibitsu naru zuan*, 1927) suffers from a too direct emphasis on personal motifs.[12] It is when Ibuse lets go of this outside frame of reference and relies on his instinctive grasp of place and people that he becomes fully convincing. The young narrator enjoys an innocent flirtation with Taeto, and her erotic appeal plays a considerable role in the story. Yet again, it comes across most charmingly when expressed in a roundabout, casual way. As she goes about her chores,

[11] IM: "Kuchisuke no iru tanima." In: *Yofuke to ume no hana*. Tokyo, Shinchôsha 1930, p. 21.
[12] IM: „Ibitsu naru zuan." In: *IMZ I*. Tokyo, Chikuma shobô 1996, pp. 101–107.

Taeto sings charming work songs in English. The young narrator translates them back into Japanese:

> Apparently she did not realize that I was observing her. She began to sing her own little song. It made me smile. The words were in a foreign language, but easy to translate. It went something like this: 'I am hungry, I am sweating. My back is all wet, and even the soles of my feet are soaked.' (11)

When her work is done and Kuchisuke and his young friend have taken their bath, Taeto enters the *o-furo*:

> Taeto finished her harvesting and now took her turn in the bath. Amid the sounds of water spilling and splashing, there was suddenly a shrill scream from a terror-stricken voice. What could have happened? Taeto, without a stitch on, came flying from the bath toward me.
>
> 'Caterpillars!' (12)

It is in these scenes where Ibuse lets his characters present themselves through their own words and actions, no matter how naive and insignificant they may appear to the city sophisticate's eye, that their existence acquires a natural dignity and the bittersweet pathos that is typical for his mature writing. The author could have made a strong value judgment about what is being done to 'his valley', but as we follow the text line by line, we can almost see Ibuse's pen shying away from any direct comment:

> The rain lasted a full four days. The following morning the skies cleared and the valley shone a brilliant green.
>
> The lumbermen had finished the job by the fourth day, and the sound of their axes did not echo under the blue skies of the fifth... The mountainsides had been

cleared up to the exact height of the dam without a single tree left behind. The denuded area depicted a lake utterly drained of its water; this was how we would last see the valley... (17)

The narrator does share Kuchisuke's sense of identity with the trees, but he does not make any emotional judgments about their destruction. Yet by skillfully placing the line "the skies cleared and the valley shone a brilliant green" before the laconic statement "without a single tree left behind," the author shows the trees to the reader in all their glory after the long rain and makes him sympathize with their plight. Similarly, the young man can give his old guardian little more than sympathy and understanding. The old man, of course, keeps daydreaming about his city friend, hoping that he is a sharp, eloquent lawyer who will deliver a fluent defense on his behalf in a last ditch effort to save his place. But even if he has no such power or skill, it is clear that the young man's feelings are not too different from the old peasant's; he says this pond has none of the charms associated with a lake and seems more like someone's eye wide open in anger. Kuchisuke echoes this view by saying: "Maybe this is where the monster will rise up." (56–57)

In the broadest sense then, the story's theme dramatizes the confrontation between modern progress and mobility and the old-fashioned sense of belonging to a Place and its unhurried, graceful humanity – rural stasis and modern flux, roots and uprootedness, a theme *par excellence* that will always be present in Ibuse's major works. To express this theme, Ibuse starts here a systematic development of a stylistic technique that

Mikhail Bakhtin calls "double-voiced" or "dialogized" discourse:

> The double-voicedness one finds in prose is of another sort altogether. There – on the rich soil of novelistic prose – double-voicedness draws its energy, its dialogized ambiguity, not from *individual* dissonances, misunderstandings or contradictions (however tragic, however firmly grounded in individual destinies), in the novel, this double-voicedness sinks its roots deep into a fundamental, socio-linguistic speech diversity...[13]

In a linguistic milieu that tends to be doubly hermetic – firstly for its insularity and secondly for its highly canonized poetic language – this discovery of living double-voicedness (or *heteroglossia*) is very important. Rather than a superficial rhetorical polemic between persons, Ibuse's dialogic mode means a full awareness and a stylistic harnessing of the energy of socially and historically stratified language and its organic becoming in a particular work's context. The dialogue between the young narrator and the elderly protagonist of the story may look a bit stagey and must appear so for its dramatic purpose. But it is also internally dialogized: just as the narrator who functions as a dialogic bridge, could put himself in the old peasant's shoes and speak his language, the author's relativistic prose-consciousness contains the full potential and the nuances of both sides of the discourse.

In a narrower, more specific symbolic sense, there is another dimension to the story we should examine.

[13] Bakhtin, Mikhail: *The Dialogic Imagination. Four essays*. Trans. Emerson, Caryl and Holquist, Michael. Holquist, Michael Ed. Austin, University of Texas Press 1981, pp. 325–326.

I have said that old Kuchisuke is the first successful portrayal of Ibuse's favourite old man (*rôjin*) figure. We will see later how this figure matures and develops with the author's own advancing years. But what is also worth mentioning is that this old man often lives with a young woman whose characteristics are remarkably similar in several other major works, most notably Ibuse's most important novel, *Black Rain*. As in "Kuchisuke's Valley," the elderly Shigematsu of *Black Rain* takes care of his niece Yasuko who has also lost her parents. In fact, the most memorable couples Ibuse has created are neither husband and wife, nor a couple of young lovers, but an elderly man and his young virgin ward. Even in those stories, such as "Isle-on-the-Billows" (*Wabisuke*), where the man is not really old but middle-aged – though we must bear in mind that by country standards one was entering old age by forty– the man may be attracted by the girl's erotic charm, but his attitude to her is always marked by gentle protectiveness.

From a purely technical point of view we might say that the personality of an old man who has lived a long life and accumulated a store of experience the young writer does not yet have, is most challenging. Even if Ibuse's old man is not always the wise old man of myth, he represents something that the young city writer is obviously not. As an archetypal figure the old man embodies a form of human existence rooted in nature and her ways. Hence his ambiguity: like nature, he can appear helpless and vulnerable when faced with modern pseudo-rationality and technology, and yet at other times he may bounce back with unexpected resilience. But he is basically man within nature, an oriental awareness of nature realized through ancient wisdom, the 'green core' personified and codified by traditional culture. The most familiar representation of this figure is the *okina* (old man) character of Noh or the folkloric old man of the mountain (*yama dossan*).

In archetypal terms, the young woman corresponds to the *anima* figure and thus represents virgin nature, an unconscious, more hidden aspect of nature that is even less accessible to the male mind than the 'nature' of the old man. Because she embodies the forces of unconscious nature, this figure has destructive aspects in western folklore (the Jungian negative *anima*). The Japanese *anima* figure, on the other hand shows remarkably few negative traits and is frequently personified in one particular form, called *mizu no onna* (water woman, water maiden) by Orikuchi Shinobu.This water maiden or *wakaminuma* of ancient myth appears in oldest texts such as the *Histories of Natural Features* (*Fudoki*) or the "Prayers to the Gods" (*Kamuyogoto*). Since in Japan certain prehistoric religious forms survived longer than in the West, the existence of this figure is only partly mythical, for she also has historical descendants in the shamanistic practices of folk religion. In the old texts she is probably a water goddess (*mizu no megami*), in derived or parallel cults of this deity she may be a sorceress called *noro* or a shamaness (*miko*) or a divine midwife called *toriage no shinjo*. But whether goddess or shamaness, her home is in the water's depths and she is familiar with its mysteries. This qualifies her to perform the most important of water rites – purification or *misogi*. As *toriage onna* (midwife) she delivers children

– especially children of nobility – administering their first and vital *ubuyu* (child's first bath).[14]

In many local traditions the water maiden becomes a divine bride (*kami no yome*), pure and clean like water itself. Having access to the water gods, she has the power to tie and untie the *mizu no o-himo* (literally the water cord), an earlier version of the *en no musubi* (marital, sexual tie), dealing with Eros at a sublime and sacred level. According to Orikuchi, in ancient times these vestal virgins would manifest their purity of body and soul by entering the water with a firmly tied *obi* (sash) or *himo* (cord, string) and untie it only in the water, thereby consummating the union with the water god. To the early Japanese imagination the divine realm, even Paradise itself is located in the water's depths rather than in Heaven.

With this information in mind, another glance at "Kuchisuke's Valley" and many other Ibuse stories will reveal unnoticed resonances. The girl Taeto has returned from a kind of nether land (*tokoyo no kuni*) both in a personal and a deeper mythical sense. She is associated with water throughout the story, though in a lighthanded and humorous fashion. Sharing the freshness and the cleanness of purifying *wakamizu,* she can protect her grandfather from the dirty waters of the dam. Without her, he would probably stay in his house and be swallowed with it. But she instinctively knows that the polluted waters of this 'demon pond' cannot be their home. In the end, *she* becomes the old man's strength and support:

[14] Orikuchi, Shinobu: "Mizu no onna." In: *Kodai kenkyû. Orikuchi Shinobu zenshû II*. Tokyo, Chûôkôronsha 1984, pp. 80–97.

172

Taeto patiently waited for us to rise. There was a look in her auburn eyes that told me she would never, ever, leave Kuchisuke behind on the dam. (20)

One also detects a personal note here, for the tapestry of Ibuse's best stories always results from a subtle blend of the deeper mythopoeic motifs and reliable, even painful personal experience. Perhaps the light-filled world of Ibuse's youth and his memory of the beautiful maiden Okichi lie at the bottom of another great dam made by the River Kronos; the task of his imagination is to recover this precious memory and save it from being swallowed up by the waters of time without trace. And so the small boy's memory of the girl whose existence was abruptly stopped is unaffected by the flow of time while she remains forever young and attractive. The keeper of the memory, on the other hand, is growing old and becoming more and more like the old men of his stories. There, in the most essential sense, is the eternal couple of Ibuse's imagination.

### "LIFE AT MR. TANGE'S"

I wrote *Tange-shi-tei* in January of 1931 and published it in the February issue of *Kaizô*. I had no intention of writing a so-called 'rural story'. As a child I used to associate with an old man whose character and sentiments I suddenly recalled. From this nostalgic, more or less fictional mood of reminiscence I created the story. At the time of its writing I was fascinated by Kôrin's paintings and considered his sparse line and colouring extremely pleasing. I was also fond of the elegant Southern school of Chinese painters and I even had the ambition of introducing their graceful sense of line into writing.

I am still attracted by anything that has to do with painting.[15]

Less than two years had elapsed between the writing of "Kuchisuke's Valley" and "Life at Mr. Tange's," but every line of this superb story shows what a long way Ibuse has come. Again, as in "Carp," we are dealing with a dense text of poetic intensity, but this time the critic's task is even harder, for the style has matured and become smoother, there are fewer visible idiosyncrasies, and the articulation of character through manner of speech more subtle. It is also clear that the writer has gained considerable confidence in his technique and the appeal of his subject matter, and feels no compulsion to 'explain himself' or justify the choice of his rustic material with stylistic tour de force.

In his preface to this story and elsewhere Ibuse stresses that he had no desire to write so called rural literature. I think he means that the motivating force of his village stories lies deeper than in the fashionable rural nostalgia, or the romantic apotheosis of a vanishing way of life. Two critical questions arise here: what is the nature of Ibuse's 'popular interest', and how truthfully can he, the educated son of a landlord, present the mentality of common country people? There is indeed an ongoing polemic among Japanese critics as to how *shominteki* (popular or common people's) a writer Ibuse really is. According to their ideological predilections, some critics of the progressive bent will see him as something of a passive bystander who basically approves of the political status quo, while conservatives

[15] IM: Preface to "Tange-shi-tei." In: Nagata, Ryûtarô Ed. *IM bungaku shoshi*. Tokyo, Nagata shobô 1972, p. 80.

will often appropriate him as 'their man', a proponent of the 'good old Japanese way'. I think they are both missing the point.

If there is any one outstanding, constant quality in Ibuse's writing, it is his sense of poise, the way he manages to maintain an equilibrium – poetic, stylistic, philosophical – and even things out. When the literary establishment swings left, Ibuse stays quietly aloof. When the whole country swings right, Ibuse remains critical and 'neutral', even going a little left of centre, as his postwar stories show. One is tempted to call this sense of balance his 'Taoist equilibrium'. This is not an empty label. I think to Ibuse literature still genuinely means a *way of life* in the very sense of the old oriental *dô* disciplines.

It is one of literary history's great ironies that Ibuse, one of Japan's most truthful novelists should have been called the 'bragging fibber' (*horafuki no usotsuki*) by one of his close literary friends, Makino Shin'ichi.[16] If it were simply *bundan* gossip of the kind that so often preoccupies Japanese critics, it would hardly be worth mentioning. But it is of importance here, for it is related to a serious critical question. Ibuse started out from the same school of writing as Makino, namely the influential *watakushi shôsetsu* (I novel). He is always present in his texts, even if the narrator is not necessarily the author himself. It is the aesthetic sum total of the work that is Ibuse and the narrator only plays one of the roles in this ensemble. By restraining the personal

[16] Matsumoto, Tsuruo: "Makino Shin'ichi no kanata e." In: *IM ron*. Tokyo, Tojusha 1978, pp. 119–138. In this chapter, Matsumoto provides a detailed discussion of the Ibuse-Makino conflict.

elements and by distancing the narrating persona from his emotional states, Ibuse blatantly disregards one of the basic requirements of the *watakushi shôsetsu:* a 'sincere' revelation of the self. The emotional sincerity of the I-novel has been much admired and there is no question that some of its writers have been able to cultivate a truthful, convincing voice of great intensity. But the Japanese concern, not to say obsession with sincerity, has also its tricky side.

In cases like Makino's, or the better known Dazai Osamu's, the sensitive artist becomes a kind of living fantasy-fulfilment for his audience, somewhat like the *sumô* wrestler of old who was allowed a diet undreamed of by the common man. There was a price to be paid in return, though. He had to put his body on display and often face heart failure at the age of fifty-five or so. And so it is with the 'sincere' *watakushi shôsetsu* writer. He is allowed a life of extraordinary freedom for a regimented society like Japan's, but he must pay the price. Vicariously participating in his pleasures and dissipations, his audience demands: "Let's see the true nature of your suffering! Show us how sincere your torment is!" For torment is always expected, and if not delivered it will be exacted in so many subtle ways. The final self-destruction of this type of artist is almost inevitable.

Life is sad enough without these juvenile games, Ibuse seems to say, putting himself on the side of common sense. As Isogai Hideo points out,[17] common sense may have rather pejorative connotations for the Japanese literary intelligentsia. It often means worldly compromise, even 'selling out' to the establishment.

[17] "IM no ichi." In: *IM kenkyû,* p. 12.

But in Ibuse's case it is rather a "crystallization of life's traditional wisdom,"[18] anchored in the basic values of his country ancestors. Some may call them 'feudal' but it was the Japanese middle and upper class peasantry who preserved such 'common sense' values: a natural sense of justice, modesty, restraint and tolerant generosity.

Other critics - for example, Kumagai Takashi - point out[19] that in his own modest way Ibuse is also something of a heretic. While performing the 'normal', expected civic role, even writing entertaining works of wide popular appeal such as *No Consultations Today*, Ibuse emerges as a rather stoic philosopher from the more exclusive works, especially the ambitious historical novels. In one of his longer historical works, *The Karusan Mansion (Karusan yashiki*, 1953), the Jesuit father Organtino looks at Nobunaga and says: "That man is living out a lonely philosophy."[20] As Kumagai suggests, the same could be said about the author himself. It was not only his handwriting and his style that looked like an old man's to Ôgai. From the very outset, Ibuse's voice was marked with a certain moral pessimism normally associated with old age. He not only paid very little attention to romantic themes such as Love, the heroic quest and the like, but soon rejected the typical Japanese romantic projection of self in the *watakushi shôsetsu* tradition. The writing, increasingly 'adult' in the manner of Ôgai's stoic, sober view of reality, is tempered with humour and compassion, but it also

[18] Ibid.
[19] Kumagai, Takashi: *IM. Postscript*. Tokyo, Hato no mori shobô 1978, p. 312.
[20] Ibid.

shows a growing discomfort with fabrication of any kind. "If I must write," we almost hear the writer sigh at times, "why must I invent?" It is these very qualities that make some of Ibuse's mature works less attractive for the 'popular reader'.

In the earlier works, there is obviously a considerable degree of aesthetic deformation, but it is always based on accurate observation. The convincing detail of seemingly trifling little facts or events gives Ibuse's episode its uncanny credibility. As Isogai Hideo points out, Ibuse will always prefer "a truth that looks like a lie to a lie that looks like the truth."[21]

Truthfulness to Ibuse means rejecting romantic illusions on the one hand (and this no doubt estranged him from many Japanese), and paying tremendous respect to the verity of the text on the other. The ultimate 'truth' is the stylistic authenticity and the rhetorical weight of the text. Yet if the author is genuinely convinced that an exploration of his own self is of little interest to the reader, and the soul of others really unknown territory, how can he continue writing fiction? The final answer is obvious. Yet before giving up fiction – at least in the common sense of the term – altogether, Ibuse managed to strike some remarkable compromises between his idea of novelistic truth and good, interesting story-telling. "Life at Mr. Tange's," I believe, represents such a successful compromise.

It is a strange *ménage* we are introduced to in this story. Two old men, one of whose wife or family is

[21] Isogai, Hideo: "Ibuse bungaku no riarizumu." In: *Kokubungaku kaishaku to kanshô* 50, 4, April 1985, p. 28.

never mentioned, the other whose wife comes to visit only to scold him. From a modern, democratic point of view the situation presented here is terrible. The master, ten years older than his servant and an extraordinary eccentric, apparently has feudal rights over him. The servant is a foundling, a man who never knew any better and who belongs to his master body and soul. They are father and child in terms of their original 'historical relationship' and yet in the present narrative situation they are deliberately presented – by ignoring their other relationships or by underscoring their absurdity, as with the Ei-Otatsu 'marriage' – as a couple, two people who live closely with each other, and go through the usual emotional ups and downs of married life. The first thing we have to realize about the story then, is that it is not a realistic portrayal of any kind of historical past, but a deft caricature of the author's emotional memory. Since it is based on truthful emotional experience, the portrayal may enable us a few unconventional insights into the nature of Japanese 'feudal relationships' in rural areas, but that is not Ibuse's emphasis at all.

In one of his essays, he says:

I am basically a sentimental person. As I write, I often feel the urge to make a lyrical statement. Then I get embarassed and try to move on to a scene in a different mood as fast as possible.[22]

This is one of the clearest summaries of the emotional dynamics behind his writing style that Ibuse ever offered. In his early stories, the "lyrical statement"

---

[22] Quoted in Noji, Junya: "IM no sakuhin no chûgokuben." In: *Gengo seikatsu* 10. *Tokushû,* October 1956, p. 31.

stands out quite clearly and the ensuing switch to a different mood often amounts to a linguistic tour de force. But in this story, the progress from mood to mood is subtle, the tensions behind the lines almost imperceptible. I have mentioned that Ibuse's style has matured considerably in the two years between writing "Kuchisuke's Valley" and "Life at Mr. Tange's." Let us see how.

The opening of the story already shows a far more skillful and productive blend of dialect and standard Japanese than the earlier stories. In Japanese, the first sentence goes:

*Tange-shi wa otokushû wo gyôgi shita.*[23]

Mr. Tange chastised his manservant.

One notes the dramatic brevity of the opening line, although something quite unusual is being announced here. In the original, it is expressed by an interesting verbal compound. Normally the two Chinese characters would be read *sekkan* (to chastise), but the verb is focussed by an unusual *furigana* gloss that instructs the reader to pronounce it *gyôgi*. Even to the Western ear, it is a softer sounding word, which means 'manners' in standard Japanese and is not used with the auxiliary verb *suru* (to do). But in the Bingo dialect, it functions as a verb and has the meaning of 'teaching someone manners'. It is softer, less severe than 'chastise', stating in brief, as it were, the overall atmosphere of the story and hinting to the perceptive reader that he is going

[23] IM: "Tange-shi-tei." In: *IMZ I,* p. 123. IM: "Life at Mr. Tange's." In: *Salamander and other Stories*. Trans Bester, John. Tokyo, New York and San Francisco, Kôdansha International 1981, p. 97. Hereafter, bracketed numbers after quotes refer to the pages of this edition.

to witness a contrast – and a meeting – of two distinct mentalities, represented by the narrator and the local people.

According to Kumagai Takashi, it gives the *kanji* a charming local colour. The bracketed laconic announcement that follows, "(Mr. Tange is sixty-seven and his manservant fifty-seven)" then 'normalizes' the strange news of the first sentence, adding a sense of documentary reality and providing the necessary distance between the reporter and his material.

The whole opening dialogue between the two men, master and servant, takes place in a homely, familiar setting and yet its tone is quite inflated. Mr. Tange delivers his instructions to the servant in a solemn tone, speaking as if he were on stage:

'You will lie down here on your back and smoke your pipe while we watch. That's what you always do, isn't it – you put your left heel up on the knot of the persimmon tree, and you lie back, and you rest your right heel on the shin of your left leg, and you go on smoking happily until it begins to get dark. So now we're going to stand here and watch you grandly smoking your pipe. Do you dare refuse to get down there quickly when I tell you?' (97)

As his anger subsides and he gets a bit ashamed of his own rhetoric, Mr. Tange gradually slips into the local dialect. This of course brings him closer to the servant, and to his everyday reality. Comparing the first 1931 version of the story (*Shigotobeya*) with the revised text in the collected works, I noticed an interesting thing. While the earlier version had a fair amount of Chinese compounds even in the narrated passages, in the later text they were mostly changed to softer and more colloquial *yamatokotoba*. In other words, the revisions show that Ibuse had made a conscious decision to use Chinese words (*kango*) as a stylistic device of characterization. While high-flown *kango* was used somewhat indiscriminately in the previous stories, here it is employed very selectively – in fact it is reserved for expressing Mr. Tange's character and his cultural aspirations. What Bester renders as:

> Our family was so well off that my revered teacher Rôro Sakatani actually wrote praising the pictures, calligraphy, and antiques in our possession. Ah, dear old Rôro, how the years do pass us by… (107)

has a much greater visual and aural appeal in the original Japanese. The name Rôro itself is unusual and 'Chinese' sounding, but it is the dense, graphically compact clusters of Chinese characters such as *"Ah, Rôro sensei, shunpû shûu…,"* literally "Ah, Rôro sensei, spring breezes, autumn showers…" that suggest an aura of Chinese poetry and Chinese learning. Nobody would of course use such lofty literary phrases in normal speech, and they add more than a touch of caricature to the old man's portrayal. The difficult Chinese Ibuse had heard his grandfather recite in a theatrical voice during his childhood serves an excellent purpose here. It can elevate the character's voice to a high level of classical-sounding oratory, comic and touching at the same time. It also provides an effective rhetoric contrast to his more colloquial utterances, for example when he recalls the pathetic story of his foundling Ei. As his voice warms up with emotion, he begins to slip into thicker dialect:

*'Dono yô ni mo washira wa, ano ko ni wa nan ni mo hoka ni tsukushite yarananda yô de, omoeba tsui ni tamaranyô degasu.'*[24]

'I can't help feeling that I've never really done any-thing else for the boy. I feel terrible when I think of it.' (107)

In a brief sentence of two lines, there are at least four touches of dialect! Thus without saying a word about the old man's subtle changes of mood, Ibuse modulates the volume of his emotions by the nuances of his speech, especially the verbal endings.

Another interesting technique of manipulating emotional distance involves referring to the same character by his various titles. This is of course an old convention of Japanese prose, especially the classical *monogatari*. Its progatonists belonged to Heian nobility and most were avid collectors of impressive titles and honours. But in this story, Mr Tange's various titles are skillfully used to create distance:

> Gazing over the wall and down into the valley, I observed Mr. Tange walking down the main road with urgent steps. He wore his hat pushed back on his head, and went both uphill and down at exactly the same pace. It takes a man born and bred in a country valley to maintain such an even pace on slopes.
>
> I attracted the attention of the old servant still lying on the mat.
>
> 'I think it's safe to get up now. The Revenue Officer is just going. I don't expect he'll be back until dusk.' (100)

By assuring the servant that the Revenue Officer is just going, the narrator not only propels Mr. Tange towards his distant office, he removes him emotion-

[24] "Tange-shi-tei," p. 136.

ally from the scene, bringing old Ei and himself closer together. Though fairly stylized, at times even improbable, the description reveals a deep knowledge of the place and its customs, for example in the line about Mr. Tange's even pace of walking on the slopes. Sometimes the translator leaves out a characteristic detail that is important for country mentality, e.g. "the Revenue Officer is just going" is a contraction of the original "the Revenue Officer is just passing by the cotton field". The cotton field should be mentioned not only because it plays a role in the imagistic structure of the story, this way of referring to a particular detail in the scenery is typical for country people and their concrete awareness of the physical features of their place.

But the way Ibuse sets people into their landscape has another important stylistic dimension in the original which does not translate well. When Mr. Tange meets the lumber broker Yônoji on the road and they start their slow, ritualized gesticulations, the reader sees the two small figures through the narrator's eye from the distant vantage point of the wall around Mr. Tange's house. One is reminded of a slow-motion puppet play, or a somewhat caricatured landscape painting. Ei's uncanny familiarity with his master's dealings helps him guess from the body movement and gestures of the two men on the road what they may be talking about:

> 'It looks as though Yônoji's just getting down to arranging the deal, doesn't it? I'm sure he's trying to arrange a sale for the pinewood at Takitsuse in Shigawa.'

> The two small figures on the distant road had begun bargaining over the price, using the method of putting

their hands alternately up each other's sleeves. Putting his hand up the other's sleeve, Mr. Tange bent backwards from the waist. Doubtless he was laughing. Next, the broker too put his hand inside Mr. Tange's sleeve and bent backwards, then he wiped his forehead with his towel. The two of them went through the same motions any number of times, until finally they drew themselves up rather more formally and began to clap hands in time with each other.

'Clap, clap, clap... Clap, clap, clap... Clap, clap, clap,' went their hands in rhythmical groups of three. We did not hear the last three until the figures in the distant scene had finished clapping. The road ran straight and unbroken along the bottom of the deep valley.

The two distant figures adopted the same positions as a while ago, with their hands stretching down to their knees, then set off walking in opposite directions. (101–102)

Even in English, this passage has a strange objectivity, combined with a puppet-like, 'wooden' funniness and a certain 'framed in' charm of a miniature. The 'frame' is created by two identical expressions – *"mukô no ôkan de wa"* (literally "on the road over there") – which open and close the description. In terms of the story's dramatic structure, this is extremely effective. While in the opening scene Mr. Tange was almost disturbingly larger than life, here he is cut to much less than life-size, and the emotional balance is subtly redressed. In the original, another interesting thing happens. What Bester renders as "two small figures," "the figures in the distant scene" and "the two distant figures" appears in the original once as *tenkei jinbutsu* and twice as *enkei jinbutsu*. Now *tenkei jinbutsu* is a technical term of oriental landscape painting and means literally "items of human interest in a landscape tableau." *Enkei* is another such term, meaning "distant view," "distant scenery." Thus by engaging the reader in a pretended game of viewing a landscape painting, Ibuse provides a vantage point from which one can observe not only the described scenery, but the *description itself*. Perhaps he did not quite manage to introduce the "graceful sense of line" of the Southern school of painting into his prose, but he certainly did give it richer stylistic appeal.

In a casual aside, the narrator tells us that he came to the valley to unearth some "extremely highly valued articles of Himetani pottery." So a suggestion is dropped that the soil of the valley conceals something precious and there may be something 'closed' or impenetrable about its inhabitants as well. What the visitor painstakingly discovers is not necessarily considered useful or valuable by the local people.:

> After two weeks' efforts, I had dug up a single pitcher. It was decorated with an arabesque pattern in monochrome and was so massive that when I showed it to Mr. Tange and the manservant, the manservant said in disgust: 'That's a terribly clumsy-looking sake bottle you've got there!' (108)

This leitmotif of 'closedness' or impenetrability is then subtly orchestrated throughout the story. When the narrator learns about the strange marriage of Otatsu and Ei, he is shocked "at the almost monastic life that the manservant had led" and asks the old master why he had never given the couple their own household.

'Why, you see!' he said almost proudly, 'you might say it's their own private affair. Who can tell the motives behind other people's abstinences?' (107)

How can my narrator hope to touch the servant's soul, Ibuse seems to say, when the man is still a mystery to someone with whom he'd lived most of his life? In a perceptive essay[25] on the story, Itô Shin'ichirô singles out one particular image:

In the cotton fields, stalks and leaves were brown and withered, and the pure white balls of cotton rested on calyxes that were equally brown. The balls were fluffy and full, and time and again I felt the urge to stretch out my hand and touch them. (108)

Pointing out that the last line of this passage is the only instance in the entire story where the narrator expresses his lyrical feeling directly, Itô suggests that perhaps the souls of the valley people are as tempting to touch as the "pure white balls of cotton," but they are equally fragile and elusive. I fully agree, but I'd like to relate this important 'botanical metaphor' to the story's overall imagistic structure. Reading the text carefully, one cannot fail to notice how much attention is being paid to the valley's vegetation, and how crucial a role plants play in its aesthetic makeup. This is hardly surprising. A writer who grew up amidst the valley's lush vegetation would naturally reach for images of trees and flowers when setting a story in such a locale. Moreover, as William La Fleur convincingly argues in his preface to an anthology of Saigyô's[26]

[25] Itô, Shin'ichirô: "Tange-shi-tei kô." In: *IM kenkyû*, pp. 248–249.
[26] LaFleur, William: *Mirror for the Moon*. Introduction. New York, New Directions 1978, p. XVIII.

poems and in *The Karma of Words*, the botanical metaphor belongs to one of the most productive devices of literary symbolism in Japanese poetry and prose, both classical and modern. But I think there is an added dimension in Ibuse's usage of the ancient technique.

It is not merely the country child's rapport with the world of plants which is so characteristic for Ibuse's vision. That is just a matrix of feeling from which his senses touch the life of vegetation. Growing from this matrix is a detailed, almost scientific interest of an adult, extremely curious mind that wants to *know*, not just to feel. Someone may even feel that this concern with the naturalistic detail is a bit too obsessive, and has little relation to the aesthetic structure of Ibuse's stories. Competent and gifted translators such as John Bester, obviously thinking that the small naturalistic detail is of little import, often translate something as concrete and meaningful as:

> *Several akebia vines* were twisting their way up the largest oak tree, and from them hung dozens of oval fruit, still green and solid.[27] (Italics mine)

in a too general, unfocused way:

> Several vines climbed up the largest tree of all… (108)

In fact it is – besides the characterization through idiosyncratic diction we have discussed – almost exclusively through plants that people's deeper emotion and the nuances of their inner makeup are expressed. This may be considered an obstacle, even a weakness of literature rooted in local soil, and yet it gives the writer subtle tools with which to reveal his people's feelings in a concrete way.

[27] "Tange-shi-tei," p. 137.

The akebia vine of the previous image provides an excellent example. To translate it as 'several vines' might do for the hazier lyricism of the classical tradition. Yet even there, as we see it happen so often in *The Tale of Genji*, it is the particular flower – e.g. the *yûgao* or moon-flower of the Lady Yûgao chapter – that reflects and focusses hidden aspects of human character and portends certain fateful developments. Often the familiar symbolic meaning of these classical botanical metaphors is canonized by repeated usage in prose and poetry and they become rhetoric devices with their own poetic history rather than realistic natural images. In Ibuse's case, it is rather the other way round. Thus the akebia image blends smoothly into its narrative context, and at first sight signalizes no special symbolic relationship with the story's theme or its characters.

The *akebi* or akebia is a creeping vine, growing in mountainous terrain. Hence its other, more poetic name of *yamahime* or mountain maiden, mountain goddess. It has dainty five-petalled flowers of purple colour, blossoming in April. Its 10 cm long, oval fruit ripen in autumn, bursting open and displaying semi-transparent 'meat' of whitish colour with rows of little black seeds. The 'meat' is edible, tasting sweet and delicious.

If, as I believe, the story's leitmotif is the closedness of the valley and its characters, then the *akebi* image and its placing make eminent poetic sense. The fact that the image closes a movement of the story devoted entirely to the old servant, his childhood, all that is visible about him, and that the oval fruit of the *akebi* are 'still green and solid' provide the typical 'trailing note' (*yoin*) of Ibuse's description at its best: just as the *akebi* fruit, closed and solid in their own existence, the soul of the old man remains closed to the visitor. The *akebi* fruit will open when their season comes, but the narrator will be long gone from the valley, unable to taste their sweet, white 'meat'. The etymology of the word *akebi,* probably related to the verb *akeru,* to open, provides even sharper contrast to the closedness of the fruit.

Another important aspect of the story's human relationship that is echoed in the life of these plants is the motif of symbiosis. We note that the *akebi* vine climbs up the largest oak tree; no matter how tough its wood – and it is very tough wood, used for making *geta* etc. – it still needs the tree to reach for the sun. Yet if the botanical metaphor reflects something essential about the two old men's symbiosis at one point, it may also echo the changing moods of their relationship. Thus in the opening scene, when Mr. Tange certainly displays his 'large oak' qualities to the fullest, the servant "had no idea of defying his cruel master" and just brushes his cheek against the leaves of a plant of the orchid family that grows on the persimmon tree. At this point, he is as weak and vulnerable as the tender orchid, and the balance of the symbiosis is of a different kind.

For this is a story about symbiosis, and I don't hesitate to say it is Ibuse's version of a love story. We know that he has no patience with the love story of romantic convention, and has written several highly unorthodox 'love stories' before: in "Carp" we saw the love of two boys and a carp, in "Sawan on the Roof" he depicted a relationship between a man and a wild goose, and here we have the strange love affair of two old men. But if I say 'love affair', I give the relationship an awkward human twist which it does not have in the original. Let's just say the two old eccentrics exist in a state of symbiosis, quite like the *akebi* and the old oak tree.

The leitmotif of closedness or elusiveness is carried not only by the plant images (the *akebi,* the fluffy cotton balls), but by several skillfully placed images of shy animals. We notice that near the opening of the story Mr. Tange complains about someone having teased his prized carp while he was away, and "[they] had grown *timid* lately and fled to the bottom of the pond whenever *they heard a footstep...*" (99) A few lines before the narrator comes to see 'the pure white balls' in the cotton field, he passes by a millet field, and recalls that "the last time I had passed by the field, I had seen a field mouse that had clambered up a stalk jump down *in alarm at my footfall.*" (108; italics mine)

All this builds up to a wonderful ironic counterpoint towards the end. The manservant, enraged by the stupidity of his wife's present to the true master of his heart, Mr. Tange, starts pounding a bundle of straw with a wooden mallet:

> Otatsu must have been ashamed of the paltry present she had brought. Without consulting Mr. Tange, she rummaged about in the back entrance and the shed and produced a battered old wicker cage; she placed it at the foot of the persimmon tree and transferred her present to it. Alarmed by the sound of the manservant wielding his mallet, the six chicks, each like a ball of pure white

cotton, rushed hither and thither raising faint cries of distress. (110)

The parallel between the real cotton balls and their metaphoric counterparts – the chicks – is deliberate, I believe. But why a complete reversal of the emotional flow? While in the first image of the cotton balls we felt a receptive mood as the narrator's emotion flowed towards the 'fluffy balls', here the brutal sound of Ei's mallet suggests a mood of rejection, a harsh denial of all the shy pussyfooting around such lyrical objects and the desire to identify with them. And we realize with some admiration that this is the ultimate, even cruel touch of truthfulness in Ibuse's tableau. Precisely because he knows more about ordinary people than most city intellectuals, he never succumbs to their customary fallacy of underestimating the common man and thinking that because he is uneducated and lacks words, he also lacks emotional complexity. Ei may not have the words, but he wields his mallet. If, as Itô Shin'ichirô had suggested, the pure white cotton balls the narrator so desired to touch were like the souls of these country people, here the whole pattern is dramatically reversed. Ei feels that the present is absurd and does not belong in their place. It has arrived from the world outside of his village just as the visiting narrator has. And so this time the tables are turned and old Ei enjoys the luxury of standing vis-à-vis a 'lyrical object', perhaps even, figuratively speaking, vis-a-vis the 'souls of others'. But it is the objective author and we, the readers, who perceive the reversed situation and its considerable irony. The lyrical, verbal definition was not Ei's to begin with – he speaks the best way he can, with his mallet. Its banging announces to the world: "I am I, I'm different from you, and there's only so much you can know about me."

And the narrator realizes that too. Retiring to his guesthouse, he looks once more at the valley:

> The moon was rising over the hills beyond – a large, red moon as it so often is these days, shining from the sky directly above, illuminating the upper layer of the mists that shrouded the valley below. (111)

The valley is closed once again, and will remain so even to the prying eye of the moon. The author's humour did touch something quite deep in its soul, but the valley has its own 'humours' (in the original sense of the word) that will protect it from the outsider and his fancy illuminations. Perhaps the colour of the moon is Ibuse's subtle poke at the ideology that professed to know all about the soul of the common man.

## IV. THE DRIFTERS AND THE ROOTED

### WAVES: A WAR DIARY, TAJINKO VILLAGE

*This is how I feel: on the one hand I'd like to return to the country as fast as possible, and on the other I want to cling to Tokyo to the last.*[1]

Ibuse Masuji

There is more than mere nostalgia for the rural home-land in this statement. Just like so many others in the twentieth century, Ibuse had to leave his native place. Yet his home weighed on his heart and he couldn't forget it, because it was and always would be the basic source of his identity. The author anticipated the most urgent theme of modern times: the loss of home, life in exile, uprootedness. What did it matter that his native village is in the same country and he could visit it any time he wished; his imagination was vivid enough and the gap between the patriarchal village of his youth and the modern metropolis so great that he could easily imagine far more dramatic and less voluntary displacements – the common fate of millions of people in the twentieth century. This was also one of the reasons why I had a good rapport with him, for he felt how intimately this central theme of his work addresses someone who had to spend most of his life in exile. Ibuse perceived the symbolic symmetry: just as

[1] IM: "Nigatsu kokonoka shokan." In: *IMZ IX,* p. 324.

his young hero of the novella *Waves: A War Diary* (hereafter *Waves* for brevity),[2] I had to leave my "Capital" of Prague, invaded by Eastern barbarians and seek refuge in the West.

Among his longer narratives, it is above all *Waves* that has a special place in Ibuse's writing. It stands out not only as the first and quite likely the best among his stories on historical themes, but it is a work that took him over ten years to complete – much longer than serious novels three or four times its length. Although the first three instalments of *Waves* came out between March and July of 1930, Ibuse started working on it around 1927 and eventually needed nine instalments – the longest interval between them being three years – to finish this ambitious work by 1938:

> Compared to those who live a peaceful life, someone caught in the maelstrom of war has to grow up awfully fast... The writing style of a youth who is forced to grow up so quickly would by necessity mature equally fast. I thought I'd follow such progress as the days and months go by. That is how *Waves* came to be written.[3]

Elsewhere, Ibuse adds in a postscript:

> It was my plan to portray a protagonist who has to grow up very quickly amidst the turmoil of war, making use of whatever experience I managed to accumulate of my own.[4]

---

[2] The original *sazanami* of the title (*Sazanami gunki*) which literally translates as 'ripples' is a well-known *makurakotoba* (poetic epithet) referring to a vanished ancient capital on the shores of Lake Biwa. It has the melancholic appeal of ruined glory and appears a number of times in *Manyôshû* and other classics.

[3] IM: "Sazanami gunki no shiryô." *Bungaku* 21, 2, February 1953, pp. 70–71.

[4] Quoted in Yokoyama, Nobuyuki: "Sazanami gunki ron." In: *IM kenkyû*. Isogai, Hideo Ed. Hiroshima, Keisuisha 1984, p. 293.

It is a favourite technique of historical fiction writers in Japan to borrow or paraphrase a fragment of an older text, sometimes a simulated document with a touch of antiquity. To add authenticity to his *Waves*, Ibuse freely uses straight or slightly paraphrased quotes and expressions from the classical *gunki monogatari*, and occasionally a fragment from an ancient Chinese text, such as Sun Tzu's *Art of War*[5] or an elegant poem by Wang Wei. His learned warrior-monk character, Izumidera no Kakutan, will sometimes speak in the very words of an old *monogatari*:

> Tametomo was our enemy, but fearless enough to quell the Lord of Darkness himself. At Sutoku's palace, one of his arrows went clear through Itoroku's cuirass and lodged in one of the pauldrons of Itogo's armor; tough three-year knotted bamboo it was, and fletched with mountain-pheasant tails – a big, powerful beggar. Another one, a turnip-shaped 'howler', took away a good part of Oba Heita's left knee before it punched a hole all the way through the barrel of his pony.[6]

This passage comes originally from *Tales of Hôgen* (*Hôgen monogatari*), which Ibuse had translated into modern Japanese. These martial tales were often composed by monks of Kakutan's type, and Ibuse quite credibly portrays him as the author of his own

---

[5] Émile Zola points out the danger of using authentic documents in a historical drama or novel, saying that unless the author's style and that of the factual material are perfectly matched, "the truth may appear to put holes through the invented plot of a work." "Le Naturalisme au théatre." In: *Oeuvres complètes XI*. Paris, Cercle du livre précieux 1881, p. 427.

[6] IM: *Waves: A War Diary*. Trans. Aylward, David and Liman, Anthony. Tokyo, New York and San Francisco, Kôdansha International 1986, pp. 52–53. Hereafter, bracketed numbers after quotes refer to the page numbers of this edition.

*Juei Journal*. In this modern version of a classical story, we are watching, as it were, the possible creator of its ancient models. While the style of these inflated rhetorical passages comes close to that of the old tales, in his descriptive prose Ibuse avoids the most blatant conventions of *The Tale of the Heike:* where the courtiers' and the court ladies' costumes would be described in great detail in the classic tales, Ibuse either uses the 'fashion show' description as parody (as in the scene of the dullwitted servant fighting for Vice-Councillor Tomomori) or as a device of characterization suggesting old-fashioned thinking, as in the portrayal of Miyaji Kotarô. We note that the most efficient warrior of all, Kakutan, looks like a "down-at-heels bonze" most of the time, and that there are practically none of the lavish descriptions of court ladies' costumes that abound in *The Tale of the Heike*. In the original *Heike* tales, emotion is situational rather than an intrinsic part of a character's inner makeup and belongs to the scene rather than the individual character, who is almost interchangeable. In *Waves*, character portrayal is more consistent with the demands of modern realism, and the emotional logic of the main characters – the boy, Kakutan, old Miyaji – is carefully developed.

To reach for this particular historical material – so familiar to the Japanese from the classical martial chronicles (*gunki monogatari*) such as the *Hôgen, Heiji* and *Heike monogatari* and their popular stage derivations – and refashion it into contemporary literature presents a tremendous challenge. A long tradition of dramatizing the principal actors and even the minor episodes of the Heike-Genji conflict has not only created a detailed awareness of the era, but has conditioned the Japanese reader and theatre-goer (for a good deal of the puppet and Noh repertoire derives from the Heike story) to a fairly orthodox response to their poetic conventions. The high moments of these texts are as well known to the Japanese audience as the popular climactic lines from *Hamlet* or *King Lear* are to the English; to ignore the rhythm and the flavour of these archaic sounds altogether would make little sense even to the most modern-minded reader.

A contemporary writer who decides to paraphrase this material is obviously interested in more than just expressing his admiration of a particular narrative rhythm. Using the familiar theme and some of the well-worn ancient imagery, he must express his own concerns, resetting the archaic verbal icons into a stylistic context that is entirely his own. Two questions arise here: why of all the classical *monogatari* was Ibuse most attracted to *The Tale of the Heike*, and why did he switch to the historical genre at all? In "The Historical material of *Waves*– About The Heike and Myself" (*Sazanami gunki no shiryô – Heike to jibun ni kansuru koto*) he says "I never read through the classics except for *The Tale of the Heike*. I read its popular text (*rufubon*) carefully from cover to cover."[7]

The reason Ibuse gives for reading this classic more carefully than the others is that he intended to base his own novella on it. It is of course hardly thinkable that a major modern novelist could have ignored the great *monogatari* of the 'feminine' tradition, most notably *The Tale of Genji*, altogether. But it seems he was more in-

[7] "Sazanami gunki no shiryô," p. 70.

terested in the harsh objective world of men and their affairs than in the intimate inner world of the Heian court ladies. His own style came to draw increasingly more energy from the spoken, colloquial language and the strong rhythm of the *Heike* tales (taken from oral recitations), must have appealed to his ear.

The reason why he switched to historical writing, and why the *Heike* theme appealed to him so much was twofold: given his sharp eye for the social scene, Ibuse felt acutely the increasing anxiety of the early thirties, and the darkening, hopeless days and months that lay ahead. He wanted to write about war, for war was in the air, and he wanted to express the feeling of the dark, hopeless age he was living in. He knew it must be an authentic, personal account, but he definitely did not want to do it from the position of a helpless modern intellectual, for his voice would have easily slipped into the wailing tone of the *watakushi shôsetsu*. It was also becoming increasingly dangerous to voice any kind of direct critique of Japan's 'national interest', and a strong antimilitary sentiment wasn't likely to be welcome in an atmosphere of growing patriotic jingoism. As other writers of historical fiction did before him, Ibuse turned to the historical theme not to escape the pressing problems of today and find an ideal world in the past, but to cast a most urgent, most personal contemporary theme into a classical context where it would acquire a depth of resonance, an epic breadth and a sheen of elegance that could hardly be matched in a contemporary work.

Like other skillful historical writers, he chose to keep the better-known historical personalities in the

wings of the story's stage. He knew that to let someone like Yoshitsune become the central character
would mean sacrificing either his creative freedom
or his deep respect for historical reality as handed
down to him by literary tradition. Instead, he let the
historically marginal figure of his young narrator,
Taira no Tomoakira, observe the main events and their
protagonists from the sidelines, as it were, allowing
them to provide a very rough time-frame and some
dramatic punctuation of the narrative. The existence
of the young hero is historical, but otherwise little is
known of him except that he gave his own life to save
his father Tomomori in the rout of Ichinotani. Ibuse
shows him as a gently reared teenager forced by the
fires of war to change from the ways of the court to
those of a cynical sea-pirate. Like many other writers
of historical fiction, most recently Umberto Eco in his
*Name of the Rose*, Ibuse employed the ruse of buttress-
ing the credibility of his young diarist-narrator by
introducing the story proper with a translator's note,
and stating in a postscript that his friend's sister had a
schoolmate, who came from a family descended from
the original Heike fugitives and possessed a treasured
old diary that corresponds to his account. The aim is,
of course, to create the illusion of reality extending
into fiction or to obscure the boundaries of historical
reality and give a sharper focus to what is realistic and
possible in contrast to the wild flights of fantasy in
historical romances.

The basic outline and the setting of the story are
given: it happens between the flight from the capital
in the seventh month (lunar calendar) of 1183 and the

debacle of Ichinotani in the second month of the following year, and follows the natural escape route to the 'West Country' (i.e. Shikoku and Kyûshû) along the Inland Sea coast and the many islands dotting it. Yet within these given limits of time and place, the author has a completely free hand. Similar to the technique of some earlier stories and novellas, (e.g. "The River"), the plot develops like an unfolding scroll: one colourful episode follows another, often without the causal relation required by Western aesthetics. Young Tomoakira, although he shares the tastes and preoccupations of his class, is by no means the stereotyped Heian courtier, but rather an alter ego who expresses his creator's feelings and opinions, making the story attractive to the modern reader.

When we look carefully at the hero's coming of age and the painful choices this process involves, we can see how much of the writer's own dilemma is symbolically represented. The boy is forced to become a man faster than he likes and he badly needs a father-figure to identify with. As frequently happens in real life, his own father is disqualified by his unattractive qualities and Tomoakira has to turn either to the staunch and brave, but hopelessly rustic (almost foolish in his sincerity) Miyaji Kotarô, or to his opposite, the well-read and ingenious, if somewhat cynical monk, Izumidera no Kakutan. Two models of courage, two 'ways of the warrior' to follow: will young Tomoakira choose the good-natured, conservative representative of the good old countryside or will he follow the cooler, more efficient 'city intellectual' Kakutan? Precisely the kind of decision young Ibuse had to make himself as a young man: should he remain in his native village (note that Innoshima, Miyaji's native island is very close to Ibuse's birthplace and one of his favorite islands) and become a provincial gentleman-farmer who dabbles in the arts, or should he give it all up and go to the cold foreign land of the Tokyo *bohème* and become a modern artist? As a larger metaphor, the hero's choice between these two possible models of identity may be seen as symbolic of the Japanese situation at the outset of World War II, which was definitely a historical crossroads for that country. Just as the young boy – whether he likes it or not – eventually comes to act like Kakutan, because his is the more efficient, modern, and flexible way, while gallant, unbending old Miyaji dies a heroic death, so Japan emerged from the war with a cooler and more cynical sense of identity than the slightly naive and static prewar one. If it is a *Bildungsroman* about the private world of an individual, the novella also provides an insight into the shifting identity of an entire nation.

The reason it took Ibuse so long to complete this story is that he had a theme and a stylistic opportunity of such extraordinary potential that he had to develop both as an artist and as a human being to handle it adequately. From the very beginning, he intended to dramatize a young boy's initiation into a cruel world at war (let's bear in mind that he started writing this novella just before the Manchurian incident and finished it on the eve of the Pacific War), and to show how quickly one has to grow up in such an abnormal situation. And young Tomoakira does age fast, almost too fast considering that the story spans only ten months or so. From a pampered aristocratic youth whose toughest pastime used to be a game of *kemari* (a ritualized slow-motion Japanese version of soccer), he is forced to become a leader of desperate marauders, running away from the familiar cultivated world of the capital to a wilderness of rough fishing villages and camps in the forest.

While at the outset of his ordeal, the boy is terrified by the Genji ruffian who comes to challenge his father, towards the end of the story he calmly admires "the elegant display of skill" with which the monk Kakutan "sends five heads flying." Not that Ibuse is suggesting this manly toughness is admirable – note how differently the boy reacts during his two encounters with young girls, both named Chinu: the one at Tomonotsu who offers him some juicy pears in her garden and the girl Chinu of Ohashi's estate. With the first one, he is still alive emotionally and perhaps still too sensitive for his own good:

'Why is it, I wonder, that I so much love a man I shall never see again?'

Speaking thus boldly, she stares curiously at my sword hilt; then, asking if the spray will not rust it, begs me to let her draw it out a little.

I should be impressed by her pure heart, but the smell of her clothes and hair moves me to rapture. I put my hand on her shoulder again, feel her pleasure in it, hope she will whisper some little pleasantries in my ear. How strange I so desire the favour of a person below my station! (38)

At the time of his flirt with the other, he can hardly remember that a town called Tomonotsu existed – it's just another harbour town, one of the many that the exigencies of war made him raze to the ground:

> After the sun went down a little while ago, Chinu showed by her manner that she was attracted to me – a gesture of courtesy to my men, as well as their commander. I suppose a general can hardly help being admired by beautiful young girls wherever he goes. I wanted to hint, with a restraint becoming my rank, that her interest was not unacceptable. When next she came near, with eyes demurely downcast, I put my hand on her shoulder... (101)

Yet even while young Tomoakira loses some of his fine courtly sensibility, he certainly does not become blind to the great social upheaval he sees around him. From the very beginning, he is somewhat aloof – perhaps to write his diary he needs a considerable distance from the older leaders of his clan, which lets him see the weakness of his own class more critically. At times, one feels, he sees it too critically for a teenager of his social background so that it is not so much his voice that we hear, but the author's. By investing his young diarist with a social conscience – something we know quite positively the Heike family did not possess – Ibuse also makes it easier for the modern reader to identify with the allegedly medieval mentality that narrates the story. This is where Ibuse's imagination enjoys freest play and where it most departs from classical models such as *The Tale of the Heike*. Nowhere in the Heike epic would we find a sarcastic parody of a senior Heike general's cowardice, as in the following scene where the hero's father Tomomori is challenged by a Genji ruffian and sends out a dull-witted proxy to fight for him and even tries to teach him an 'extemporaneous *tanka*' required by court etiquette:

> In this kind of situation, it was naturally up to my father to accept the challenge, but instead, with a distracted expression, he called a certain Saburôji to him. Promising to give his younger brother four rolls of Hachijô silk if anything happened, he persuaded the poor devil to don his master's armour. Saburôji, being a little slow of wit, asked my father – who was trying to teach him an 'extemporaneous tanka' – again and again for instructions while the armour was being put on. (28)

The senseless brutality of war is always somewhat stylized and beautified in the classical *gunki monogatari*. When someone criticized him for not respecting the beauty of the older text, Ibuse replied:

> Reading the *Heike* I feel the events and the people are portrayed faithfully enough, but there is a lot of stylistic embellishment. It's the same when you look at the scrolls – they are very beautiful, and yet war must have been a pretty brutal affair in those days, too.[8]

Ibuse not only satirizes the older accounts' stereotyped sentimental conventions, but presents a realistic view of war that must have been far more brutal than the pretty ritual portrayed in the early *emakimono* (mostly handscrolls illustrating the tales) and the *gunki monogatari*. Setting the perceptions of the common people (or perhaps simply their common sense) against the narrow mentality of the ruling establishment shapes Ibuse's imagery in a certain way: time and again we note that the boy not only sympathizes with the people's view, he'd like to identify with them

[8] Ban, Toshihiko: "Ibuse-san kara kiita koto, sono 2." In: *IMZ III, Geppô* 4, p. 2.

if he could. Because of this mixed view, Ibuse shows us a brutal parody with the raw punch of a rural puppet show rather than the elegant, dance-like ritual of warfare we see in the *haute culture* of the epic tales or the scrolls, as in the bare-backed rider episode:

> He was announcing himself in a very inflated manner, but it was with just such phrases as my father would use on the field of honour. Saburôji twice looked back at us while he was speaking. As soon as he had finished, the two of them engaged. The other was the more powerful by far. He gripped one shoulder with his left hand and Saburôji's helmet with the right, and wrenching it around, actually tore his head off! A tremendous spurt of blood gushed out of the stump fully four feet into the air, drenching the trunk in red and splattering the ground about. The victor picked up Saburôji's sword and tied it to his horse's reins. The black horse stood steady, as though its will were lost with its master, so keeping the headless body in the saddle. (29)

Yet even the starkest of these images is conveyed by a highly polished and sophisticated style. Ibuse did not spend the long waiting years between the writing of *Waves* in vain: what really makes the young diarist's rapid emotional change credible is the maturing style of the narration itself. In the beginning, the boy's writing is fairly subjective, at times even sentimental. He still sees the world through the hazy veil of youthful memory, which makes the present but a shadow of things past:

> All I know is that we arrived at the old temporary capital of Fukuhara late last evening. Until three summers ago, it was my home, too. In those days, I thought of noth-

ing but running up and down its stone-paved streets. I remember my shoes made a sliding sound that echoed pleasantly from the earthen walls lining both sides. How I loved to kick my ball down those streets and run after it! Only a short time ago, but now moss coats all the flagstones and every type of grass imaginable has sprung up in the cracks. Cranesbill, plantain, *susuki*, and patrinia are flourishing. (32–33)

Many a time he sees things as they might have been, had the world not changed so drastically. Yet change it did, and the tone of the boy's reflections midway through the narrative starts to change too, though very subtly. We note that by the end there are few frills in his laconic entries and no 'poetry', only a tremendous fatigue and a clearheaded, pragmatic estimate of the resources left to him:

Occupied a place called Kitahama on Shiraishijima. Got a dozen boats and three hundred sacks of grain. Wounded in the right arm, and can't hold my brush. I am dictating this to Fukasu. In none of my engagements since the retreat from the capital have I known defeat, yet on this remote island, to be caught by vulgar bandits! My own fault. (102–103)

Reading Ibuse's polished and thoughtful style – even its somewhat faded reflection in English – we must watch for the nuances, for he is not a writer who rushes ahead on the crest of a wave of words along a clear linear plot. Quite the contrary – he will dwell on the shape and depth of every sentence until he feels it's perfect, even at the risk of a sluggish pacing. But where does the excitement and strong sense of rhythm come from? The writing is sparse and there are lacunae be-

tween the sentences where a lot remains unsaid. Some
lines, especially when Ibuse draws a stylized caricature,
are energetic and robust; yet others are fine, almost
invisible by contrast. It is this interplay and harmony
of shaded line that is difficult to perceive, because
to the casual reader only the thick line of caricature
stands out. What we tend to call 'vignettes' are often
important sections of the narrative scroll, contribut-
ing to its variety and consequently to the fullness of
our reading experience. Take for example the episode
about General Shigehira's old groom cutting grass for
his master's horse:

> A little apart from this bustle, General Shigehira's old
> groom crouches by himself. With a stout black helmet on
> his head and a small blade in one hand, he is solemnly
> cutting dry grass for his master's horse. A clump of grass
> is left where a broken arrow sticks in the ground. Anx-
> ious to avoid the missile, he has carefully cut all around
> it. (44)

While the image of an old man cutting carefully
around the broken arrow – instead of simply pulling
it out and throwing it away – bears the unmistakable touch of Ibuse's caricature, it tells the reader
a lot about the old man's mentality: he respects his
master's tools of war so much that he dare not touch
them, preferring his own tools and not wanting anything to do with the sinister place where the arrow
has struck.

Even when Ibuse parodies the lyrical accounts of
the Heike's glory and tones down the pathos of their
downfall, the ancient images still carry enough weight
and lustre to give an essentially modern story the sad

elegance of bygone days. Furthermore, the historical disguise – the theme's safe distance from the topical issues of the present – allows the contemporary author to maintain an aesthetic control and perhaps even overcome some of his bad habits. It would be easy to dismiss the pressures of leftism and the appeal of the *watakushi shôsetsu* mode in the literary establishment as irrelevant to a truly independent artist. But Ibuse is Japanese and as such struggles for his independence in ways different from a Westerner. He had tried his hand at Western techniques of storytelling before *Waves* and even managed to work out an interesting compromise between traditional Japanese ways of handling the first person narrative and those used in the West. Yet he is too serious an artist to imitate foreign modes when there are viable native ones that can be modified to modern expectations. He couldn't dismiss the confessional mode altogether, for he felt it provided an authentic, credible voice, a voice that could speak most intimately to a reader living in a confused age where the objective, wide-focus narration of the omniscient writer has lost much of its authority.

Unlike the self-pitying I-novelists of the orthodox school, Ibuse manages to preserve a considerable distance between his own self and the projected 'I' of his young narrator – note the skillful insertion of another 'I' (the 'translator' and editor) between the two – while maintaining the close focus, acute perception and convincing subjective experience of the Japanese first-person narrative. In a thoughtful article on "Fictional versus Historical Lives", Dorrit Cohn tries to define the distance between author and narrator in fictional autobiography. The general theoretical assumption seems to be that:

> First, autobiography – no less than biography – is a referential genre, a discourse that refers to the past of a real speaker; and second, that the first-person novel, at least in its classical guise of fictional autobiography, is the deliberate artificial simulation of this referential genre.[9]

A diary has a different purpose than autobiography – rather than systematically revealing and summing up one's life and personality, the diary is a closer, serialized chronicle of this personality, this 'I' as it copes with life's concrete situations. The difference then lies in selection and organization: autobiography looks at a life in its totality, diary as a day-to-day series of closely focussed events within a shorter span of time. The structuring of Ibuse's narrative with seemingly random diary entries is based on a flow of time, but the content and the colour of each episode is far more important than the passage of chronological time. When nothing interesting happens, there may be a gap of two weeks in Tomoakira's report, when events pile up, he writes as often as three times a day. The days he decided to save from oblivion are important to him personally as well as to the aestetic structure created by the author.

Yet Japanese diaries are often close to autobiography and what Cohn terms "a double pact" of fictional autobiography would seem to apply to the fictional diary as well:

> In effect all fictional autobiographies offer us a telescoped *double* pact, an autobiographical pact impacted within a

[9] Cohn, Dorrit: "Fictional versus Historical Lives: Borderlines and Borderline Cases." *The Journal of Narrative Technique* 19, 1, Winter 1989, p. 12.

fictional pact. I see in this literally equivocal origin of its discourse *the* decisive factor that (more or less consciously) shapes our reading experience of a novel cast in first-person form and sets it apart from the experience of reading a real autobiography.[10]

In *Waves,* a fictional diary of a marginal historical personality, we enter into a more complex 'double pact' with the author. On the one hand we are aware that the historical Tomoakira could hardly have written the way our young diarist does and that the life presented to us is fictional, and yet we also know that the man on whom our narrator was modelled was once undoubtedly flesh and blood, not an entirely imaginary character. While his diary is a simulated, fictional one, its elevated, deliberately archaic tone also gives it that strange aura of 'true' medieval illumination and consequently a greater measure of authenticity than one would find in a contemporary work. Moreover, by placing his story – so remote in terms of time – into the familiar landscape of his childhood, the author can indulge in a sort of lyrical excursion into the favourite scenery of his own past, without being too obviously nostalgic. The merging of Time and Place that Bakhtin calls *chronotope* is expressed most naturally here and instead of a strong plot we get a rich, detailed evocation of character and a strong ambience of place.

The old poem by Tu Fu, later paraphrased by Bashô in *The Narrow Road to the Deep North* – "In defeat, we have

[10] Ibid., p. 14. In: *Travellers of a Hundred Ages.* New York, Columbia University Press 1999, p. 8, Donald Keene says about the Japanese diary form: "To keep a diary is to preserve time, to save from oblivion days that from the point of view of the historian might seem of little importance" which applies to Ibuse's narrative.

still our mountains and rivers"(96) (*Kuni yaburete sanga ari*) is not quoted as a mere archaic ornament in *Waves*. It expresses Ibuse's deeper philosophy and his own brand of a modest historical optimism. Yes, we do live in a dark age, very much like the 'latter days of the Law', the dark *mappô*[11] era of the Gempei civil war. But while the flow of historical events and the changing of times can't be stopped, the wise man of Kakutan's mettle rebuilds his 'village' in his heart and in his mind, drawing energy and support not only from the permanent word of the great texts of classical antiquity, but from the eternal, life-giving rhythm of the familiar scenery around him.

The lofty historical theme and the diary format not only helped Ibuse bypass the pitfalls of the I-novel, they also enabled him to develop the classical poise and the aesthetic control needed to restrain the emotional turmoil he must have felt when virtually all his literary friends joined the popular proletarian literature movement in the late twenties, leaving him – ironically enough the only one among these intellectuals who had a genuine interest in the common people – in complete isolation. One does feel the loneliness and the longing for communication with human beings outside his own class throughout *Waves*, yet these feelings are mostly well-integrated into the story and do not become self-serving ideological motifs:

> Our carpenter was felling pines up the mountain. This man also had a sketch for me, of something like a

[11] *Mappô jidai*, according to Buddhist belief, is a dark period of the 11th–12th century when the previous Buddha is gone and the new one not yet born.

thatched hut. We might have to leave this beach tomorrow, but already he was leveling off ground under an old oak at the foot of a cliff. He had put up a branch of the sacred sakaki to placate the spirits of the earth he was building on. Once in a while, he would hum an air in time to his woodcutting, and as I watched his absorbed, contented figure I was seized with envy... (63)

Ibuse's central theme is expressed most effectively here. The mighty rulers of yesterday – the Heike – representing a special fixed law and order have turned into castaways almost overnight. If there is anything stable left in their world, anything the young courtier can cling to, it is the ongoing sense of everyday life preserved almost instinctively by the villagers. The closing coda of the novella, one of the most beautiful Ibuse has ever written, brings all the antagonistic forces of the narrative together in one final, peaceful chord:

There is a great old matriarchal oak in the garden; of the many arrows that have skimmed past her trunk, only one has pierced the bark. It is evening, and the island across the bay is dyed a deep purple. (103)

The straying men come and go (the original has *nagareya* or stray arrow), but the deeply rooted world of women – and of the villagers – remains. The emphasis on the feminine aspects of the oak is clearer in the original where the word *ubamegashi* is used. It means literally 'matron's oak', for it was this tree from which the dye for blackening married women's teeth was extracted. Thus the finale is not necessarily pessimistic. The young diarist was forced to leave behind all romantic dreams of youth and take a sceptical, clearheaded view of reality. The author, in his turn, took another significant step from what René Girard calls *"la mensonge romantique"*[12] towards his own version of *"vérité romanesque."*

*Waves* is one of those rare, completely successful works of art which happens once or twice in an artist's lifetime. A tremendous wealth of meaning blends with precise, realistic detail, colourful images of the heroic past are imbued with contemporary significance, and an entire poetic tradition is subjected to loving parody and thus to a critical re-interpretation, welding the best in the elegant tradition of the past with modern, enlightened scepticism.

## TAJINKO VILLAGE

In *Tajinko Village* I used a country policeman's record of miscellaneous incidents.

It was a long record, so I took up a part of his bulky chronicle and added a touch of fiction to it, changing things around. Thus when he says 'I like sentimental ballads (*naniwabushi*)', I'd write that he hates them and so forth...

Although it is a policeman's record, to keep it wasn't part of his official duties. Writing was a hobby for him and he invented quite freely. As a rule the resident policeman would have been married, but the narrator of this record is a single man. He must have collected his yarns from other stations all over Shikoku, since so many incidents could hardly have happened at one police station.

---

[12] Girard, René: *Mensonge romantique et vérité romanesque.* Paris, Editions Bernard Grasset 1961.

So I took a somewhat inflated manuscript, changed its tales and reworked its composition.[13]

The first great best-seller of Ibuse's writing career, this short novel also became a lasting irritant to 'progressive' Japanese critics. It has happened to other writers, of course, that the more their reading public enjoyed one of their novels, the less acceptable it became to professional critics. One can understand why the story was an immediate success when published on the eve of the Pacific War, and why it kept selling so well throughout the war years. At first sight it looks as if the story gave the common reader exactly what he wanted at this tragic historical juncture: a nostalgic evocation of a genteel world about to be swept away by a harsher and more cruel age. Yet the common reader is by no means a fool, and is not really gratified by a writer who flatters him too obviously. What the reader does appreciate is to recognize himself in a novel and be able to identify with its characters in a direct, emotional way. But it seems to me that this novella had a special, and not just pleasing appeal. Just when Japanese readers, looking into its mirror, thought they recognized a familiar face, the image started blurring, fading, and a somewhat frightening perception took place: "this is us" – but "this isn't us anymore." A vanishing face in the mirror, and a blank void afterwards. Although the space of the novella looks familiar enough, it really takes place between the historical present and a dark, ominous future. The great divide between the two, of course, is the war. Only after reading the story several times does one realize how large the shadow of war

[13] Hagiwara, Tokushi: *IM kikigaki*. Tokyo, Seikyûsha 1994, pp. 25–26.

looms over this seemingly placid story. It begins with a poetic, strategically placed quote:

> There is a verse by a certain poet that runs: 'Rippling waves / On the ebbtide shore; / Then into the village / Where the plum's in bloom.' The plum of course is not in bloom yet, but soon it will be, and then the verse will be a perfect description of the scene in one part of Tajinko Village.[14]

This is the village's natural past, with its typical ambience of Place and an easy-going compromise between man-made and natural environment. The soft-sounding name *Tajinko* means an edible plant, sorrel (*itadori*) in the Shikoku dialect. It grows wild in the mountains, and people collect it for the soursweet taste of its stem and the medicinal properties of its roots. It is a most fitting metaphor for the novella, as it too is characterized by a soursweet tone. The very first chapter-heading (left out in Bester's translation) says: "Emergency Warning at the End of the Year" (*"Saimatsu hijô keikai"*). We are told, in no uncertain terms, that a time-span, a year, perhaps a whole era is coming to an end and the 'blossoms' are just a memory belonging to the past. The awareness of a rich, multi-layered past is cultivated throughout the story by references to popular kabuki figures (e.g. the villain Sadakuro), ancient Chinese poems and sayings, and most notably in the entry of March 22. It is called, significantly, "Waiting for a Holiday" and shows the whole village on a fine day, holding a ceremony to pray for the welfare of new

---

[14] IM: "Tajinko Village." In: *Lieutenant Lookeast and Other Stories.* Trans Bester, John. Tokyo and Palo Alto, Kôdansha International 1971, p. 135. Hereafter, bracketed numbers after quotes refer to the page numbers of this edition.

draftees. But Kôda, the policeman-narrator, decides to realize "a long-standing ambition and visit the site of the old castle in the next village." (221) While the villagers are sending their sons to distant battlefields of the near future, the policeman goes to watch and imbibe the aura of other battlefields in the distant past.

'While my husband was alive', says the priest's mother at the Rokunomaru castle, 'you could hear them [the voices of the dead] in the autumn, crying up there at the pond. But my son says it's all a lot of nonsense and since he took over you don't hear the voices anymore.' (225)

How much of our own present will stay and how much will be swept away, how long will our own voices be heard, wonders the policeman. Perhaps all that will remain, as in the ancient castle, is something like a blackened grain of wheat. The voices can be heard only as long as someone believes in their existence, and then, like all outdated tradition, they become 'a lot of nonsense'. At present, there is just an emergency warning; it's dark and a cold wind is blowing at six in the morning; the crowds must be controlled by the police as they are seeing off troops leaving for the front.

Among the many negative views of the novella, Terada Tôru's and Sugiura Minpei's are most typical. Terada,[15] a humanist of somewhat Christian orientation, dislikes the story because the writer displays too much "worldly interest" – he is motivated by social sentiment rather than a genuine love for human beings. Sugiura, a more outspoken leftist, dismisses the story because he feels it is "A halfhearted modernization of the sentimental ballad (naniwabushi) of the philan-

[15] Terada, Tôru: "IM ron." In: IM-Fukazawa Shichirô. Tokyo, Yûseidô 1977, p. 35.

thropic Tokugawa Mitsukuni (*Mito kômon*), a glorified collusion of sentiment and established power."[16] In Sugiura's view, the story completely failed "to embody aspects of a deeper tragedy, suggesting through the sequence of events happening in a little country town during the Sino-Japanese war the larger cataclysm of Japanese society."[17] Isn't that precisely what the story does? If it is an elegy for the last days of tradition in a rural past, it is also a penetrating insight into how Japanese society works, and how – with some minor changes – it will probably continue to work in the foreseeable future. There are certainly many passages with a touch of naiveté, examples of the typical childish sentiment of prewar Japanese society: the departing soldiers, for example, sound like "children going off to a picnic" as they call joyfully "Be seeing you!" (*"Itte kimasu, itte kimasu!"*) boarding the train to Manchuria. Yet even if the narrator of this scene does not realize how few of these young men he'll be seeing again, the man behind the narrative does. Through a careful reading of the story, I'd like to show that there is a keen critical intelligence working between its lines, and that it is more productive to see a work in the writer's own context rather than in terms of superimposed ideological or philosophical systems. The novella will then emerge rather as a realistic insight into the life of a prewar Japanese village community and its lasting patterns of existence than as an elegiac pastoral romance as it has been conventionally perceived.

[16] Sugiura, Minpei: "IM." In: *Gendai nihon no sakka*. Tokyo, Miraisha 1964, p. 256.
[17] Ibid

218

The crucial question here is: how much of his critical awareness can the writer reveal when presenting his story through the diary of a man whose consciousness is defined by his narrow social context and therefore severely limited? So first we have to ask: who is this country policeman by the name of Kôda? Is he the tip of the long arm of the Japanese power establishment, as many Japanese critics suggest? Is he a *deus ex machina* who pulls the strings of events, manipulating people's lives, or is he more of a pivot of the narration – a rock in the flow of events, if you will – who happens to be in the most advantageous position inside the narrative and in whose hands the threads of all the village stories naturally gather?

Some of the stories are nasty, even gruesome. Before this man's eyes, all of humanity's foibles, vices and tragedies parade, if on a miniature village scale. Gambling, wenching, boozing, cockfighting, quarreling (very high on the policeman's agenda), violent fights, racism, robbery, theft, murder, lunacy, suicide, illness and accident; there is hardly one human vice – or tragedy – that is not represented in this supposedly sentimental story. It is a gallery of human types and life's dramatic situations, yet interestingly enough, two are conspicuously missing: innocent love and childbirth. What is being born here is a new age in the shadow of war, a world of growing bitterness and anxiety.

Tajinko is an island within an island, a small model of the great world outside, and its society – in fact any human society, Ibuse seems to suggest – is a gathering of lonely porcupines. They must live in close company, yet the closer they get, the more they will feel the prickly touch of the others' quills.

Kôda is a cool man – no wonder Ibuse has him dislike *naniwabushi* ballads and presents him with the nickname *Kantai san* or 'Mr. Frigid'. Like Kakutan or Manjirô, he is a man of contemplated action, being equally skillful with his sword as with his pen. Needless to say, to be skillful with the pen, he has to distance himself from the events he has taken a major part in. Unlike many wonderful *raconteurs* who lose their gift of words as soon as they leave the warmth of their favourite bars and their creative temperature drops, this man can operate in both zones, the frigid and the balmy ('warm' or *ontai* in the original). Two central places in the village (his own station and the neighbouring village office) are nicknamed frigid and warm for their micro-climates, suggesting not only a convenient spatial division, but also a psychological one. He speaks the local dialect, drinks and banters freely with the peasants, and yet he uses fairly literary words such as 'feel lacrymose' (*rakurui suru*) instead of the plain 'shed tears' (*namida o kobosu*) or *shôrai* for the more common *matsukaze* (wind in the pines). The recent expense in his household ledger shows that he bought two second-hand foreign novels – *Life with the Cossack Army* and *Les Misérables*.[18] Quite a well-read man for a country cop from a small Shikoku village before the war. Perhaps his voice is a trifle too literate here and there, given the limits of his junior high school education, thus betray-

---

[18] The selection of the policeman's reading is interesting: in Tolstoy's work we witness a policing action against 'reactionaries' and in Hugo's novel one of the most disturbing portrayals of a policeman ever written.

ing the writer's hand behind his own which helps him to wield the pen. But more often than not the blend results in a smooth, interesting stylistic compromise and the narrative voice successfully fulfills some of Ibuse's long-standing ambitions: to observe the common people with some objectivity (as a policeman must), yet remain an active, close participant in their daily affairs. He is not only able to speak their local dialect – still stylized, but more realistic this time – and thus close the gap that so troubled the young narrator of *Waves*, but also knows how to put down turbulent, even messy emotional affairs in a cool, descriptive, at times almost documentary style.

The narrator does not say much about himself, though he reveals his personality early in the novella:

> One of the neighbours with whom I've got friendly lately brought along a basket containing three crucian carp at least a foot long. 'I caught some carp,' he said. 'Would you like some?' He'd netted them beneath the reeds in the stream. Leaden-hued scales, silver bellies, a lively way of swimming – I put them in a bucket, enjoying the feel of the scales as I did so. At the same time, I began to get murderous thoughts, and went and fetched the kitchen knife to prepare them for eating. (137)

This reminds me of an experience I had on a local train in southern Shikoku years ago: it was a warm day, the train slow with many stops in small villages most of which still looked like Tajinko. At one of the country stations, a large butterfly flew in through the open window and alighted on the soiled floor, lifting its colourful wings gracefully. An old peasant in working trousers (*monpe*) and *tabi* sandals, sitting on the seat opposite me, looked at the elegant creature for a while – admiring its beauty, I naively thought –, then lifted his foot and stomped on the speck of beauty on the floor. Ibuse used to make me uncomfortable by always seeing both: the beauty of the butterfly, but also the occasional necessity of the peasant stamping his foot on it. The butterfly, one suspects, may have been putting some pernicious larvae into the old man's field and it is *their reality* he reacts to.

It is only natural that people of an ancient culture would prefer to show the outside visitor the surface beauty of their world rather than the brutal realities lurking beneath it. The Japanese are master-salesmen of an illusion: their world, they'd like us to believe, is based on social harmony, love of nature, the gentleness of a refined poetic tradition – an illusion we in the West are only too eager to buy, as a contrast to the opposite, and equally erroneous stereotype of the yellow peril, the inhumanity of the feudal system and the like.

We notice that one of the most brutal thugs in the story, a violent break-and-entry man is also an accomplished singer of sentimental *naniwabushi* ballads. It has been said that brutality is the flip side of the sentimentality coin, and if indeed this novella focuses on Japanese sentimentality, we must explore how it copes with the other side of the coin. Sugiura, Terada and other critics who would like us to believe that it does not cope with it at all, make the dangerous mistake of not differentiating carefully between *figural views* (views and sentiments expressed by literary characters) and *narrative views* (underlying opinions of the author, expressed indirectly through the way he presents his material).

There are quite a few brutal and unpleasant incidents in the novella, but two are in particular chillingly frightening: Granny Okinu hanging herself because she doesn't want any more favours from the village, and the priest Gankai dancing away the young Hiramoto to war. The latter is much less obviously so, and yet I believe it represents the most devastating indictment of the sentimentality/brutality package lurking beneath the placid surface of Japanese society. Perhaps it cuts a little too close to the bone to allow a clear realization even by critics as perceptive as Terada or Sugiura. In a postwar interview, Ibuse recalled the writing of *Tajinko Village*, emphasizing the threatening atmosphere of war surrounding it:

> The war was getting fiercer by the day, and one couldn't write careless things anymore. I still remember the acute mental anguish I felt when putting down the scenes of new draftees departing for the front... I took tremendous care what to write. Such restraint is no good of course, but there was nothing we could do. The Japanese people felt very differently in those days...[19]

The Japanese people at large may have felt it was their war, but I don't think Ibuse did. What he says about his mental anguish (*"totemo shinkei wo tsukatta yo"*) is unusually emphatic for him, so much so that I'd say he is indirectly reacting here to all the negative critiques of this work. Although his critical rejection of the war may be a little roundabout, it is there in the text to be perceived by the attentive reader.

On the surface of it, the farewell party for young Hiramoto is a very conventional, jovial affair. But

[19] *IM kikigaki*, p. 26.

I've always felt there was something deadly lurking beneath the placid surface of this scene. The village's elite has assembled to say goodbye to the eldest son of one of its 'pillars', the jûdo master Hiramoto, and Reverend Gankai, the local Zen priest, performs a brief dance to his own sentimental accompaniment:

'Gladly they [the young men] leave in answer to the call,' he sang. He bowed his head slightly, turned to look behind him, and shaded his eyes with his hand as though bidding farewell to his home. There was a slight burst of applause at this point, and Gankai, encouraged, went on in a more resonant voice:

'Not for them the tears of women and children!'

Slowly, he turned to face the front again and made gestures as though brushing aside women and children who approached him from right and left.

'With a smile they go to die for their sovereign lord.' (172)

Why does the smiling face of this lean, bald figure haunt one? Gankai, as his name suggests, is the 'inheritor of vision', for he is the seventeenth in succession to the famous founder of the local Zen temple, Gankô. "Instilling the spirit of compassion into the rude countryfolk of the area," Gankô's name means literally 'Bright eye', but also 'penetrating vision', suggesting an ability to read between the lines. Gankai's Buddhist name, a subtle variation of the original Gan (sight, vision) means 'scope of vision' or 'outlook'. On the day of the farewell party, the policeman goes to see him, for he feels a little guilty for having arrested a bunch of youngsters the previous day. When he asks the priest if he had committed a grave sin by taking so many young boys in charge, Gankai promptly replies: "Oh, undoubtedly." Not a conventional answer, but the proper one according to Zen. In this and other instances Gankai shows a sharp understanding of people and situations, and one might simply conclude that his dance, true to the spirit of compassion conveyed to the rude countryfolk by his great predecessor, eases the boy's departure to war, dressing the painful moment in a kind of familiar sentimental garb.

Were he just another song and dance man, not a learned Zen priest, we would not have to question Gankai's ambiguous role in the narrative. Kôda, the narrator, may not have noticed the strange connection between the meaning of the priest's words in the morning – "Undoubtedly you've committed a grave sin by arresting these young boys" – and the words he sings so nonchalantly in the evening: "With a smile they go to die for their sovereign lord." But we do, and we can't help wondering how true the priest is to his vocation. Whether Catholic or Buddhist, it is undoubtedly the role of a priest to ease the departure of the living into the great void, but certainly not dance them away to the battlefield while they are in the prime of their lives.

Amidst all the jovial drunkenness of the farewell party, Gankai's gaunt figure stands out as the shadow of the Grim Reaper in Gothic pictures, wielding his scythe and presiding over the merriment. We might also be reminded of the terrible Shiva demanding human sacrifice, as he dances the living away in his aspect of Nataraja, the Dance King. Am I reading a critical spirit into a text that was not deliberately intended by its author? I believe there is enough textual evidence to show that there is a critical judgment – as inconspicuous and subtle as it may be – between the lines. Before he is asked to dance, Gankai plies the young draftee with sake, and quotes a poem to him. He recites it in a low voice, and Kôda asks him to write it down in pencil in his own diary. This of course draws the reader's attention to the poem by giving it emphasis. The poem goes:

High o'er the road to remote Yang-kuan,

The smoke of barbarian fires, the dust from their forts.

It is spring, yet at times the wild goose flies;

In a thousand leagues, the wayfarers are few.

The clover came in with the Persian steeds,

The grapes were brought by messengers of Han:

Let your might strike awe into the foreign heart,

And never seek to make of him your friend. (171)

Kôda feels that the verse is a new one, and asks Gankai:

'Who wrote that – it was you, wasn't it?'

'Eh?' he explained in surprise. 'It's ancient Chinese!' (171)

Again, a subtle point is made by suggesting to the reader that the poem only *looks* as if expressing Gankai's own, contemporary viewpoint, while in fact it belongs to the ancient Chinese. Gankai naively provides all the background information, without making the obvious conclusions:

A man called Wang-Wei, who lived during the T'ang dynasty, wrote it. He came from Ta-yuan, a walled town which the *Japanese forces have now occupied;* they say there's a *Japanese-owned factory there.* His hobby was writing poetry, and he left a good number of farewell poems. He

226

even wrote one to say goodbye to Abe no Nakamaro, a Japanese who served as a scribe at the T'ang court.... It [Wang's poem] seems to express perfectly what I feel about young Hiramoto here. (171; italics mine)

But surely not what the author feels. The irony is unmistakable: the smoke of barbarian fires from the original – and contemporary – Chinese point of view is now the smoke of the Japanese invaders' fires, the dust rises from their forts and their factories. The Chinese were generous and friendly to us in the past, Ibuse suggests by mentioning the envoy Abe no Nakamaro, and this is how we repay their kindness – we come now as the enemies and the barbarians of the old poem. Had he wanted to avoid the obvious conclusion a thoughtful reader would draw, Ibuse might have chosen another Chinese poet, quoted different farewell lines. But Gankai doesn't see the obvious irony, and thus, exactly as his name suggests, is a man of 'limited vision'. His view is circumscribed by his social and cultural orbit: while within it, he sees clearly and correctly; beyond it he is blind. The author's implied irony is considerable – Gankô, a man of penetrating vision who could read between the lines; Gankai, his lesser successor, a man who can't even read the lines.

And so, what at first sight looks like a casual collection of sentimental yarns begins to reveal its deeper aesthetic cohesion. The opinions of the man who writes the diary may be as limited as the other 'figural views' he relates, yet the narrative viewpoint expressed by the author clearly transcends these limitations. So it is with the way the various episodes are told, how they are introduced and organized. When I first read the story's second heading of December 30, which says: "The Madman, the Badger and the Household Ledger," I thought this must be Dada composition. And yet, just as the first heading ("The Emergency Warning at the End of the Year") sets the historical scene, the where and when of the narrative, the second contains in a nutshell *how* it will be told, and suggests not only its thematic range and variety, but its metaphysical span.

Significantly, the episode begins with Kôda awaking from deep sleep and musing about the predictability of events. According to a theory forwarded by one of his colleagues, you could tell people's general type of business by their voices: an abrupt "Officer!" suggested trouble, a child's voice meant it had found some lost property, a young woman's meant a request for a prostitute's licence and so forth. Theory proposes an ordered and predictable world, and the voices of these visitors do seek order, directions, maintenance of a status quo. Yet there is another world out there, which is completely beyond human control, a world of lunacy and unmanageable wildness. It is not necessarily pathological or 'abnormal' by modern flexible standards, for those who know the lunatic of this episode well admit that he is seventy percent normal. We understand that the wild dog who had to be destroyed did nothing worse than biting the calf of a somewhat hysterical woman. It's easy enough, even without contracting rabies or raving madness, the author suggests, to become a wild dangerous creature, threatening the ordered 'normality' of Japanese society.

What is really interesting here is not establishing the degree of the boy's clinical madness. By modern metropolitan standards, changing clothes three to four times a day or jabbing young women in the rear would hardly be considered 'mad' in any but a metaphorical sense. It is the way the other villagers perceive this wildness that draws the contemporary reader's attention: "You'd think he'd got some special power," they say, and: "Hardly human, I call it." (148) Leaping like a frog and running as fast as a wild animal, the lunatic lives on the borderline of humanity and wildness, ironically the freest existence in this village of conventions.

Such wildness, Japanese culture decrees, must be contained: tame it by tradition, draw it into the human orbit (as the great lore of fox and badger stories does), relegate it to the fringes of the village or beyond – as with the original banishment of the naughty Susanoo in the myths – confine it in the lunatic asylum. And if all else fails, let the stamping foot fall and reach for strychnine or rat poison. Crude and somewhat rural poisons, these potions against wildness – or perhaps they are emblems of wildness itself. Note how often rat poison is mentioned – and used – in the story. Unmanageable passion in humans seems to equal the wildness of nature, and requires similar treatment. That the poison does not have to be force-fed to the culprit simply shows how deeply social convention can be internalized. Although, as the priest suggests, there are many other ways out of one unfortunate girl's situation, she reaches for the almost prescribed solution to a desperate love affair – rat poison. There are two ways of looking at the poison: either as an extreme opposite of culture and the individual's desperate refuge from it, or, more pessimistically, as an internalized prescription of the culture itself against wildness or abnormality of any sort. This ambivalence shows clearly in another rat poison incident, when a girl takes it to follow her fiancé who has been killed in the war. Kôda thinks there is something beautiful about it; but Ariga wonders, more sceptically, if she wasn't being forced into marriage with another man. Whether the rat poison is an antidote to culture's more subtle intoxication, or simply a drastic extension of it, there is another potion that flows most freely through the entire story and plays a very important dramatic role in it – sake. When the sensitive 'madman' is caught and transported to the hospital, it is the local busybody-drunk, Boozer, who provides eager assistance:

'You're not well, so you've got to get better soon,' said Boozer.

'I don't like hospital!' said the madman.

'Don't be silly, you've got to get better quickly to please your mother.'

'Well, then, I'll go there once...' he said. 'I've got a train running in my head, so I don't like cars.' he added.

'There, officer,' said Boozer, looking at me and laughing.

'Just listen to the cunning things he says to try and get away!' (150)

By now, however, the madman had finally decided that it was really Boozer who was off his head. "Boozer, please get better soon, I'm praying for you," he said. "Be good now, won't you, Boozer, until I come to fetch you?" One wonders – is the madman right? It is clear from the passage that the boy still has a gentle, human voice, though he may occasionally "leap like a frog" when frightened. Although a little fluid, the boy's existence and its wildness still belong to culture – he likes to dress in human clothes, and speaks a human language. The true lunatics of the insane ward don't:

> …on the other side of the iron bars in the ward, I could see a lunatic running about *stripped to the waist* in spite of the cold. At the corner of the corridor, another madman stood on one leg without moving, *like a weary duck*. Someone else… was making a sound *like the cry of a pheasant*. (150; italics mine)

Here is true wildness beyond the human ken. It may be as brutal as giving him a drink of rat poison, the narrative seems to suggest, to expose the tame wildness of this boy's mind to the frightening animal world of the ward, a world of "wordless, unintelligible muttering." It is interesting to note that Ibuse interweaves the mad boy's story with a seemingly innocent year-end drinking party. It is attended by some soldiers soon to leave for the front, and the omnipresent Boozer, who never misses an opportunity to get a free drink. They are all "rather far gone," and the soldiers' representative indulges in some high oratory:

> 'We're very much obliged for all you've done for us,' he was saying, 'but we're off to the wars at last. The weather's cold these days, so I hope you'll all take care of yourselves. For a man, the chance to fight for his country is the honour of a lifetime, so we're all on our mettle. Whatever we do, we're determined to give it everything we've got!'

'That's the stuff, Kan boy!' shouted Boozer. (148–149)

It is these drunken youngsters with Boozer at their head who go out to catch the 'mad' boy, and one can't help wondering – isn't Ibuse hinting that there is a greater collective madness in the making here, an intoxication by culture and its ritualized poison that might be even more frightening than the visible 'abnormality' of one individual? That sake is poison, if not taken according to proper cultural rituals, is suggested time and again in a number of episodes. The judo master, Hiramoto, takes it *cold* after his son's farewell party, and barely survives a heart-failure. The thief drinks it *alone* after a major job and gets caught. Otaguro, a mild and diligent man, turns violent and uncontrollable when he's had *too much* of it. As the policeman sums it up: "Too much drink poisons the system, you know." Milder than rat poison, sake still performs its two possible functions, if on a more ritualized, genteel level: it can intensify 'culture' and the mind's intoxication with it, but it can also provide the individual a refuge from his culture.

In the context of all this, the switch to the badger motif makes eminent aesthetic sense. When the policeman hears that someone saw a badger in the state-owned forest nearby, he asks an old man why the villagers don't catch these animals:

'Oh, so it wasn't enough to kill a stray dog yesterday, officer?' he [the old man] said sarcastically.

'Now you want to go hunting animals in the hills, I suppose. Hunting wild dogs is at least some use to the public, but a government employee hunting badgers – there's a fine idea for you!' (151)

The old man admits that very far back the village did hunt for badgers, but those were austere days of starvation, and they killed the animals for food, not for their furs. At this point, another old man, the former village headman, comes along and chimes in with some charming badger tales:

> 'One of the most amazing badgers of all,' he said, 'is the kind called a 'thousand-cushion badger,' that turns itself into cushions along the road as far as you can see.'
>
> 'Whether badgers can turn themselves into things or not, I wouldn't be sure,' I put in, 'but they do say that wild animals hate any newfangled installations.'
>
> 'Ah, I don't doubt it,' agreed the former headman. 'Way back, when the village first got a post office and telegraph poles, the postman was often tricked. I expect the badgers had a grudge against modern facilities like post offices and telegraph poles. Why, I myself have seen the postman knocking at the telegraph pole, thinking it was a door.'
>
> 'How about radios, then?' I asked. 'I expect the badgers resent them particularly, don't they?'
>
> 'I'm quite sure they do,' said the former headman. (152)

The point is obvious: halfway between the extreme world of raw, untamed nature where human spirit can only run wild in circles of lunacy and the too predictable, too geometrical domestic order of the policeman's household ledger lies a zone of compromise. A meeting point, where nature's wildness has been contained, but not extinguished, by human imagination and where mute animals are endowed with human character and human voices and thus can speak for a whole graceful tradition of the past. A little crazy as it may sound, the folktale badger has every reason to resent radios. They bring an oral culture of a different kind, speaking for lofty issues of education and wartime propaganda, and obliterating this charming creature's imaginative existence. Instead of a "thousand-cushion badger" that can turn itself into cushions along the road as far as you can see, modernity has lined the roads with regular lines of telegraph poles, as neat and predictable as the rows of figures in the policeman's household ledger. This is why the ledger appears in the heading along with the madman and the badger, and why it closes their stories. That the narrator gives a fair amount of thought to the order of things, to the predictability and randomness of events, is confirmed again in the entry of March 20:

> I have the feeling that incidents tend to follow a fixed pattern. There's nothing at all for a while, and then, suddenly, they start again in a rush. Very often, too, they're the same general type of incident. I often used to notice while watching people go past the police box in the town that there were moments when the flow of people would suddenly dry up completely, and others when everybody who went past was a young woman. In just the same way, you get two or three days with nothing happening at all, then a whole crop of small incidents hardly worth paying any attention to. (207–208)

We might say that the author's 'theory of narrative' is reflected on a domestic, familiar level in the everyday views of his narrator and forms an organic, yet visible part of the narrative. The motif of another kind of poison runs throughout the story. Less violent than rat poison, and not nearly as exhilarating as sake, it is nonetheless quite lethal. Looking at the ruins of Roku-nomaru Castle, the priest quotes Bashô's version of Tu Fu's famous poem: "The nations pass, as they say, but the mountain stream flows for ever." (227) A nostalgic sigh, but not reality anymore. Rivers are being filled in, mountains reclaimed and leveled, although as Kôda says, filling in the village's stream is "almost as bad as breaching the banks of the Yangtze river." But pollution, he correctly recognizes, spreads from the human mind, and it is when the mind is poisoned that other things die. When two rival gangs of middle-school students confront each other in a violent brawl which results in murder, he concludes:

> Personally, I'm not fond of the idea of 'rounding up' schoolboys, but the fact is that the bad ones among them are aping university students in Tokyo by hanging around the cafés, smoking and drinking, and carrying on shamelessly with schoolgirls wherever the fancy takes them. Some university student or other, who was back home for the vacation, apparently came to headquarters to complain that to blame them for such things was 'old-fashioned and uncivilized.' But I wonder what would happen if the countryside was full of university and middle-school students like them? Most likely, every-thing in the fields and woods would be dead within the year. (167)

A consistent view is expressed throughout the narra-tive: there is a fairly innocent, if harsh and 'uncivilized' world of the patriarchal village, where people used to live like a family, and the world of the modern city from where the newfangled installations and manners spread. The nostalgic world of the village is not entirely real, and not necessarily the author's own, for it is presented mostly through the hazy veil of elderly people's youthful memories, or as a frail melody of little girls' songs. Interestingly, the most idealistic view of the village and its 'nature' is voiced indirectly through a city-policeman's report, and it sounds rather like wishful thinking from the midst of urban squalor:

> He would be better advised to give up ideas of coming to Osaka and engaging in manual labour of such an unsteady nature, and to continue his leisurely life in the country, there to cherish his spiritual resources and, from time to time, seek solace for his mind in the pleasures of Nature and the passing seasons. End of report. (229)

In the policeman's advice how a wise man should live we hear a reflection of the ancient ideal of Chinese poets, men like Wang Wei, Li Po and especially the author of the utopian fable *Peach Blossom Spring* T'ao Ch'ien. The city, and even a modest provincial town dumps its unwanted pets into the village's backyard and puts contaminated seeds of wildness into its youngsters' minds. Perhaps a novel theme in 1939, to the contemporary reader it is hardly original. The *yakuza* toughs of Café Lulu and their tarts are morally no different from their present-day counterparts, yet they look a little mild to the reader of the early twenty-first century, whose image of a gangster is fashioned by *The Godfather*.

But there is another, less visible motif that emerges from this contrast of country and city, one that relates directly to Ibuse's larger theme of stasis and flow, rootedness and drifting. While in "The River" the course and 'becoming' of the stream were given and the flights of imagination were articulated vertically, in *Tajinko Village* it is mostly the horizontal movement that is developed. The human episodes that dotted the river's stream in the earlier story have here become the narrative's central current, contained by the walls of convention and ritual. At first sight it looks as if the wave of modernity from the city might wash away the old mainstays of identity. The 'modern boys' are all flux and no substance, and to attempt to put some spirit in them would be like "trying to put backbone in a lump of custard," as Kôda realizes. Because they have so little confidence in their inner resources, they want to identify with others of the same mold:

His hair was glistening with pomade and he wore a double-breasted suit with a red tie. His newly shaven cheeks gave off a smell of cold cream. Young men dressed in this way are known in the village as 'modern boys'; the effect was very similar to that of the young man who had come with the tart this morning. There was nothing strange about the coincidence; in town, there are any number of young fellows from the same mold. What is strange is that they should all, to my eyes at least, *seem to conform so closely to that mold.* (192; italics mine)

The old villagers, on the other hand, are like the badgers of their folktales – able to assume different identities on the surface, but underneath their various disguises, the same wily old creatures. We note that even the two pivots of normality and order, the policemen Kôda and Ariga, look like burglars themselves when they dress up for one of their night missions. The deranged boy, less convention-bound than everybody else, changes identities as freely as his clothes; yet even he has more personality than the 'modern boys.' Hiramoto, the judo master, who can "take people apart", can also put them together as a skilled bonesetter, and the most vicious robber can sing beautiful *naniwabushi* ballads. These people are solidly rooted in one sense and yet quite fluid in another.

A human identity without backbone is not necessarily an evil one to Ibuse; a man with a 'custard spine' is just less useful to his society and less interesting to the writer. The identity of the old badgers may be fluid and interchangeable on the surface, but there is a firm core underneath and they exist within the 'embankment' of custom and ritual. By contrast, the identity of the modern boys is that of a jellyfish – liquid and soft throughout.

The story ends, quite convincingly, with the flow of the most basic kind – water. Perhaps in this finale (called "The Case of the Water Disputes") the figural views do blend with the narrative view and the sentiments expressed here are the writer's own. But we must not forget that this entry was added after a very long break in the narrative, lasting two months, while the pauses between the other entries were no longer than two or three weeks. On April 5, the policeman goes to see Dr. Nanba, for "ringing noises and pain in his ears." No wonder – this man has been the village's ear for a long time, and now his ear says: enough, let's hear no more. And indeed, for a long while he doesn't hear anything; the first case is the water dispute of June 7. It would seem Ibuse needed a final chord of harmony after all the turmoil of the previous incidents. What could better serve this purpose than the most essential, life-giving element of Japanese mythology: water? If he were a sentimental writer, he might have sent Kôda on a poetic trip to a beautiful waterfall in the mountains and have its purifying power wash away his fatigue and the grime of his soul. But Ibuse is a sceptic and deals with water as a source of discord, not of harmony and purification. The final harmony comes not from the mythical power of water itself, but from human willingness to compromise. The ancient idiom, *mizu wo mukeru* (literally to direct water, but metaphorically to reach an agreement) applies perfectly here. As in the previous village stories, there is of course a fair amount of mythical belief and superstition:

> On the way back, I caught sight of a bonfire in front of the shrine to the water god. I went to look, and found a large number of people pouring oil on a pile of blazing brushwood. A bamboo fence had been set up round it, with sprigs of fresh bamboo grass at the corners, and an ascetic was blowing lustily on a conch shell, writhing about in a kind of frenzy as he did so. In time with him, a large number of people were worshipping the fire, fingering their prayer beads or rubbing the palms of their hands together before their faces. But it looked as though their prayers for rain would be entirely wasted, for the sky was covered with stars, with not a breath of wind from either sea or hills. (241)

In contrast with the earlier stories such as "Kuchisuke's Valley," these mythical beliefs are less obviously satirized, but simply presented. They belong to an older world, where water disputes were solved not with police intervention, but by rules as ancient as the rice-planting songs of the season. But at this time of national emergency, the people are willing to compromise their local interest for a larger issue. Should we blame Ibuse for putting his finger on this phenomenon just on the eve of his people's total immersion in what seemed then as a genuine national cause? Should we blame him for suggesting that this willingness to compromise may be as eternal, as basic to this particular culture as the flow of water?

If I understand Sugiura correctly, he admits that criticizing Ibuse for the way he wrote this story might be the same as blaming the Japanese people for what they are.[20] And that – to paraphrase the poem Gankai copies in his calligraphy – would be as futile as scolding the rain, and reviling the wind of their native islands.

---

[20] Sugiura, Minpei: "IM." p. 250: "One might say that Ibuse Masuji's literature is a mirror that reflects the life of the Japanese people. He not only employs the above-mentioned themes from everyday life, they clearly define the tone of his style as well. The writing reflects not only the laughter and the gloom of the common people's lives, but one feels it is saturated with the lucidity, the humanity and even the anarchistic tendencies of the popular psyche in this country."

"ISLE-ON-THE-BILLOWS," "LIEUTENANT LOOKEAST"

*An extravagant business, war is.*

Corporal Tomomura in "Lt. Lookeast"[1]

In December 1941, the theme of war, forced exile, shipwreck and drifting that had haunted Ibuse for the previous decade suddenly became a frightening personal reality. Drafted into the Imperial Army on November 22 as a war correspondent in a propaganda unit, Ibuse was shipped out of Kôbe harbour ten days later on board the steamer *Afurika-maru,* headed for an unknown destination somewhere in the Southern Seas. The telegram that had summoned him came from the Imperial Headquarters itself and was based on the recently passed General Mobilization Law[2] which made it possible to draft practically anybody, with the exception of the very old, the very young and the very infirm.

The propaganda unit – most probably modelled on Dr. Goebbels' pen units that accompanied the Wehrmacht – was divided into four squads: 120 men were

---

[1] IM: "Lieutenant Lookeast." In: *Salamander And Other Stories.* Trans. Bester, John. Tokyo, New York and San Francisco, Kôdansha International 1981, p. 35.

[2] Wakuta, Yû: *Shichû IM.* Tokyo, Meiji Shoin 1981, p. 143.

being dispatched to the Philippines, 120 (including Ibuse) to Malay, 80 men to Burma and another 120 to Java. Nobody had the faintest idea what exactly these intellectuals – painters, writers, photographers, cameramen, musicians, editors, Buddhist priests, and even a few scholars of Islam – were supposed to do at the front. Most of their commanding officers were not sure what to do with them either, but the army has old techniques to fall back on when orders are not clear. Mustering his troops on the deck, the escorting Lieutenant-Colonel began with a roar: "Atten-shun!... I am your commanding officer. Your lives are in my hands now. Any complaints and I'll cut you to pieces!"[3] A visible tremor went through the assembled ranks, and one man even fainted. But there was also one who mumbled: "Go ahead and try."

Before the rollcall was over, the Commander, who sported a huge drooping moustache, had acquired the nickname 'Moustache' or *Hige*. He was a bit surprised that his pep-talk had such a limited effect on his bohemians, and concluded:

> Your bunch is infected by anti-military thought, and I'd better watch my step on this ship. I won't come to the deck unless it's absolutely inevitable. With you people on board, one might end up in the ocean. (157)

In a sense he kept his word and showed up on the deck only when the news of Japan's war effort was good, to assemble his troops and order them to 'worship toward the East', a kind of ceremonious

---

[3] IM: *Chôyôchû no koto*. Tokyo, Kôdansha 1996, p. 157. First published in serialized form in *Umi,* September 9, 1977–January 1, 1980. Hereafter, bracketed numbers after quotes refer to the page numbers of this edition.

thanksgiving in the direction of the Imperial Palace. Since 'good news' was sometimes no more than a safe passage of a single Japanese plane over the ship, 'worshipping toward the East' became a frequent, daily ritual. So frequent, in fact, that the Commander of the Burma squad once said to 'Moustache': "Aren't you overdoing that Eastern worship of yours?" (158)

First impressions, whether pleasant or terrible, are usually the longest remembered. Fourteen years later Ibuse would immortalize the commander's line "Any complaints and I'll cut you to pieces!" (*"Guzu-guzu iu mono wa, buttagiru zo!"*) in his best known satirical story about the army and its drills, "Lieutenant Lookeast" (*Yôhai taichô*, 1950). The 'far-worshipping' (*yôhai*) of the title also suggests how vividly the exaggerated ritual stuck in Ibuse's mind.

It is interesting to compare Ibuse's wartime diary, called "Sailing South" (*Nankô taigaiki,* 1943) with a later memoir, *During My Draft* (*Chôyôchû no koto*) that was published in twenty-nine instalments from September 1977 to January 1980. What couldn't be spelled out in "Sailing South," for obvious reasons of strict wartime censorship, is retold in expanded form and much greater detail in the later chronicle. The fact that it is the longest serialized work of Ibuse's late years and shows a great deal of concentration and skill in organizing the elusive material of memories, suggests how seriously the author was concerned about leaving behind a truthful, objective account of the most painful period not only in his own life, but in the life of his people.

In the first journal, we get a fairly sketchy outline of the main events, but little comment – at least not the kind of critical or satirical comment that the suspicious eye of an army censor would pick out. The seasoned Ibuse reader, whose ear is attuned to the little silences between the lines, and the way Ibuse's pen juxtaposes seemingly neutral events, will probably know how the writer felt in the given circumstances. *During My Draft* tells a different story. Although in no way an emotional outburst of Ibuse's wrath – which had found expression long before in stories such as "Isle-on-the-Billows" (*Wabisuke*) or "Lieutenant Lookeast" – it still sounds like an indictment, but rather one reminiscent of a calm, dry summary by an old judge passing sentence on a stupid and dangerous prank of anti-social adolescents. Ibuse had no illusions about the army when he was forced to join it:

> People said to me: 'In the army it's essential to know the ropes. To remember the basic rules of the game is vital', they stressed. There were cases of soldiers who lost their army-issue shirt and deserted, for it was against the rules. So, I concluded, the army is a rather frightening place to be. (155)

As Wakuta Yû points out,[4] the war diaries are Ibuse's own *Sazanami gunki*. It is to an almost uncanny degree that the prewar novella anticipates the events that would so deeply influence Ibuse's life and postwar writing. Like the young diarist of *Waves*, who is frightened and often deeply upset by the brutal events that threaten to engulf his life, Ibuse's eye searches for some signs of normality in his surroundings, something lasting and familiar that might give him a little solace. The boy Tomoakira, at least at the outset of his ordeal,

[4] Wakuta, Yû: *Shichû IM*. Tokyo, Meiji shoin 1981, p. 147.

watched the common people of small fishing villages along the Heike clan's escape route, envying them their peaceful existence, or sympathizing with them when the war took it away. In moments of despair, he would turn his eye to the ocean or to the familiar flowers and trees around him, be it the "smallest leaf of the fragrant orchid growing on the *nagi* tree in our garden."[5] It is the same minute and loving attention to the living things of an environment threatened by death that characterizes Ibuse's perception in his wartime diaries. Typically, his own discomforts and fears – and there must have been many – are passed over in a line or two, while a visit to Singapore's botanical garden towards the end of "Sailing South" takes half a page:

> Rain, rain from early morning… With an English diction-ary under my arm, I'm off to the botanical garden. Every variety of the Chinese rose is just in bloom: red, pink, white, 'dyed' (*shibori*), double flowered, bell-shaped (*fūrin bussôge*). I saw two varieties of Indian jasmine – one red-blossomed, the other white. I realized that the large tree I had seen by the roadside in Singola was a true *bodaiju*. The ones growing in Osaka's Tennôji must be Linden trees, or the *Lindenbaum* variety. If that's so, then these trees are really Buddha's original trees, not the *Linden* of Schubert's song. Indeed, the dictionary says 'Indian *bodaiju*'. It has narrow, pointed leaves, attached to the branch as if they were on a string, and they give one the feeling of freshness. Droplets of water were sliding down the leaves – what a sight! If I didn't catch dengue fever in this rain, I'd call it a great outing.[6]

5 *Waves*, p. 30.
6 IM: "Nankô taigaiki." In: *IMZ X,* p. 54.

And just as the boy in *Waves* realizes that fighting men – above all his mentors Kakutan and Miyaji – are not necessarily heartless killers, Ibuse speaks with respect about an elite outfit of combat soldiers that joined the propaganda squad in Saigon.[7] After a week in a pleasant city with pronounced French cultural overtones, they board a larger steamer and on December 25, 1941 are finally off to Malaya. The crack troops belong to a heavy artillery regiment from Kumamoto which went through its baptism of fire on the Asian continent. Most of the soldiers wear elaborate tattoos and sport all kinds of whiskers and moustaches. Yet fierce as they look, they are kind and polite to the correspondents. When one of the ship's rough crew-members starts teasing these relatively helpless city intellectuals, the soldiers beat him up. The matter is reported to their commander, but all he says is: "Well done. Next time – cut him down."[8] Needless to say, there is no next time, and the rest of the passage is peaceful.

When Ibuse receives the draft-order, his lifetime friend and literary colleague, Kawamori Yoshizô comes to see him on a *mimai*, the visit one pays to a friend stricken by sudden illness or disaster. Yet to Kawamori's surprise, a day or two later he receives a thank-you note from Ibuse that says: "I have no intention of dying for the Fatherland. I am definitely coming back."[9]

Ibuse's survival policy was simple.[10] "I'll do my best

[7] IM: "Gisei." In: *IMZ V*, p. 82.

[8] Ibid., pp. 82–83.

[9] Kawamori, Yoshizô: *IM zuimon*. Tokyo, Shinchôsha 1986, p. 263.

[10] He was also lucky that when he was ordered to transfer from the relative safety of Singapore to the battlefield of Northern Borneo, two more experienced men, Sakai Seiichirô and Satomura Kinzô, were sent on this mission instead of him.

not to get in the way of my comrades-in-arms, and stay out of trouble,"[11] he writes in the original introduction to "Sailing South." The six weeks after debarking at Singola (December 27, 1941), a small Thai port on the Malayan peninsula, were probably the most dangerous ones. Although he was not attached to a combat regiment, but a supply unit that operated behind the lines, Ibuse still had to travel hundreds of miles through the jungle, where the stragglers of the British army – especially the tough bush-wise Australians – were still hiding. There were frequent air-raids by allied planes and the trucks would roll into occupied towns just hours after they had fallen, often while gunfire could still be heard. He saw bombed bridges rebuilt by engineers and blasted to piece again. The unit was also supposed to make propaganda speeches in Chinese or Malayan to the local population about racial harmony, the 'World Under One Roof Principle', and the 'Greater East Asia Co-Prosperity Sphere', but Ibuse tried to stay in the background as much as he could. On January 18 they reached a small town and railway junction called Gemas where a major battle had raged for four days:

> Departure at 9:00 A.M. Arrived at Gemas, a small town on the border of the Johore province. Saw evidence of fierce fighting in the town's outskirts. Grave-markers for the fallen soldiers are standing on a mild slope by the road. On both sides of the road, where the grass and the concrete meet, fragments of cloth, towels and leaves are

Sakai reports this in a 1975 article called *"Ibuse-shi no migawari"* ("Changing Places with Mr. Ibuse"). Quoted in *Shichû*, pp. 147–148.

[11] IM: "Nankô taigaiki." In: *Hana no machi*. Tokyo, Bungei shunjûsha 1943, p. 175. I am using the first edition here, since it has a slightly different text.

drifting like fluffs of cotton in the wind. Even the palm leaves of the camouflage have been trampled paper thin. One guesses this must have been a furious battle. Trampled by the people, crushed by the tanks, all matter has turned into a grey, cotton-like substance.[12]

Ibuse had given a telling title to one of his early prewar collections of short stories: *My Precious Reality* (*Natsukashiki genjitsu*, 1930). In this 'city of death' he realizes that modern war not only destroys people's lives, it can obliterate the very face of everyday reality, changing the distinct 'thingness' of those myriad objects that Ibuse's eye cherishes so much, into a "grey, cotton-like substance." And yet there is a tenacity to Ibuse's way of perceiving the world that does not allow it to be deprived of its shape and colour even in these extreme circumstances. Three days later we find the following entry in his journal:

> Light control. Did my laundry. Worked on my manuscript for a while. Got acquainted with a popular Malayan thief of this neighbourhood. His name is Jimmie Nelson and he's the boss of a large gang. They say he's a chivalrous robber though, and someone nicknamed him *Nezumi* (Rat) Boy.[13]

In his recent memoir, *During My Draft*, Ibuse likens this local Robin Hood, who apparently never stole from his fellow Asians but only from rich Englishmen, to *Nezumi kozô*, the legendary Japanese robber. (118–119) After mentioning Jimmie Nelson in "Sailing South" Ibuse talks about an interesting specimen of scorpion that he saw in the doctor's office and lists the where-

[12] "Nankô taigaiki," p. 45.
[13] Ibid., p. 46.

abouts of these creatures. On the way to take some pictures of local customs, he witnesses a lively quarrel between a Malayan and Chinese housewife over a stray chicken that looks and sounds exactly like a scene out of Ibuse's own "The River". It is this openness to the smallest events, the seemingly trivial anecdotes, in short all the local colour of a given environment which is so important in the author's aesthetics, especially his major postwar novel, *Black Rain*. Ibuse knows if the yarn is good, it will have an intrinsic literary quality and it will matter very little whether it is real or imagined:

> February 7. Went to see some soldiers wounded in the jungle fighting. They were using monkeys to gather coconuts.
>
> Since enemy sharpshooters are always on the ready, they'd put a steel helmet on the monkey's head. The monkey grabs the fruit with one hand, or its hind leg as it moves on, but always looks down to make sure where it's falling. If there are people under the tree, it's supposed to sense the danger.[14]

On February 15 the greatest piece of news of the whole Malayan campaign reached Ibuse's unit: Singapore had fallen, and the Japanese army under General Yamashita had achieved the most glorious military victory of its entire existence. Here is what Ibuse put down in his journal on that day:

> This is an auspicious day to be remembered. Singapore has fallen. At 7:15 P.M., the enemy accepted unconditional surrender. The cheering of everyone at home can almost be heard all the way here.[15]

[14] Ibid., p. 48.
[15] Ibid., p. 50.

It is obvious that in a journal published in 1943, at the height of the war effort, Ibuse had to say something about an event of such magnitude. But one notices that it was accorded less space than the anecdote about monkeys picking coconuts, and certainly less personal emotion than the visit to the botanical gardens. As Tôgô Katsumi points out,[16] this was a patriotic moment of the highest intensity, and even people as sober and reticent as Shiga Naoya wrote gushy eulogies about its historical significance. Putting Ibuse's diary entry side by side with such sentimental outbursts, it strikes one as relatively cool and unconcerned.

Yet the fall of Singapore did bring a significant change in Ibuse's personal life. On February 16, a day after the surrender, the propaganda squad was transferred to the city and assigned more permanent tasks than the rather aimless wandering behind combat troops through the jungle. They were stationed in a stately, but rather run-down suburban villa on Orchard Road, near the back entrance to the botanical gardens. Although he downplays this assignment in his journals and essays, Ibuse was given a fairly important task: he was to become editor-in-chief of the daily *Shônan Times*, as the former Singapore paper *Straits Times* was renamed:

> Singapore fell on the 15th of February 1942 and we marched into the city on the 16th. I learned that the city was renamed Shônan on the 17th of February. On the 18th the army confiscated the English newspaper company *Straits Times* and on the next day it summoned

[16] Tôgô, Katsumi: "Sensôka no IM." In: *IM to Fukazawa Shichirô*. Tokyo, Yûseidô 1977, p. 199.

all the remaining editors, reporters, office-workers and printers, and ordered me to become the editor-in-chief of the *Shônan Times*, a daily organ to be published by the military. It was just as if someone who doesn't know a thing about baseball had been ordered to become the catcher of a professional team. (18)

One can imagine how many pressing chores lay ahead of the newly appointed editor if he was to make a half-decent job of his assignment.[17] Ibuse went about it in his usual pragmatic manner. First he paid a visit to the *Straits Times* building in the city and checked the condition of its printing facilities, the company's stock of paper, etc. There he met with the paper's Chinese photographer, Ben Lion, and some administrative workers, and asked for the rest of the staff – especially the reporters and the editors – to come and see him at the Orchard Road dormitory. On February 20, the POWs were still clearing the debris from the streets and a requiem to pacify the souls of Japanese soldiers killed in action was being held at the former Raffles University. Ibuse went to his office and worked out the paper's basic format with his Japanese interpreter and the staff. Its contents were divided roughly into four sections: local news, radio news (i.e. news from abroad), proclamations and ads, and a Japanese language column.

---

[17] When I discussed the problem of Ibuse's wartime responsibility with the historian Grant K. Goodman, he suggested that the writer was a collaborationist with the military regime. Perhaps he did more than he had to, but we have to be very careful about applying Western criteria to the consensus-minded Japanese. Besides, refusing an order during wartime meant immediate reprisal by the *kenpeitai*.

The stock of newsprint was abundant, the printing facilities in perfect order, and the staff – mostly Eurasians, one Burmese, an Indian and some Chinese – fully cooperative, for they had no choice. Within a week, the new editor-in-chief had the paper going, and he began to relax: the inept catcher might do after all. But then on March 11 the first hardball came his way. A couple of army air force officers arrived at his office to interrogate the native employees of the paper about the source of some photographs that were published in the former weekly magazine *Eastern Graph*. On the same day, Ibuse and his interpreter were taken by the dreaded *Kenpeitai* to the notorious Changi prison. In his wartime journal, "Sailing South," he had to skim over the affair in a brief paragraph, only to end the diary half a page later on the following note:

> March 18. Had supper at the HQ's mess-hall tonight. The talk doesn't penetrate my brain. There's a tired, fuzzy feeling inside my head.[18]

No wonder. The *Kenpeitai*, sometimes misleadingly called Field Gendarmerie or Military Police, were really a combination of the SS and the Gestapo, with all their gruesome functions, and to have anything to do with them was like stepping into a viper's nest.

In *During My Draft* Ibuse unveils the incident in full detail. The photographs that had caused the uproar had appeared in the company's picture magazine, *Eastern Graph*, several weeks before, and one of them depicted two proud New Zealand pilots displaying a tailplane from a shot-down Japanese plane. The captions rang with the usual patriotic fervour, and

[18] "Nankô taigaiki," p. 56.

the whole thing, as the young lieutenant from the Peregrine flying squadron explained, was absolutely intolerable to the officers and the men of his unit. During this unpleasant affair Ibuse witnesses a brutal interrogation of the former English president of *Straits Times* by the army, and learns some details about the fate of a fellow writer, the Chinese Yu Dafu. Though Yu Dafu did become a sworn enemy of Japan, perhaps even a central figure in the Chinese opposition to its colonial ambitions, Ibuse is rather troubled by the fact that both the Englishman and the Chinese had been sincere Japanophiles until the war. Throughout *During My Draft* Ibuse returns to Yu Dafu's story, and one gathers it must have been weighing upon his mind. He learned later that Yu did make it safely to Sumatra and managed to live out most of the Japanese occupation, manufacturing Japanese-style paper from bamboo and brewing sake from imported Japanese rice. He was suspected by the *Kenpeitai* of being a spy, although he kept his amicable contacts with the Japanese community at Sumatra. Towards the end of the war he seems to have joined the Indonesian guerillas, and was killed either by the *Kenpeitai*, or a regular Japanese soldier. Ibuse is not given to using strong words of condemnation, whether he talks about the atrocities of the *Kenpeitai*, or about the atomic bombing of Hiroshima. One feels that what concerns him most is not to make a comfortable moralistic distinction between right and wrong, or to separate neatly 'human' from 'inhuman' behaviour, but rather to understand as clearly as possible what made ordinary human beings behave the way they did. Still, the following excerpt shows how much the tragic fate of Yu Dafu[19] must have troubled him. The passage describes a visit to an eerie mountain shrine, hidden inside a deep cave in the jungle:

> Above the entrance to the grotto on the right, a nail had been driven into the cliff-wall and a time-worn scroll painting of Heaven and Hell is hanging from it. Someone must have brought it here from an antique shop. The Hell section depicts a wailing man with the Devil clutching his back in his claw. A stream is flowing behind them, probably the River of Hades. On the opposite bank stands a composed-looking gentleman. He's reminiscent of a young nobleman and his features bear an uncanny resemblance to those of Yu Dafu when I'd met him in Japan some years ago. The fat face of the man in the Devil's claws looks like my own. (258)

Of course Ibuse was aware of many more incidents in which the local Chinese population was brutalized by his countrymen – and he does list them with remarkable objectivity in the 28th instalment of his memoir. Wakuta Yû even suggests that it was on the days of executions that Ibuse was unable to write anything. Yu Dafu's case was special and struck even closer to home: he had been a personal acquaintance, a respected fellow-writer and one of Japan's truest friends. War is by definition a brutal business and a writer should be truthful about it. But that does not mean that he can portray all its horrors in graphic detail. Ibuse clearly realizes the dilemma:

---

[19] For more detailed information on Yu Dafu see Ou-fan Lee, Leo: *The Romantic Generation of Modern Chinese Writers*. Cambridge, Harvard University Press 1973.

There is an old caveat: 'Don't speak about the trenches.' Some say it's the basic wisdom of those who've experienced war. It seems this statement takes for granted that war is by definition a gruesome affair. But the words also contain a warning: 'Shut up about everything you're going to see here.' The taboo seems to work, although there is something uncanny about it. Keeping all that in mind, I'd like to report what I saw and heard during my draft. Curbing my words a little and with some moderation, I will tell my story.[20]

Did he really tell his full story? We detect a certain hesitation on the author's part and he did later rewrite or delete some passages from his wartime memoirs. The painful memories of a troubled era and a lasting guilty feeling did not go away with the passage of time. Though unable to revolt openly, Ibuse tried to live as decently as possible during the occupation, managing the paper in an easygoing way, making friends, writing 'certificates of good citizenship' for the local people and giving talks on Japanese history and culture at a Sunday school. In "Shônan Diary" (*Shônan nikki*, 1942), a somewhat more relaxed account of his everyday life in Singapore during the summer of 1942, he reports a visit to the home of one of his Chinese friends. The occasion was the Chinese festival of June 18, or the 5th day of the 5th month according to the old lunar calendar. When he arrives at his friend's house, Ibuse notices a bouquet of iris flowers arranged at the entrance, and realizes that the festival, in all its details, closely resembles *Ayame no sekku,* the iris (or blue-flag) festival of the Japanese. These people, even

[20] "Gisei," p. 81.

the oldest among them, are second or third-generation descendants of Chinese immigrants, and yet they have staunchly preserved their cultural heritage:

> Hearing the whole family intone *Na-mu-ami-to-fù,* I thought it sounded exactly like the *Namu-Amida* chant in Japan. Biri's grandmother got up, quite excited and said: 'Is this what you do in Japan? Wait, I have something to show you!' and she fetched an ancient-looking book from her Buddhist altar... It was a wood-block print of the Kannon Sutra. The granny couldn't read Chinese script, but she had memorized the whole text as a child the way she used to hear her grandmother recite it. The old lady intoned the sutra in her Chinese pronunciation, I was following the Chinese characters and reading them in the Japanese way. Our diction, its rhythm and its intonation weren't all that different. It gave me a wonderful feeling.[21]

Ibuse's superiors among the Japanese military hardly shared his feelings about the local population and their culture. How very differently men like General Yamashita felt is best shown in an essay called, most fittingly, "Nightmare" (*Akumu,* 1947). After the fall of Singapore, Yamashita apparently found time a little heavy on his hands and took to reading an army paper called *Camp News* (*Jinchû yomimono*). A short paper one could read in fifteen minutes from first to last page, yet the Commander spent several hours over it every day, obviously re-reading it five or six times. One day he flew out of his room, raving mad. Clutching the paper in his hands, he ordered an immediate inspection tour of its editorial premises. Since they were located

[21] "Shônan nikki." In: *IMZ X*, pp. 59–60.

on the same floor of the press building as Ibuse's office, he could clearly hear the General roaring in the Propaganda squad-leader's room:

> 'You call this sissy drivel poetry? Such nonsense should never have been published! A Malayan girl picking grass, and making it a side-dish of her breakfast! What's wrong with that? No need to write about it. To call this poetry is an insult! The sheer nerve of it!'[22]

The staff gathered that what had so upset the General must have been the fact that a Japanese would dare to write a poem, expressing sympathy with the poverty of the local people. As Yamashita said, if they ate weeds, that's the way it should be. Although Ibuse heard the General and his entourage tramp down the corridor a while later, he didn't expect him to enter his modest office. And so he kept sitting, with his back to the door, when Yamashita peeped in. As if he didn't believe his eyes, the General stepped back into the corridor. Ibuse kept pasting some newspaper clippings into his scrapbook. Then the Tiger burst into the room in earnest:

> There, right in front of me stands the looming figure of the Supreme Commander. He's surrounded on both flanks by a train of staff officers. His cheeks are purple, and his bulging, beady eyes bore right through me. From his wide open mouth comes a deafening roar: 'What an undisciplined slob!' Then he yells at the young soldier by my side: 'What is this? I want this man out of here!' The soldier manages to stutter: 'This is a draftee.' General Yamashita tramples the floor and roars again: 'A draftee is still a soldier! Hasn't he sworn an oath? So he's a sol-

[22] "Akumu." In: *IMZ X*, p. 164.

dier. And to a soldier, discipline is everything! Don't you understand, ill-behaved slob'?[23]

The tirade went on and on, in the best barracks manner, and Ibuse confesses he was so perplexed that all he could do was to mumble an occasional "Yes, sir". What made him feel even more miserable was the realization that his voice sounded exactly as that of his eldest son when he had been scolded by his father. The fact that the scolding came to be known as the scandal of the Propaganda squad, or that one of the non-commissioned officers said to him, "Oh, if I had the luck to be dressed down, at least once in my life, by his Excellency the Supreme Commander!" (389) didn't make Ibuse feel any better about it. Still, the unpleasant experience did yield impressive literary material, and there is many a scene in his angry postwar stories which depicts a hapless, lowly individual being dressed down by a roaring official of one kind or another. The incident may also have been instrumental in another important development: someone in Yamashita's entourage did take the General's displeasure seriously and decided to demobilize the undisciplined draftee. Having left *Shônan Times* for reasons of health a little earlier, Ibuse did not have much to do anyway, except for occasional editorial help in the press building of the Propaganda squad and teaching ancient Japanese history at the local Japanese school. He did write the serialized novella *City of Flowers* (*Hana no machi*) from August to October, but that might as well have been done in Japan.

And so on November 22, 1942, a year to the day on which he had been drafted, Ibuse was back home.

[23] Ibid., pp. 165–166.

If there had been any lingering thoughts in his mind of gallantry in battle, manly virtues such as those displayed by his earlier heroes of Izumidera no Kakutan's mettle when he was leaving Japan, now there was only one burning thought in his mind: war is a cruel and extravagant form of stupidity.

### "ISLE-ON-THE-BILLOWS"

In his postscript to the revised edition of this story,[24] published in 1970, Ibuse recalls that he finished it in the spring of 1946, a day before the first American jeep rolled into his native village; he had been staying in his parents' house to wait out the raids, the famine and the turmoil of the postwar months in Tokyo. That he wrote the story at this particular moment is quite significant: the long war had come to an end at last, but most Japanese cities were smoldering heaps of rubble, the exhausted population was at starvation point, and the shock waves of what had happened in Hiroshima on the morning of August 6, 1945, were still being painfully felt throughout Ibuse's native prefecture. There were few villages in the larger Hiroshima area, even small, remote ones like his own, that didn't have someone in the city on that fateful day. Ibuse did not experience the bombing, but he had seen enough of the war – at very close range – as a war correspondent during the Fall of Singapore and the Malayan campaign. He came back a very angry man, critical not only of the military clique but of the whole ruling bureaucracy of established institutions, be it the army, the Buddhist clergy or the political oligarchy.

[24] IM: *Teihon Wabisuke*. Tokyo, Seiga shobô 1970, p. 94.

This anger, at times almost an urge to see 'official Japan' wiped off the face of the earth, found expression in several powerful stories written at this time. Continuing the resistance theme of several wartime stories (e.g."Day of Mourning for the Bell", *Kane kuyô no hi,* 1943), they nearly turned into a rejection of the culture itself. "Lieutenant Lookeast" is best known among them for its biting satire of the Imperial Army and its dehumanizing discipline. "Isle-on-the-Billows" (*Wabisuke*) is less of an obvious satire on the army and its tyranny over the common people, yet through its seemingly detached historical theme, it presents a no less compelling caricature of the feudal bureaucracy. Ibuse's growing conviction that the common people's world had almost nothing to do with the one in which their superiors lived is symbolically expressed here by a more dramatic polarization than in the other story. There are many untranslated intimations in the imagery of "Isle" that suggest this. Take the name of the island, Hadakajima: it is written with three characters meaning "High-Wave Island," but in its spoken form it conveys the double entendre of "Naked Island" (as Shindô's famous film was called), suggesting that this penal colony is a miniature version of Japanese society, with its complex power structure exposed in a more boldly obvious form. From the top of the social hierarchy where the well-meaning shogun and his religious advisor issue a somewhat overzealous law of "Compassion with Fellow Creatures", all the way down to the ambitious warden of a small penal colony, stretches a chain of imitation; by aping the mannerisms of their superiors, these social climbers hope to reach the same exalted status. In contrast to this *ersatz* world of interchangeable bureaucrats – note that the warden hasn't a single skill he can call his own – the common people (and especially their representative in the story, Wabisuke the Bird-Catcher) each have a craft that makes them individually unique. Anybody can become a warden and copy the refined way of beating prisoners by 'drumming' on their backs, but nobody can catch four sparrows with one thrust of a fowling rod, or tell at a glance what kind of bird is nesting high in the branches of a tree, as Wabisuke can. What Wabisuke lacks in verbal culture, he makes up in manual skills. He doesn't lack real poetic sensitivity either – we note that when he climbs the gnarled old pine tree on the mountain, he lingers a few moments to take in "the moan of the wind through the pine needles." Another favourite image of classical poetry, but how many court poets had gone to its source?

Although the author does not idealize him in any way – he's an earthy working man, inarticulate and socially clumsy at times – his name combines a wealth of connotations that suggest he is more than simply 'everyman'. Wabisuke not only translates as 'companion in solitude', it is the name of a small, modest, yet elegant variety of camellia.

A contemporary Western reader who has had no experience of life in an authoritarian society may find some passages a little hard to take: for example, why do Uetoku the gardener and his friend the estate guard not vent their anger more openly when one of them gets flogged by the steward? They are obviously out of ear-shot in the guard's hut and yet they talk about the caning as if admiring some display of skill. We find here one of Ibuse's favorite stylistic techniques: what might be called 'oblique criticism through irony'; but it is also a realistic portrayal of the Japanese reluctance to criticize one's superiors too bluntly and openly. There is always a chance that of the two people entering a discussion one will turn informer, or someone else will overhear them – little wonder in a close-packed country with no solid walls in the Western sense. Words of mock admiration for the master's skill at punishment provide a safe expedient: the peasants are supposed to be inherently stupid and incapable of irony; to admit overtly that their communication has more subtle levels than its face value would be intolerable for the official class. A careful exchange of sarcasm allows the two men to feel each other out, and when they realize they have both tasted the rod they become more openly critical of their superiors.

Throughout the story Ibuse not only parodies the hypocrisy of samurai officials and Buddhist bonzes (to whom the well-meant Law of Compassion comes to serve as a vehicle for personal advantage and a tool for pestering the common people) but questions the very essence of aesthetic tradition. He seems to be saying that the aristocratic cult of nature, with its moon-viewing parties and picnics under blossoming cherry trees where genteel poems are exchanged, belongs to a narrow, privileged world to which peasants and artisans have no access. When Warden Onohachi sends an amorous haiku to Osugi, neither she nor the crafty

Tôkichi know what to do with it. Tôkichi dismisses it as a joke: "Can you see me making a haiku?" Osugi is a real farm girl of flesh and blood, not the stereotyped 'country lass' of poetic convention, and, like Wabisuke, has to cope with natural forces more tangible than the elegant images of court poetry. Yet if they don't appreciate such idealized lyrical images, it doesn't mean that these people are less sensitive to 'nature' than their superiors. It's just that their perceptions are less filtered through the *haute culture* of established poetry and that they put more trust in what their senses tell them; they make their living, after all, not by reading poems, but by reading the 'language' of nature directly through smell, touch and sound.

What might at first sight look simply as a realistic satire of Japanese society, past and present, is on closer reading one of Ibuse's richest and symbolically most consistent works. Having deep roots in popular life and an unusual intimacy not only with its most essential problems but with a rich spectrum of folkways and popular oral traditions, Ibuse achieved in this story a balanced, easygoing blend of documentary and fairy tale elements. The remarkable mythopoeic structure of the story is thus contained solely in its stylistic elaboration, almost hiding behind the factual dryness of the narration and the quasi-historical, documentary form. In an essay on the historical novel, Alfred Döblin says:

> The present day novel, not only the historical novel, is subject to two currents – the one derives from the fairy tale; the other from the report. Their source is not the ether of aesthetics, but the reality of our life... The novel

is caught up in a struggle between the two tendencies: fairy tale constructions with a maximum of elaboration and a minimum of material and novel constructions with a maximum of material and a minimum of elaboration.[25]

So in "Isle-on-the-Billows" we have these two basic 'currents' blending and contrasting throughout the story: the external, cool documentary enumeration of facts, and the warmer, more oral and tactile style of the narration of everyday detail. Both are of course mediated by the author, who stands, as it were, between the people and their everyday stories and yarns, and the objective flow of larger historical time, with its ponderous official chronicles and records. The final destruction of the island and its penal colony is described twice towards the story's finale, once in the cool, objective style of an official report, once in the narrative voice which approximates the inmates' rendering:

Since the First Month of this year, a succession of minor tremors has been observed, and people are spreading irreponsible rumours that Mt. Asama is going to erupt. On the afternoon of the fourth day of the Sixth Month there was a major earthquake...

The great disaster struck in the afternoon, a little after four. When the prisoners who were still at work clearing new land at the hillside saw the Fuji river shrouded in spray, they froze in their tracks, unable to move or speak. By sheer chance, Wabisuke's eyes took in the scene seconds before the island slipped away. Then the river seemed to flow in reverse. In the same instant, the

[25] Quoted in Lukacs, Georg: *The Historical Novel*. Trans. Mitchell, Hannah and Stanley. Harmondsworth, Penguin Books 1969, p. 329.

entire island turned into a whirling, snow-white water-spout…[26]

Sometimes the fairy tale motifs are introduced very nonchalantly, e.g. when the big fisher girl Omon, while taking a last goodbye from her pets, the trained cormorants, can't resist plucking out a wing feather from her favourite bird called "Nightlight." A common gesture of fairy tales, where a hero or heroine create a fetish-like bond with their animal helpmate by accepting and cherishing a part of his body, usually the most essential to its survival and thus symbolic of the qualities that its human friend may need to borrow. In this case, it is of course the suggestion of flight and freedom, echoed in so many images throughout the story, most notably in the prisoners' ribald worksong:

'I wish I could be
A dog but I know
It's too much for me
To hope for, and so
Perhaps if I die
In heaven I'll be
A bird in the sky
And flying go free.
To kick my own eggs
Without any fear
Of feeling the lash
I keep getting here.
A heron's behind's

---

[26] IM: "Isle-on-the-Billows." In: *Waves*. Trans. Alylward, David and Liman, Anthony. Tokyo, New York and San Francisco, Kôdansha International 1986, pp. 141–142. Hereafter, bracketed numbers after quotes refer to the page numbers of this edition.

As bald as his face.
If I was a feather
I'd fit into place!' (133–134)

The portrayal of Wabisuke's female companions is realistic enough, especially that of Omon; yet comparing the two women we may wonder what the author's purpose is in bringing together such contrasting types. Omon couldn't be more down-to-earth, but let us look more closely at Osugi. As always in Ibuse, Osugi's tragic story is presented with humorous overtones. We learn that her convulsive crying fit was brought on by seeing traces of a recent forest fire, and that she has good reason to fear such a fire. What made her 'crime' really grave is not the fact that her so-called negligence caused considerable damage to her fellow farmers' property, but rather that a family of badgers died on her mountain, and went unreported into the bargain. This is the ironic, conscious surface of the text, but underneath we can hear the deeper symbolic connections suggested by Ibuse's unique turn of phrase: Osugi's weeping fit is described as having a "glowing charm (艶なるもの)," and an "almost smoldering quality (焦げくさい)." Such terms are unusual, yet the image brings together the two elements of fire and water, echoing the real fire and flood that shaped Osugi's life; the eruption of Osugi's "blood storm" and her tears reenact the fire and the flood from the broken dam in her home district. This flood of tears washes away all her fear and frustration and, far from irritating Wabisuke, calms him and purges his own anger and fear – the 'grime of his soul' – in a sort of symbolic purification:

To Wabisuke's eye, the storm in her body had reached high tide. It was like the frenzy of a woman wild drunk from too much sake. It didn't seem funny, nor yet make him sad. Strange to tell, it gave her a glowing charm, an almost smoldering quality. (129)

When Wabisuke tells her the terrifying story about the shogun's extravagant treatment of dogs, the poor country girl refuses to believe him, and gasps "You just made that up... It's some bogey tale to frighten kids – not about the shogun." (127) In the original, this passage goes *"Saimon katari ga iu, Sanshô dayû no yô na sora osoroshii..."* or "This is a frightening tale, the kind that ballad-singers tell about Sanshô the Bailiff..." Now Sanshô the Bailiff is the proverbial ogre of Japanese folk and fairy tales, and it is interesting to note how this motif from the popular oral tradition is used to contrast, and to comment upon, the historical material. No doubt to a modest farm-girl from the mountainous area of Kôshû, the lavish, whimsical waste of the shogun and his court must seem as frightening and irrational as the grotesque behaviour of the legendary villain Sanshô.

While the language of the officials is stilted, at times bombastic, the common people speak a rich colloquial Japanese, and the passages describing their daily activities abound in dynamic, colourful verbs. Occasionally Ibuse will use a striking metaphor, such as "Osugi was still wailing into the earth as if trying to break it open." Again, we see that while the samurai bureaucracy moves about in a shallow, puppet-like world, the people are in touch – not through words but through their very existence – with the elemental forces of the Japanese soil. Osugi wails into the ground on the mountain where they work, and deep in the entrails of another mountain, this time the great Fuji itself, a larger "blood storm" is gathering.

I can hardly think of another Ibuse story where the deep rapport of the Japanese peasant with his cosmos is orchestrated on a similar dramatic scale and with equally passionate conviction. Two life-styles and two rhythms are juxtaposed through the story: the artificial and basically empty world of officials, contained by false 'refinement' and rendered inauthentic by obsessive imitation, and the earthy world of the common people, ruled by the forces of nature – mainly fire and water – and existentially contained only by the sky and the limits of their own life-force. They don't entirely lack in style either, yet it is not dictated by imitation, but rather by the nature of a concrete job at hand; so it's the birds themselves who teach Wabisuke how to be caught and the texture of a tree's bark and the disposition of its branches that tell him how to climb it.

As in any good fairy tale, we perceive a number of universal mythical motifs here. Wabisuke dwells in a men's world, his existential sphere is the air, its spiritual mood the song of freedom, the flying birds. He nearly becomes a bird himself when he prepares to climb the tree:

> But first he had to climb high up the tree with a bamboo tube of birdlime and water dangling at his hip and a handful of straw hanging from his sash like a tail. He handed the fowling rod to Osugi, and lightened his load to one sheaf of straw and the birdlime case. He then tied a pale yellow towel around his face, and relieved himself nearby. His preparations were complete. (123)

Every word of this brief passage radiates a wealth of deeper meaning. The birdman must be as light as the airy creatures he's after, and as 'pure'. Relieving himself on the ground, he has, as it were, left his everyday material body behind. Masking his face, he has assumed another identity. Part shaman, part bird with his straw tail he now ascends the tree, ready to partake in the quality of his totem creatures. Moreover, he links the earth (where he left his physical signature) with the air through the trunk and the branches of the tree where he will spread his birdlime. All of this is concrete and functional, almost a simple job-description, and yet at the same time full of mythical resonance. What Döblin called "a struggle of two currents," has become one graceful, uninterrupted flow in the hands of a master.

Ibuse has his whole stylistic repertoire under full control by now and can afford to dramatize most effectively his recurrent theme of stasis and flow, or containment and release. His own flow had been stopped, one might say, for the end of the war and all it brought about was so overwhelming that 1945 was the only year in the author's long writing career when he didn't publish any new works. Nature's response to containment, whether man-made or accidental, is a catastrophic release of flood proportions. You cannot stop the natural flow of water any more than you can stop the flow of language, Ibuse seems to be saying. Yet the officials have placed a strict taboo on 'wild rumour': one mustn't speak about earthquakes, one mustn't gossip, one must offer prayers to the gods and the officials themselves for providing the daily bread, etc. They have imposed a cruel embargo on one of the people's most natural urges, that of storytelling. While Wabisuke and Osugi are almost mute, their tongues freed only very gradually in unison with the flow of nature around them, (especially the sight of rebirth after the forest fire), the earthy fisherwoman Omon heartily defies all such confinements. Representing a healthy release, almost an overflow of language, she babbles on end, farts, yawns, gossips about her betters and loves telling lengthy stories that present them as ridiculous and pretentious fools.

When the underground anger erupts towards the end it takes away the whole "living hell" of the island, along with the warden and his henchmen. And when the angry waters of the Fuji river swallow the Isle, washing away what the Japanese of those days would have called its *kegare* (ritual impurity), we witness another purification rite, this time on a cosmic scale. We note that "all that could be seen were high waves washing the river's banks" just where the sinister Mole of Hell juts out above the water. Every time Wabisuke climbs the mountain, he longingly watches the distant figure of an official or a boatman fishing for trout from this cliff. He wouldn't mind fishing himself, but he is never given the time. Hours before the island sinks into the river, Wabisuke once again watches this hateful place from the top of the mountain, shading his eyes against the sunlight. Suddenly he realizes that his posture is that of prisoners who have been released from the isle and are returning home. But he is also described looking like Urashima Tarô, the legendary young fisherman who had spent a pleasant year in the Dragon King's palace at the bottom of the ocean and is taking leave from the beautiful naiad Otohime. Now there is no reason why Wabisuke should hope to return home at this particular moment. His eyes are not looking at the Princess Otohime, but at the hateful island. Yet his mind's eye, perhaps sensing what is coming, looks into the Dragon King's palace and urges the ruler of the underwater kingdom: "Come fast and take this horrible place away." And when the waters do just that, we can sense both the power of the water deities and their generosity in the description of the Isle's destruction. In this context, the fact that the girl Omon, prosaic as she may be, comes from "Dragon King's Village" is not a mere coincidence, for she is also in touch with the depths, not least through her trained cormorants that dive in the river for fish.

Again, all the female commoners in the story, whether real or legendary, act in deep accord with the mythopoeic roles they are often given in fairy tales. Unlike the absurd 'show-offs' of the upper classes, these women have an intimate rapport with the chthonic realms, especially the underwater kingdom and its creatures – the waterfowl and the fish – who in turn are in touch with the bottom of the earth through their sensitive skins:

> The murmur of the river was melancholy as always. When the work crews had time, they would fish, but lately they'd been puzzled by the strange behavior of the trout.
>
> Once on the hook, they would pull down and dash away like lightning. You could tell by the pull on the rod they were heading right for the bottom. The slight earth tremors noticeable the last few days might have had something to do with it. (134)

When Wabisuke sings his 'freedom song' about the heron's tail feather he'd like to be in the life to come for Osugi after her weeping fit, Ibuse uses another striking metaphor about the way the song sounds: "It came out like a sutra chanted at the bottom of a river." (134) A humorous and subtle hint is made here that the circle is closing, and Wabisuke, the creature of heights, is being offered a connection with the watery depths by the woman. *Tajinko Village*, as we saw, had been criticized for too much complacency towards the Japanese power establishment. The eruption of Ibuse's anger in this story leaves no doubt that a considerable change has occurred in the writer's psychic makeup during the war years. And yet there isn't even a hint of the neat ideological formula the critics had been calling for; Ibuse's popular heroes are still by and large incapable of revolutionary action, life is still full of reversals and ironies and everything in the human order is relative. What to the birds is a "richly wooded paradise blessed with warm temperatures" is a living hell to humans. A man catches animals and gets caught himself, for such is the inescapable karma of life which can never be pure. But the fact that those who caught and tortured him get washed away by a burst of nature's anger – not a writer's figment of imagination, but a real historical event this time – is a novel theme in the context of Ibuse's work. Whereas calamities in previous stories merely added hardship and pain to the common people's lives, this one acts on their behalf. Perhaps the war had been too much for Ibuse to take and he needed this release to preserve his own sanity. Perhaps he felt, and I think quite justifiedly, that a people who had always deeply revered the gods of its streams, its mountains, and forests, might be entitled once in a long historic while to trust that their *kami* would come to the rescue. What we witness in the dramatic finale of the story then, is a tableau of 'sinking Japan', or rather 'official Japan' being wiped off the map. Why else would Ibuse close his story with Wabisuke's eyes holding the deeply imprinted image of the red poppies against the snow-white water spout that swallowed the Isle? There is no mistaking the familiar colors of the sun-disc flag of Japan.

### "LIEUTENANT LOOKEAST"

In "Life at Mr. Tange's" we saw dialect define individual characters and express the gamut of their changing emotions; in "Lieutenant Lookeast " it defines a locale and the unique character of its close-knit community vis-à-vis the universal outside world. By deftly placed fragments of dialect, the playful opening of Ibuse's "Lieutenant Lookeast" takes us down from the transparent, universal level of standard Japanese to a more opaque and illogical, but all the more palpable world of the mad lieutenant and his postwar village:

> In the dialect of our part of the country, anything that disturbs the life of the village is referred to as 'ruptions in the village', while anything that upsets one's small section of the community is called 'ruptions over here'.[27]

---

[27] IM: "Lieutenant Lookeast."Trans. Bester, John. In: *Salamander and Other Stories.* Kôdansha International, Tokyo, New York and San Francisco 1981, p. 23. Hereafter, bracketed numbers after quotes refer to the page numbers of this edition.

Bester's sensitive translation tries to convey all of the text's illogical densities or, precisely speaking, its smooth blend of the narrator's lucid voice with carefully selected oral quotes from this 'other' opaque reality. But it is above all the sound of these authentic verbal tokens in the original text that gives them a special appeal. Thus a long, vernacular *kôchi* (over here) instead of the crisp brevity of the standard *kochi* or *kochira* conveys a tangible feeling of murky softness, drawing the reader inside the story's narrowing inner space.

When later one of the focal points of its locale, the Hattabira pond, is mentioned and a discussion of its dialect pronunciation, Hattabyura, ensues, one feels even more strongly the contrast between the crisp dryness of a universal Hattabira that resounds through clear air like a whip's crack and the muffled, opaque sound of Hattabyura that rather reminds of someone mumbling from the water's depth. Hattabira, one might say, is the voice of an outsider naming the pond from some distance, Hattabyura the voice of those calling it from its depth. The gourd-shaped pond was made by damming up a stream and lies in the hills behind Sasayama. It is in a meadow by this pond that the village children come to cut grass or gather reeds. So the location of the pond on the small-scale map of the area is not quite 'over here', but outside of the *buraku*, and thus rather far-away for a rural child whose familiar universe is relatively small. Pulling up new shoots of grass, the children sing a simple folk song:

> Home we go, then, home we go,
> Empty baskets, home we go.
> Came to Hattabira pond,

But the jay was crying there
And the meadows were quite bare.
There we gathered grass but
All the stems that we had cut
Fell out through the wicker, so
Empty baskets, home we go. (32)

Interestingly enough, it is this 'rustic and artless' children's rhyme that becomes a kind of codeword of local identity. When one of the local men, Yojû, is being repatriated from Siberia, he meets a sergeant-major by the name of Ueda on the south-bound train. Although Ueda comes from Yamaguchi prefecture, he not only knows the 'Sasayama Children's Song', but gives Hattabira its dialect pronunciation of Hattaby-ura. Yojû, "homeward bound from Siberia as he was, naturally felt a surge of nostalgia, even about such an uninspiring scene as that presented by the pond." (32) It turns out that Ueda had picked up the song on a troop transport before the Pacific war from Lieuten-ant Okazaki Yûichi who used to sing it whenever the soldiers gave an amateur show on board the transport.

We note that the two soldiers' discussion about the dialect pronunciation of Hattabyura is introduced by a longer quote of examples than Bester chose to translate:

They [the local inhabitants] would pronounce *katabira* (summer hempen clothes) as *katabyura, hanabira* (flower petal) as *hanabyura,* and *tobira* (door) as *tobyura... Okayama* becomes *Okyayama* in their diction...[28]

---

[28] IM: "Yôhai taichô." In: *IMZ IV,* p. 306.

What is being communicated here is that while the story's 'movement' has been directed towards its centre 'over here' so far, now the flow turns outwards, away from this centre of reality and narration. The linguistic trademark of local belonging, the muffled -*byu* sound, travels overseas, as it were, and reaches men from other places, outsiders with different local identities. And yet the distinct miniature world of Sasayama, its uninspiring pond and its children's artless song, also embody the fate of all these homebound men in a most poignant, concrete way. Looking carefully at the little song's words, we notice that it expresses a sense of loss and disappointment ("empty baskets, home we go") and a vague fear of this wilder place outside of the familiar space of the *buraku* ("came to Hattabira pond, but the jay was crying there and the meadows were quite bare") (32). The Japanese jay, we should add, is a bird known for its skilfull imitation of other birds' voices and sounds, and thus suggests a sense of deception or inauthenticity. From places where meadows were certainly bare (Siberia, for example) and a bird's song was not quite what it seemed, these defeated men are now coming home like helpless children, with 'empty baskets' in every sense of the phrase.

The motif of the pond being a kind of matrix of local identity, whose water draws people in but also expands in widening circles far beyond the village's ken, is playfully repeated towards the end of the story:

> 'Tomorrow's the day for draining Hattabyura pond, isn't it?' said Shintaku... 'Autumn's come early this year, so it'll be hard on the man whose turn it is to let the water out, the water being so cold.'

'Right. And it's my turn this year, surely?' said Mu-
nejiro...

'Yes, I suppose I'll have to drain such a famous pond.'
(50–51)

Theirs is a practical yearly chore, not a religious
ritual. Yet many a local *matsuri* is orchestrated around
this kind of practical task of agrarian existence. I wonder if we can't hear echoes of such rites here: taking
turns in assisting the pond's seasonal renewal, the men
renew their own ties with it, restating their identity in
a most natural way. The carefully chosen dialect words
are thus no mere stylistic ornaments here, and they play
a far more important aesthetic role in the text than
provide a touch of authenticity, as they did in some
earlier stories. Linguistically, the dialect sets apart the
transparent world of postwar Japan, with its imported
ideologies and the fashionable jargon of the day (such
as 'fascist relic' and the like), from the older, denser
and more opaque existence of the Japanese villagers.
By ironic extension, as he goes through the story, the
reader comes to realize that the newfangled words of
'postwar democracy' can barely scratch the surface of
this older and denser reality. Thus we might say that
when the concentric waves of the story's symbolic
development have reached its centre, they spread out
again in widening symbolic echoes, suggesting that
underneath the thin surface layer of universality, every
Japanese carries his 'village' and his past, where some
reflection of the murky Hattabyura pond lingers on.

The mad lieutenant's mind, of course, embodies
the immediate past in a far more dramatic way. Suffering from an illusion that the war has never ended – an

illusion shared by a man as lucid as Lt. Onoda – his mind is caught in the spatio-temporal web of wartime, frozen in the context of an entirely different language and different emotions. Matching beautifully the *kôchi ga megeru* ("broken over here") his seems to be a broken mind, split between the physical here and now of the village and the distant battlefields of Malaya. Or perhaps it is only his body that inhabits the present postwar village, for his mind does not recognize any 'postwar'. When he is in his 'normal' state, he believes himself to be stationed at home; during one of his fits he thinks he's in action at the front. So in a sense – and this is a superb touch of irony on Ibuse's part – it is not his mental world at all that has suffered the major break of defeat, the emperor's fall from divinity, the invasion of foreign ideology, etc. In symbolic terms, the break or eruptions 'over here' do not run so much through some remote fictional village in the South, as through the Japanese Everyman's heart. Yûichi, the mad lieutenant lives in a world of complete consistency:

> ...when his mother brings home cigarettes she has bought for him, he declares that they are a special imperial gift and, turning towards the east with every sign of intense emotion, makes a profound obeisance. (23–24)

A less visible, yet by no means unreal, axis through the story's space begins to emerge here. Although the lieutenant worships towards the east – the direction of the Rising Sun of Japan – his obeisance takes into account the general direction of the Emperor's palace, and, more significantly, the Emperor's symbolic place in his nation's existence. Such a position would surely not be located at a merely geographical distance in a horizontal, eastward direction, but on a somewhat elevated plane corresponding to the rising sun's course in the eastern sky. The vertical structuring of the story's space is also expressed by a related motif of social aspirations towards status. Yûichi's mother, an ambitious widow of many schemes, has 'enormous concrete gateposts' erected at the entrance to her garden. These fancy gateposts have no relevance to the garden or the surrounding scenery, for the gate leads to neither of them. It is an entrance into the elevated social space above, the social climber's extravagant ladder upward, designed to impress the neighbours. It is through these extravagant gateposts that the widow's son begins his climb to glory and – madness. The local headman admires them so much that he recommends the boy to a cadet-training college, for as he explains, Yûichi not only is a bright pupil, but his mother is a woman of character and theirs a model family. As Yojû puts it "You'll never understand him [Yûichi] properly, until you've seen those [the gateposts]." (44) Ironically, it is the line "war is extravagant," uttered by one of his subordinates, that unwittingly hits him in his softest spot and causes his accident and his madness. This ironic motif of upward mobility is further associated in the story's finale with a more traditional image of the iron well-chain that echoes shrilly around the whole village when it is being wound up:

> The headmaster, too, had spoken as though he were interested by the sound. There was a famous passage about the sound of an iron well-chain in the national reader they used at school; one of the finest pieces by a poet called Bokusui Wakayama, he had said.

279

'When you hear the sound from a distance,' said the headman, waxing still more enthusiastic, 'it's really just like the cry of a crane. What does the Chinese poem say? The crane cries deep in the marshes, its voice ascends to the heavens.' (51)

As if trying to ascend with the crane's auspicious voice, the diligent widow would draw more water than she really needed for a long time to come. Although the classical imagery is given an ironic slant here, it still reinforces our awareness of the story's vertical spacing, suggesting that there is a larger, cosmic scale of things beyond the village's ken and perhaps well beyond the patriotic headman's grasp. The crane's cry comes from the depth of the marshes, linking the wet, murky space below with air and heaven. The well's chain reaches into subterranean waters and its sound echoes upward towards the sky. Thus the vertical thrust of the story is not simply directed upward, it also points downward, and quite significantly so. The subterranean realm of Sasayama village, unlike the fantasy underworld of *Alice in Wonderland*, is far more real in the given cultural context.

As I have tried to show in my analyses of the early stories, be it "Salamander," "Carp" or "Life at Mr. Tange's," Ibuse will use the subtlest tensions between words to express human psychology without much visible authorial intrusion. His skill with words is even more subtle in these postwar stories. What we must realize again is that modern Japanese, just like the Japanese psyche, is a repository of several incongruous historical layers of vocabulary. Since 'modernity' was imposed on Japan so quickly, and not always willingly accepted, the awareness of these layers is perhaps keener and more problematic than in other modern languages. There are the ancient words rooted in the country's indigenous culture (mainly the polysyllabic *yamatokotoba*), a somewhat later layer of the Chinese compound words (*kanjukugo*) and finally the most recent layer of mechanically translated conceptual imports like 'militarism' (*gunkokushugi*) and the like. These -ism concepts are created by adding the suffix *-shugi* to a combination of Chinese characters. When a villager who still speaks his native dialect uses a word like *shinryakushugi* (aggressionism) it sticks out of his speech with extraordinary ostentatiousness. On top of that, from the postwar period into the present a great number of loan words from entirely different cultural contexts were adopted by the Japanese. A good example is the word *fasshô,* the colloquial adaptation of fascism that is used in the story. When you call someone 'a relic of fascism' in any postwar Western country, the word will ring with distinct meaning, as it is rooted in Europe's recent dramatic history. Although Japan's wartime history is no less dramatic, the words *fasshô no ibutsu* (relic of fascism) acquire a rather comic connotation from a contemporary perspective. One may talk about the collective mania of nipponism, but it would be quite misleading to attribute weighty European connotations to this fashionable word. When during his thirtieth or fortieth fit, Yûichi pesters some casual visitor to the village, using the authoritative military phraseology of yesterday, the youngster responds in the fashionable vocabulary of today:

'Listen to him – slaughter me, indeed! He's a relic of militarism, that's what he is! A bloody corpse!'...

'Hey!' yelled Yûichi, gazing about him. 'I want an NCO. An NCO! NCO – slaughter this man!'

'Monster!' snarled the young man in the old uniform, as though loath to give up the battle. 'Fascist relic!' (26–27)

What we get here, at least in the original, is another example of Ibuse's brilliant linguistic caricature. Behind words like *buttagiru zo* ('I'll cut you to pieces!') lurks the sharp edge of the samurai sword, honed and perfected for three hundred years. No wonder that it cuts deeper than fancy imports such as 'freedom', 'fascism' or 'aggressionism'. But the young visitor in the "old army uniform" – seemingly Yûichi's extreme opposite, but in fact a *doppelgänger* of sorts – does not speak solely in this new fashionable jargon. We must note that in fact every one of his new-fangled words is paired with a more traditional or colloquial expression. Thus the first "relic of militarism" is really *gunkokushugi no bôrei* in the original. Now *bôrei* means literally 'departed soul' or spirit, and by extension 'ghost'. Needless to say, the word has deep roots in the Japanese cult of ancestor worship and provides a much sharper and more meaningful contrast to the word 'militarism' than 'relic'. Likewise, when a little later the young man snarls at Yûichi *"Bakemono me! Fasshô no ibutsu!"* ("Monster! Relic of fascism!"), he did not really say 'monster', but 'bogey', 'spook' or 'spectre'. Again, the word *bakemono* is an important keyword of the rich Japanese lore of popular ghost tales and folk tales about creatures possessing magic powers. The most prominent among these creatures is the fox who can enchant people and assumes different disguises to do so. This association is naturally suggested in the preceding paragraph:

> His [Yûichi's] face was white. His eyes were bloodshot and narrowed at the outer corners, so that his features resembled one of those fox masks that they sell at toy shops. (27)

In this way, the psychological conflict between the opaque, older level of Japanese mentality and modern abstract or ideological thinking is expressed primarily in terms of a verbal clash. Towards the end of the altercation, we can follow a kind of circular return to the natural speech pattern, where there is no more conflict between innermost feeling and its verbal expression:

> *Shinryakushugi no, hyôrokudama...* (aggressionism of a nitwit or idiot) *hyôrokudama no bakemono...* (idiotic spook)

The first word is highly abstract, not to say artificial, the rest very colloquial. Bester renders this as "stupid pawn of aggression" and "half-witted leftover," in an understandable attempt to make the passage sound as natural as possible in English. Yet by doing so, he almost loses a crucial, and very insistent suggestion: it is the strong links of the Japanese culture, and especially local village culture to the nether world (or underworld, for the two are not clearly differentiated in the popular tradition) that lie at the heart of this story. Time and again we get hints that Yûichi is a spirit, a ghost or a corpse (really skeleton or *gaikotsu* in Japanese). In a sense then, the story is a caricature of the basic Japanese belief that a dead person's spirit wanders around and affects living people who go out of their way to keep such an unruly spirit pacified.

The mad lieutenant, in a way, is everybody's ancestor, a spirit of the dead who constantly reminds the community of its past. That he belongs more to the world of the dead than that of the living is dramatically manifested in one of the most powerful scenes of the story, Yûichi's visit to the cemetery. When he rants at the living, he is usually satisfied with verbal abuse. But here at the graveyard he is truly among his own and thus the contact is of a more physical kind:

> Yûichi... was in the cemetery up on the hillside, walking up and down between the rows of gravestones. As he walked, he struck at each stone with his belt, lashing out with an enthusiasm that suggested that he saw the stones as his troops. (45-46)

On the same day that Yûichi strays into the graveyard, one of the younger villagers, Yojû, comes back home form Siberia. When his older brother Munejirô tells him that the first thing he should do is pay a visit to the grave of his ancestors and report to them the good news of his safe return from the Great War, Yojû balks. Like the youngster in the old army uniform who had confronted the mad lieutenant some time before, Yojû distrusts such old-fashioned nonsense which he considers a relic of the feudal past, and contrary to his principles. Interestingly, Ibuse does not really say 'principles' but *shugi*, or -ism and thus dissociates the narrative from the figural view. Obviously, Yojû is a spiritual sibling of the previous youngster, his thinking of very much the same mould. He uses the same fashionable vocabulary of the day: Shinto ritual is a relic of the feudal era to him, Lt. Yûichi is a 'skeleton' (*gaikotsu*). But the older villagers, knowing well that village reality is never that simple, gently coax him to go along with the ancient custom:

'Now don't say that, Yojû. When in Rome, you know… If you don't behave, you'll find yourself without a girl to marry you. Anyway, I don't see anything to stop you visiting your ancestors' grave.'

'You did as the Romans when you were over there, Yojû,' added Shintaku, 'so I don't see why you can't do the same in your own village. There are all kinds of things in everyone's life that one has to turn a blind eye to…' (46)

We detect a veiled threat in the older man's words as well, for a young repatriate from war would naturally be looking for a woman. In order to find one, he must belong. To belong, he has to plunge – in more than one sense – into the murky waters of Hattabyura pond, which is exactly what his older brother asks him to do towards the end of the story. The quiet obeisance at the graveyard goes well at first, and Yojû seems to have rediscovered some of the proper feelings. As if to underscore the motif of opening up emotionally to the "pleasingly unsophisticated" old rite, Ibuse has him carry a "sprig of sasanqua with a half-open bud." The three men who accompany him all bring the usual offerings: lighted incense, fresh water and a large "thin-skinned *manjû*" (bun stuffed with bean jam).

Suddenly there is a loud roar and Lieutenant Look-east descends on the party. The villagers, being well aware of his fondness for sweets, try to appease him by offering him the bun. Surprisingly, Yûichi responds in a manner which is very rare for him: raising the bun with both hands before his eyes in a gesture of gratitude, he bursts out crying in a voice like "the howling of a dog." The men are moved and agree among themselves to humour him this time. Lining them up and ordering them to attention, Yûichi delivers an intensely emotional, solemn address:

'Today, His Imperial Majesty has been graciously pleased to send us a gift – of cakes. His Majesty has especially singled this unit out for his gift. There can be no greater honour. Nothing remains, I submit, but tears of gratitude. You will accept the gift with proper reverence. An official will now distribute them amongst you. First, though, we will face towards the east and bow in token of our allegiance'. At Yûichi's command, the four of them faced in the direction of Hattabira pond. The weather was cloudy, but they were aiming, quite accurately, eastwards. (48)

Breaking off small pieces of the bun, Yûichi then places one in each man's mouth. Offering food and drink to the deceased ancestors is of course a common religious practice in Shinto, and the bun was brought here as a present from the living to the dead. But Yûichi has reversed the gesture, and it is now the 'spirit of the dead', the 'corpse' who feeds the living. Moreover, the travesty has chilling symbolic overtones, reminding one above all of the Catholic mass. Interestingly enough, the thin whitish 'skin' of the bun and the red jam filling sustain this feeling to an uncanny degree. Yet I don't think it was necessarily the author's intention to suggest the ritual of any particular religion. A great artist's imagery reaches far back to the dawn of the human psyche, suggesting rather some kind of essential 'rite of participation', a deep human urge to

286

hold on to the physical presence of a venerated ancestor or deity, and partake in it even after it has departed. Since the rituals of modern religion are more often than not sublimated adaptations of these half-forgotten older rites, the most recent layer simply comes to mind first.

As we have seen, Ibuse had every reason to resent the army and the kind of fanatical emotion expressed in Yûichi's speech. Yet he is too truthful an artist to raise the banner of any *-ism* and deny the older realities of his Japanese 'village', uncomfortable as they may be. We notice that the four men at the cemetery worship not merely towards an undefined East, but first of all in the direction of Hattabira pond. An important and very real reference point of their local identity is thus tied to the rather remote existence of the emperor and at the same time to the communal cemetery, another central *locus amoenus* of their existence. Furthermore, although Yojû calls the speech a "lot of rubbish," the men do feel that the mad lieutenant's ranting may not belong entirely to a "chorus by a bunch of men in jackboots":

> 'But I must say, though, he's good at pep talks. Made you feel for a moment almost as though you'd really been sent cakes by the Emperor...' (49)

Another surprising thing about this ambiguous description is the violent disgust with which all the men – except Yûichi, who ingests the largest portion of the bun – spit out the tiny morsel of food after Yûichi has been taken away by his mother. Not one of them had dared to swallow it, yet not one of them had felt like spitting it out before Yûichi's gaze.

One wonders: would hardy Japanese peasants, some of whom had seen the battlefield, and most had experienced near starvation and eaten many an unsavoury dish in the recent years, really be so repelled by the mere taint of Yûichi's "grubby paws"? I think Ibuse suggests a more subtle psychic taint here. Doesn't one feel, even if for a mere fleeting moment, that Yûichi, like a mad shaman or priest who mediates between this and the nether world, is offering them a communion with his fallen deity? To him, of course, who dwells spiritually in the nether world of departed souls, the emperor is as divine, and as eternally alive as ever. The deranged brain maintains a reality, or a truth that is hardly apparent to other, sane men at this historical juncture. They will have heard the emperor's broadcast, renouncing his divinity, and they may have seen the even more tangible proof of his fall in the famous picture of General McArthur granting Emperor Hirohito an audience: next to the relaxed, towering figure of the foreign shogun, in his open-necked khaki shirt, stands a rigid midget of a man in a formal morning coat. The stiff collar and the tie almost strangle him, his body seems paralyzed. Only the eyes are alive, and they bespeak the terrible agony of a man crucified... Yûichi does not know all this, but the other men in the story as well as the reader, do. A peculiar wording is used in the original: *"Sakki no kuroi tsuba no hô ga, mada anjisei ni tonde iru nê!"* ("That dark spittle there is rich with suggestions!") He probably means that the spittle contains symbolically all his unpleasant memories of war. What the author may mean, with another touch of irony, is that while Yûichi does not necessarily know what he is doing, his act suggests meanings and consequences that transcend an individual's limited interpretation.

Since the centre of narration – and reality – is 'over here', Ibuse slowly gathers the story of Yûichi's overseas experience in bits and pieces of rumour as they reach this centre. Before Yojû meets sergeant-major Ueda (the Lieutenant's former orderly) on the train, the villagers subscribe to all kinds of wild, contradictory theories about the cause and extent of his injuries. Some attribute his brain damage to congenital syphilis, the broken leg to a fight during a quarrel. At one point it is even believed that Yûichi's language shows no experience of army life at all. Reality, as always, is what a majority of people find most congenial, most familiar and most advantageous.

Ironically, while the war lasts, nobody really notices that a madman is moving in their midst. The author suggests that the madness was like morning mist hanging over the place and its people, whether they liked it or not. It is only when the mist lifted that everybody realized the deeper madness of Yûichi. The common soldiers are drafted villagers and they do grumble about war's extravagance and the zeal of their officers, but to the Western ear their 'protest' sounds more like the complaint of a disgruntled family member than reason's rebellion. Time and again, it is suggested that reality, especially hearsay reality, is more porous towards its periphery than the solid centre 'over here'. The sceptical army surgeon who, with a few sharp questions, cuts through the web of lies and half-truths presented to him as the reality of Yûichi's accident, might be seen as the reader's surrogate within the narrative. The insiders' line of vision runs too often through the cloudy waters of the Hattabyura pond, and the reader, just as any other outsider, must constantly question their view. The most distant spot on the story's periphery is of course the Malayan countryside where Yûichi's accident happened. This scenery is vividly described, if at second-hand, through Yojû, who hears it from sergeant-major Ueda on the train:

> There had just been a shower, and it was cool among the rubber trees. The river, curving into sight through a gap in the rubber trees opposite, cut straight across the meadows and disappeared again behind a hillock. Here and there in the meadows were great holes where bombs had fallen. They had filled with rain to form small ponds, and in one of them two water buffaloes were soaking companionably in the muddy water, with only their heads above the surface. A white heron could be seen perched on the horns of one of the buffalo. Bird and beast alike were perfectly still, as though spellbound by the sight of the engineers at work on their bridge. (34)

Watching this unfamiliar scenery, the Japanese soldiers are in turn watched by its enigmatic creatures. Some features of this landscape may remind them, if only superficially, of their native countryside: the meadows, the small ponds, the heron. But it is a closed scenery into which the Japanese intruders have no clues, for they don't know its code. Whether made by allied or Japanese bombs, the craters will fill with local water, creating an equivalent of Hattabira pond under the Malayan sky. To penetrate these waters, and be able to mumble a password such as 'Hattabyura', the insiders' name that belongs to this place alone and unlocks its secrets, is clearly beyond the power of any invader. Worse, the stream that swallows Corporal Tomomura is without even a proper common name.

It is interesting to consider the image of the water buffalo in terms of the complex and historically shifting meaning of the bull symbol. According to Cirlot: "The basic dilemma lies between the interpretation of the bull as a symbol of the earth, of the mother, and of the *wetness* principle and the view that it represents heaven and the father."[29] Some believe that the bull symbol gradually came to represent the connecting link between heaven and earth, or between the elements of fire and water. We do perceive echoes of this dilemma in the image of the water buffaloes presented in the story. The 'ponds' were made by fiery explosives and thus may represent a compromise between the igniferous and the wetness element. But the submerged water buffaloes obviously belong to earth and its wetness, while the white heron that rests peacefully on one of its horns links it with the air and heaven. It is an image of power contained, a harmonious union of opposites in a closed circle that the Japanese intruder can never hope to penetrate.

Most significantly, the Japanese are depicted fixing a bombed-out concrete bridge and later stalled in their trucks on the temporary wooden bridge. As Cirlot suggests, "the bridge is always symbolic of a transition from one state to another".[30] Furthermore, in the

[29] Cirlot, Juan E.: *A Dictionary of Symbols.* Trans. Sage, Jack. New York, Philosophical Library 1962, p. 32.
[30] Ibid.

Japanese literary tradition, most notably Chikamatsu's *michiyuki* in *Love Suicides at Amijima*, crossing a bridge symbolizes a transition of a special kind. Every bridge the lovers cross takes them farther away from the world of the living, and closer to the nether world. One of the bridges in the drama is tellingly called 'Bridge of becoming' (*O-nari*), a play on words linked to the Buddhist concept of becoming a Buddha in the afterlife (*jôbutsu*).

Like the *O-nari* bridge of Chikamatsu, this temporary bridge in Malaya leads to the nether world. As he topples off the truck into the river, the Lieutenant grabs Corporal Tomomura, pulling him to death. When he is being carried away to the field hospital, Yûichi repeatedly tries to grasp the rubber-tree branch that, according to Ibuse's memoirs, Japanese soldiers always used to mark the graves of their war pals when they had no time to make a proper wooden marker. They do so for the dead Corporal in the story, though it is only to mark his assumed last resting place, since his body was never found. He is gone, his body swallowed by the nameless river.

Yûichi, who keeps talking to the now-dead Tomomura through his delirium, is 'gone' though his body is still here. Bidding adieu to their draftees during the war, Japanese villagers often felt that the world of the living ended on the doorstep of their community. Crossing that boundary, the young men in their white headbands were departing in every sense of the word.

To retain a foothold in the murky, and from a modern viewpoint, slightly mad atmosphere of the ancestral village is increasingly difficult for the out-ward-oriented younger Japanese of today. And yet, as the company soldier leaves his 'island village' behind and faces an alien world abroad, the problem still looks similar. The deeper he penetrates the outside world's symbolic code, the more distance he puts between himself and the in-language of his 'village', putting in jeopardy his identity, and ultimately his psychic balance. In spiritual terms, the great void begins, as it did sixty years ago, at the water's edge. Without proper anchorage at the ancestral shrine or burial plot, and without lasting remembrance, a man's soul may drift, or worse, be lost forever.

## VI. THE OLD FISHERMEN AND JAPANESE IDENTITY

"WHITE HAIR," "THE HEARTH FLOWER"

*I thought of the mysterious eels with tiny snake-like eyes, running up my river on their long journey from oceans and seas. How strange – so much has vanished from my life, yet one thing will always remain: the fish. They are tied with nature and with being far away from the jerking, comical streetcar of civilization. I came to understand that most fishermen are not really after the fish; what they want is to be alone as a man could be in times long ago. Hear the call of the wild bird and the deer, the falling of autumn leaves…*

*Above all, fishing is freedom.*[1]

Ota Pavel

To grasp the deeper affinity of a literary culture with what we might call 'the culture of angling' and thus penetrate the highly refined, complex texture of Ibuse's fishing stories and *zuihitsu* requires a brief exploration of this unique subculture. The editors of an excellent anthology of fishing in literature, *The Magic Wheel,*[2] define the connection very succinctly:

> It is not just that there happens to have been some fine writing about fishing, or that some fine writers, from

[1] Pavel, Ota: *Veliký vodní tulák*. Praha, Čs. spisovatel 1980. Introduction on dust jacket.
[2] *The Magic Wheel. An Anthology of Fishing in Literature*. Profumo, David and Swift, Graham Eds. London, William Heinemann and Pan Books 1985.

Ovid to Orwell, happen to have loved fishing. It is rather that the habits and attitudes which make literature, echo to an extraordinary degree, as they do with few other specific pastimes, the habits and attitudes of fishing.[3]

Thinking about fish and angling, and how they relate to literature, one must first consider the connection between the fish's habitat, water, and literature. The symbolic meanings of water from its very first representations in man's art are endless, of course, as imagination itself seems to move more freely in the opaque twilight of the underwater realm. The rippling mirror of clear water seems to have invited a narcissistic contemplation of man's self from the moment his mind became capable of projecting and perceiving objective images beyond itself. Water and dreams, as Gaston Bachelard argues in *L'Eau et les rêves*,[4] are inseparable. Or, as Herman Melville once put it, "meditation and water are wedded for ever."[5] That water is an essential element in Romantic iconography is manifested in such critical works as W. H. Auden's classic *The Enchafed Flood*. Harold Bloom proposes a theory about a strong response to water being the absolute pre-requisite for a lyrical poet. In any artistic tradition, regardless of its cultural background, the images emerging from the deepest recesses of the unconscious mind will often take the form of aqueous metaphors. Depth, fluidity, vagueness, unpredictability, the mysterious springing of life-force, in short feminine or womb-like aspects, are all embedded in this 'wetness principle'.

[3] Ibid., p. 1.
[4] Bachelard, Gaston: *L'Eau et les rêves*. Paris, Librairie José Corti 1942.
[5] Melville, Herman: *Moby Dick or, The Whale*. Mansfield, Luther S. and Vincent, Howard P. Eds. New York, Hendricks House 1952, p. 2.

Water, or the lack of it, is always important and always present in some form, whether as a practical daily commodity or as a significant symbolic motif, in any literary tradition. But there are few, if any other cultures which have not only based their everyday life, their very survival, on the existence of abundant water, but also articulated their religious and spiritual life in terms of water-rituals as much as Japan. Travelling through the Japanese countryside in spring when the ricefields are flooded one has a feeling that this is not *terra firma* at all. Rather, it is a watery kingdom in which man has only a limited foothold on narrow paths (*azemichi*) from which he can work the wet fields, and tiny islands where he can put his bed to stay dry during the night.

The most common Shinto ritual, performed in one form or another at every shrine and village community is the rite of purification or *misogi*. In his "The Water Woman" (*Mizu no onna*)[6] Orikuchi Shinobu shows how deeply embedded in the life of the Japanese farming communities were the rituals honouring water deities. One can hardly think of another post-industrial, modern country where an ancient water-ritual such as the early spring *mizutori* of Tôdaiji at Nara is taken with such utter seriousness. This 'water drawing ceremony' at Tôdaiji is an elaborate ritual with a long tradition of 1,200 years. It absorbed pre-Buddhist 'water religion' (*mizu shinkô*), has shamanistic aspects of ascetic practice and involves two weeks of arduous religious ceremonies that go on day and night before the actual

[6] Orikuchi, Shinobu: "Mizu no onna." *Orikuchi Shinobu zenshû II.* Tokyo, Chûôkôronsha 1982, pp. 80–109.

water is drawn from the old well called well of youth (*wakasai*).

Although written with a different character than water (*mizu*), Japan in ancient times was called 'country of fresh rice stalks', or *mizuho no kuni*. The word for freshness is *mizumizushii* and obviously has etymological connections with the word *mizu*. It is the blossoming, greening fertile water that nurtures the rice stalks, and a deep intimacy with its life-giving properties that has given this culture its dominant symbolic keys: fluidity, 'wetness', and haziness. Needless to say, the womb-like space under water and its sacred inner time find expression in numerous folktales, legends, myths and fairy tales, most notably in the legend of Urashima Tarô which Ibuse called "the most beloved tale of the Japanese nation." Isn't the whole point of Japan's greatest art forms, especially that of Noh, to take one out of the hectic ticking of chronological time back into the quiet, slow inner rhythm of water? The fluid movement of the Noh dancer itself is reminiscent of underwater motion, and the elegant gesture of the Japanese fan, whether used in Noh or in a folk dance, bears an uncanny resemblance to the curling flip of the fish's tail.

It's only natural that such lasting intimacy with water would not only influence the imagination of a race, but leave a deep imprint on their language. Again, though we do find the proverbial expressions such as "water under the bridge" or "still waters run deep" in English, it would be hard to find another language where the metaphorical idioms based on water are so frequent and so expressive as they are in Japanese.

From *mizu shôbai* (literally water trade – entertainment business) to *mizuage* (literally offering water – a maiden courtesan's first reception of a guest); from *mizu mono* (literally water-thing – a very unpredictable thing) to all the expressions based on water's flow, such as *ryûkô* (fashion), *runin* (exile), *ryûmin* (drifters), *ryûgen* or *rugen* (false rumour) – what an eloquent variety of phrase! It suggests that if water is indispensable to every living creature on this planet, and if man's imagination is forever attracted by the mystery of that "tantalizing horizontal veil, the surface of water,"[7] then the ambience of the Japanese mind is by definition of a more submerged, wet, even piscine nature. Just as in the underwater realm, sound carries fast in this society and people's skin is sensitive to the slightest vibration. Like fish, who are in constant touch with their environment, the Japanese are inseparable from their surroundings.

Many Japanese authors have naturally used fish and water as an important motif in their writing – we may recall Kawabata's "Moon on the Water," (*Suigetsu*), Dazai's "Metamorphosis,"(*Gyofukuki*), Ogai's *Records of Water Foam* (*Utakata no ki*), Sôseki's *Sanshirô*, Kyôka's *Demon Pond* (*Yasha ga ike*) and many others – but I'd agree with Wakuta Yû who suggests that while these writers use water for aesthetic effect, Ibuse's writing could be called water literature.[8] Water not only forms the basic element of his created world, with mountain streams, rivers, fish and fishing or drifting from island to island as his favourite thematic choice, but the nature of water underlies his whole aesthetic philosophy. Matsumoto

---

[7] *The Magic Wheel*, p. 14.

[8] Wakuta, Yû: *Zusetsu IM*. Tokyo, Yûhô shoten shinsha 1985, p. 9.

Tsuruo even suggests that Ibuse's stylistic distortion and his unique viewpoint are those of a fish-lens.[9]

There is no question that the typical softness and fluidity of Ibuse's mature style, its resistance to rigid critical categories, suggests the flow of water, but also its power in the sense of Lao Tzu's famous dictum that "Nothing is weaker than water, but when it attacks something hard or resistant, then nothing withstands it, and nothing will alter its way!"[10] As we saw in *Tajinko Village* or *Waves*, Ibuse's favourite and most mature characters are those men who have instinctively understood that there is permanence and strength in fluidity, that "the nations pass... but the mountain stream flows forever."[11] As a Scottish angler puts it:

> What is of all things on earth the most changeable appears so the least... there is no mountain in the land which we can certify as presenting the same aspect it did five centuries ago... but waters, seas, lochs, and many rivers, are still the same.[12]

In his *Musa Piscatrix* (1896) John Buchan notes that "the celebration of angling by the poets is a very English characteristic,"[13] and it is true that while other nations may have their practising devotees, the literary tradition of angling is more prominent in England

---

[9] Matsumoto, Tsuruo: *IM ron.* Tokyo, Tojûsha 1978, p. 8. If I were to use an animal metaphor for Ibuse's viewpoint, I'd prefer another river creature – the kingfisher, whose eye can not only look up from the river's depths, but observe it from high above.

[10] Lao, Tzu: *The Way of Life.* Transl. Blakney, Raymond B. New York, New American Library 1955, p. 131.

[11] IM: *Lieutenant Lookeast and Other Stories.* Trans. Bester, John. Tokyo and Palo Alto, Kôdansha International 1971, p. 227.

[12] *The Magic Wheel*, p. 202.

[13] Ibid., p. 17.

than anywhere else in the West. Certainly the existence of Walton's *The Compleat Angler* and other treatises of angling would seem to confirm this view. What Goldsmith wrote about England might as well have been said about Japan:

> Happy England! Where the sea furnishes an abundant and luxurious repast, and the fresh waters an innocent and harmless pastime: where the angler, in cheerful solitude, strolls by the edge of the stream, and fears neither the coiled snake, nor the lurking crocodile.[14]

Even if these poetic metaphors reflect certain preferences of their respective cultural background, when we look at the way both traditions perceive the deeper meaning of fishing – or if you wish the philosophical aspects of this 'contemplative man's recreation'– we find a remarkable similarity. Walton's motto, inscribed under his portrait in the stained-glass window of Winchester cathedral, sounds surprisingly 'oriental': "Study to be quiet." When I talked to Mr. Ibuse about the great anglers he used to know, above all his revered mentor Satô Kôseki, he stressed the sterling moral qualities of these men. "What they all had in common," he said, "was a strong sense of responsibility and honesty."[15] Virginia Woolf, whose watery death is more commonly known than her great respect for anglers and their craft, puts it in almost identical terms: "Fishing teaches a stern morality, inculcates a remorseless honesty."[16]

---

[14] Goldsmith, Oliver: *A History of the Earth and Animated Nature II.* Quoted in *The Magic Wheel: An Anthology of Fishing in Literature.* p. 155.

[15] During my interviews with him at Takamori, August 1975.

[16] Woolf, Virginia: "Fishing," *The Moment and Other Essays.* London, The Hogarth Press 1947, p. 178.

Some of Ibuse's most colourful rustic characters were modelled on, or at least inspired by, the old anglers he'd met by streams: old Hogoden in "The Hearth Flower" (*Kotatsubana,* 1963), the old angler in "White Hair" (*Shiraga*), old man Isomatsu of "Bridgeside Inn" (*Hashimotoya,* 1946); others, e.g. Old Kingfisher (*Kawasemi oyaji*), or Yasaki san of the Fuefuki river, were introduced into his fishing sketches without much fictional change. The inimitable turn of phrase of these men and their colourful dialect provide much of the charm of these stories. Virginia Woolf perceptively recognizes the great energy of such language:

> ... if we have no novelist in England today whose stature is higher than the third button on Sir Walter's waistcoat ... is it not that the Cumberland poachers are dying out?... Banish from fiction all poachers' talk, the dialect, the dialogue of Scott, the publicans, the farmers of Dickens and George Eliot, and what remains? Moldy velvet; moth-eaten ermine; mahogany tables; and a few stuffed fowls. No wonder, since the poachers are gone, that fiction is failing.[17]

Another contrast which both Ibuse and the English writers employ for good dramatic effect is the difference between the fancy tackle of the City angler, and the simple gear of the Rustic; in both cases it is of course his intimate knowledge of the local conditions that gets the fish, not the superior equipment. Even Shigematsu, the protagonist of Ibuse's major novel, *Black Rain,* was closely modelled on Mr. Shigematsu Shizuma, a fishing acquaintance. Interestingly enough, as in English fishing literature, it is often the Japanese village post-

[17] Ibid., pp. 177–178.

man or barber who becomes the local 'kingfisher'. Because of their superior streamcraft, these masters will get away with any amount of eccentricity, becoming legendary characters as time goes by.

Virginia Woolf makes another interesting observation which will sound familiar to every practising angler:

> I felt receptive to every sight, every colour and every sound, as though I walked through a world from which a veil had been withdrawn.
>
> Is it possible that to remove veils from trees it is necessary to fish? – Our conscious mind must be all body, and then the unconscious mind leaps to the top and strips off veils?[18]

There is another advantage to fishing: it's a quiet sport, and stillness goes well with sensitivity. In 1884, when the noise in our cities was nowhere near its present levels, John Burroughs made an interesting remark about the relationship of sensitivity, imagination and silence:

> Indeed there is no depth of solitude that the mind does not endow with some human interest. As in a dead silence the ear is filled with its own murmur, so amid these aboriginal scenes one's feeling and sympathies become external to him, as it were, and he holds converse with them. Then a lake is the ear as well as the eye of a forest.[19]

I wonder how much the extraordinary vividness of Ibuse's scenic descriptions, the deeply carved precision

---

[18] "Fishing", p. 177.

[19] Burroughs, John: *Locusts and Wild Honey*. Quoted in *The Magic Wheel*, pp. 294–295.

of his imagery, and the economy with which he can evoke in several strokes a sharp sense of a particular locale, are owed to his fishing excursions. One might say that the great haiku poets also had this thoughtless sensitivity and their best lines are so vivid because the poem's basic images touched their deeper mind before consciousness could get hold of them; the rest is technical articulation. In an interview at his summer-house in Shinshû (August 1975), Ibuse told me how much he admires haiku but immediately added with a sigh: "Alas, I could never make a living from that. A good haiku comes to you no more than once or twice a year."

What is important to realize here is that the author clearly distinguishes between making a haiku and a haiku coming to him; it is this unexpected gift of living images that may or may not come to the poet (and the angler) he was really talking about. Thus fishing not only offered a lifelong pastime to the writer, it also helped him to capture the essence of his favorite landscape and its creatures. Reading Ibuse's fishing essays and stories one has a distinct feeling that he cultivates the same basic scenery – the river valley of his childhood – throughout his career, striving for an ever-deepening and more condensed expression of it.

"When you take the rod in your hands," Satô Kôseki used to urge Ibuse, "you must first banish all evil thought."[20] His other favourite advice was: "Dissolve in the stream, become one with the plants."[21] Not too different from Bashô's famous "What a pine

[20] IM: "Chôgyoki." In: *Kawatsuri*. Tokyo, Iwanami shoten 1975, pp. 4–5.
[21] Ibid., p. 4.

is, learn from the pine; what a bamboo is, learn from the bamboo".

By "banishing evil thought," Satô may have meant 'don't let your fishing rod become an extension of your ego'. Every angler has met obsessed men by the riverside who use their rod as a whip to subdue weaker creatures or test their strength against the life force of a huge fish; the point is, as in other Japanese *dô* disciplines, to subdue one's own ego rather than the 'opponent'. Like the master-craftsmen of old, Kôseki was a stern teacher who demanded the utmost from his pupil. When the current was too strong, he'd say: "Know what the singing frogs do in a flood? They swallow pebbles, to get heavier."[22] And he'd order Ibuse to fill his rucksack with heavy, melon-sized rocks to weigh himself down. After wading across the raging river and nearly drowning in the deep rapids, Ibuse modestly mentions that Kôseki rewarded him by saying: "Hey, you show promise, Ibuse! You do know about water, don't you?"[23] In his own essay called "Boasting a Disciple" (*Deshi jiman*), Satô uses much higher words of praise for his student:

> Ibuse has the personality of a born angler. Reading his stories and essays I felt the presence of a certain transcendent quality. Yes, I concluded, this man is worthy of teaching.[24]

Being a journalist and a writer himself, Kôseki understood the subtle parallel between developing a

[22] IM: *Tsuribito*. Tokyo, Shinchôsha 1970, p. 23.

[23] Ibid., p. 25.

[24] Satô, Kôseki: "Deshi jiman." In: IM, Dazai, Osamu, Takii, Kôsaku et al.: *Ayutsuri no ki*. Tokyo, Sakufûsha 1984, p. 159.

superior streamcraft and creating a personal style in literature:

> 'There are all kinds of *tomozuri*[25] techniques. But the one I'm teaching you is based on forty years of fishing experience and thus the best by far. As you saw a while ago, you were able to catch a fish without trouble. But next year, as you gain more experience, you'll try to add your own touch and modify the technique. The year after that you will try again and you'll get less and less fish until the third or fourth year when you may think you have no skill at all... But by the tenth year, after a decade of your own experience, you'll feel like going back to the method I'm teaching you now. Returning to the principles you learnt at the beginning, you'll feel as confident about them as if they were your own discovery. In other words, it's just like training in literary style. As much as you may try to add your own touch to style, in the end you'll come back to the point of understanding how great Bashô was.'[26]

Ibuse not only took his mentor's lessons to heart, he never really thought of streamcraft and the craft of literature as separate, or unrelated activities. Many of his shorter works, though not fishing stories in the technical sense of the word - e.g. "Pilgrim's Inn" (*Henrôyado*), "The Wasabi Thief" (*Wasabi nusubito*, 1951) etc. - were inspired by fishing trips to remote areas. Even his grasp of foreign literature and his infrequent

---

[25] *Tomozuri,* literally 'friend fishing' is a technique of intruding a bait fish of the same species into *ayu* territory. The bait fish is floated on a line, held by a ring through its nostrils with several loose hooks on short leaders attached to the main line. The *ayu* that approach the bait fish, trying to attack and chase it away, get hooked on these loosely hanging hooks. The technique resembles what is called 'jigging' in the West.

[26] Chôgyoki, pp. 3-4.

critical comments about it are often inspired by its fishing theme or imagery. In one of his diaries Ibuse recalls that in Sholokhov's *And Quiet Flows the Don* there is a scene of two farmers, father and son, fishing for carp. The son hooks a huge carp, nearly five feet long, but it's too much for him, so the old man says: "Give him a breath of wind, he'll calm down." While he was fishing for carp at Sahara, the boatman offered Ibuse the same advice: "Listen, if you give him a breath of air, the carp will float up to the surface."[27] Fishing skills are more or less the same in the West as in the East, and it's the fish who teach the anglers how they can be caught.

Several times I have observed Ibuse's reaction to critical or theoretical comments about his own or another author's writing and I think he distrusts them all. By the same token he is extremely wary of making such comments himself, especially about literature that grows from a distant cultural soil. Yet with fish and water it is different: a carp is a carp whether it lives in a Japanese or a Russian river, and its 'language' has nothing to do with cultural nuances. The east wind may have its local names – in Japan it is sometimes called *yamase,* wind from the mountains – yet when it blows, fish seem to respond in the same way the world over: they don't bite. It is this universal language of nature and its experience, always verifiable with hook and line – and a skillful human hand – that Ibuse seems to trust far more than critical jargon.

In one of his fishing *zuihitsu* he talks about Maupassant's fishing stories, one called "The Fishing

[27] IM: "Nikki." In: *IM shû.* Konuma, Tan Ed. Tokyo, Yayoi shobô 1982, p. 195.

Hole" and the other "Two Friends." The first deals with a quarrel of two anglers about a favourite fishing spot. One is a newcomer on the river, and does not realize that the spot 'belongs' to the other; when the habitué throws the newcomer into the river, the case goes to court and the judge, probably an angler himself, finds the defendant not guilty and lets him go. Remarking how fond Maupassant must have been of fishing, Ibuse then looks at the other, more famous story. It takes place during the Franco-Prussian War, in the last days of the Paris blockade. Two ardent fishermen, Monsieur Morrissot and Monsieur Sauvage, meet on a fine Sunday morning, and after a couple of absinthes decide to go out fishing, blockade or no blockade. Obtaining a permit from the commander of the French outposts, they reach their favourite fishing spot in the country and soon catch a netfull of gudgeons. They keep fishing even when they hear the booming of cannon nearby. But suddenly a patrol of German soldiers steps out of the bushes, seizes them and brings them to their commanding officer. The Prussian accuses them of being spies, and since they patriotically refuse to reveal the password, has them shot on the spot. It is after giving the story's brief synopsis, that Ibuse's comment becomes critically interesting:

> The two men were ordered to be shot. Their eyes were bound, the shots rang out, and both fell forward like logs. The fish in the creel were thrashing about....
>
> That's how I remember the plot, but I also recall that after reading the story I had a feeling that the description of the fish in the creel was a little too intense. I even

thought that the author contrived the brutal episode to give a neat finale to his story...[28]

Although Maupassant describes the fish on the grass, not in the creel, and places the scene a few moments before the execution, the image of the lively fish thrashing about is unmistakably there: "The pile of fish, which were still wriggling, glistened in a ray of sunshine."[29] Also, there is a neat, cruel circularity in the Prussian officer's cynical remark after he had the two corpses thrown in the river: "Now it is the fishes turn!" His last sentence completes the circle and gives the reader the final dramatic punch: "Fry these little things for me straight away while they are still alive. They'll be delicious."[30]

It is this harsh symmetry of the story's finale that must have bothered Ibuse. While in his essay he still admits that "the story is after all one of Maupassant's masterpieces,"[31] with increasing age his patience with this kind of dramatic story-telling grew even thinner. When I asked him about Maupassant in 1980 when he was eighty-two, he just said: "It won't do to kill people in order to advance your plot."[32]

Yet there is one line in Maupassant's story that may have influenced Ibuse quite deeply. When they hear the Prussian bombardment, the two French anglers engage in the following dialogue:

'They must be fools, killing each other like that.'

[28] IM: "Chôgyo zakki." In: *Kawatsuri,* p. 20.
[29] Maupassant, Guy de: "Two Friends." In: *Selected Short Stories*. Trans. Colet, Roger. Harmondsworth, Penguin Books 1971, p. 154.
[30] Ibid., p. 155.
[31] "Chôgyo zakki," p. 20.
[32] During my interview with him at Ogikubo, Fall 1980.

'They're worse than wild beasts,' said Monsieur Sauvage.

And Morrissot, who had just hooked a bleak, declared:

'To think that it'll always be like that as long as we have governments!'[33]

Not only do we find what Maupassant so nicely calls "the sweet reasonableness of peaceable, ignorant men" in many an Ibuse work, he will often use almost identical words. In "Lieutenant Lookeast," one of the common soldiers says: "I envy these Malays. *They have no state,* so they can leave wars to other people."[34] And in *Black Rain,* another soldier sighs: "If only we'd been born in a country, not a *damn fool state!*"[35] (Italics mine).

Another important skill that a poet may learn from fishing, as Ted Hughes suggests, is to "settle his mind on one thing:"

> So you see, fishing with a float is a sort of mental exercise in concentration on a small point, while at the same time letting your imagination work freely to collect everything that might concern that still point: in this case the still point is the float and the things that concern the float are all the fish you are busy imagining.[36]

The concentration on a still point has another beneficial effect on the angler's mind. By directing its attention elsewhere, it settles the mind's inner turmoil.

[33] "Two Friends," p. 151.

[34] IM: "Yôhai taichô." In: *IMZ IV.,* p. 315. Since J. Bester renders this as "It's not their own country," I use my translation for accuracy.

[35] IM: *Black Rain.* Trans. Bester, John. Tokyo, New York and San Francisco, Kôdansha International 1980, p. 162.

[36] Hughes, Ted: *Poetry In The Making.* London, Faber 1967, p. 61.

There is no question that his hobby helped Ibuse to maintain his mental equilibrium through very difficult times. Many anglers, especially the intellectuals among them, have noted this soothing effect. Thus Herbert Spencer wrote:

> I found fishing so admirable a sedative, serving so completely to prevent thinking, that I took to it again, and afterwards deliberately pursued it with a view to health. Nothing else served so well to rest my brain and fit it for resumption of work.[37]

In *Black Rain,* Ibuse says almost the same thing:

> While one was fishing, one's powers of thought were temporarily paralysed, so that it had the same effect on resting the cells of the brain as a deep sleep.[38]

The fishing motif in *Black Rain* and a number of other Ibuse stories suggests another interesting point. Although these stories may have themes very different from fishing, there is often an inconspicuous image of a fisherman in them, or, as in *Black Rain,* a side motif of fishing that runs through the entire work. Like some Renaissance painters who preferred placing a modest self-portrait somewhere in a crowd of faces to signing their names, Ibuse places these 'fishing signatures' in his most serious works. So in *Black Rain* we have Shigematsu and his friends, who by fishing at the pond where they raise carp, are able to kill two birds with one stone; they suffer from a light case of radiation disease, and their doctors have prescribed walks for them. But leisurely walks are unthinkable in the busy

[37] Spencer, Herbert: *An Autobiography.* Quoted in *Magic Wheel: An Anthology of Fishing in Literature,* p. 310.
[38] *Black Rain*, p. 27.

Japanese countryside, and so they engage in a practical activity, beneficial both for them and for their community.

In *Waves: A War Diary*, the fishing signature shows a blacksmith, who picks hairs from the tail of a dead horse and fishes for sea bream. Ostensibly, the goal is to obtain something to make oil from, but, as Ibuse says: "Perhaps fishing was a consolation too."[39] It is this image of fishing as consolation that often appears when Ibuse portrays the unbearable hardships of common people's lives. In "Isle-on-the-Billows" we see Wabisuke climb the mountain on his way to the work site and watch longingly the distant figure of an official or boatman fishing for *ayu* from a cliff called Mole of Hell. In a hard-working, feudal country there were no sports in the modern sense and fishing was the people's only accepted form of recreation. But the exiles hardly have any free time for this innocent pastime and this makes life in the penal colony even more unbearable.

What is even more important, is that in Ibuse's fishing stories, the presence of healthy fish in undisturbed streams is a sensitive test of a country's ecological health and the quality of fishing manners a measure of its humanity. When the author took me to one of his favorite fishing streams, the Kamanashi, in the summer of 1975, we saw a series of dams, columns of trucks roaring down the road and huge machinery grinding the river's rocky shores into gravel. "What a mud-stream," sighed Ibuse and then added: "You

[39] IM: *Waves: A War Diary*. Trans Aylward, David and Liman, Anthony. Tokyo, New York and San Francisco, Kôdansha International 1986, p. 61.

know, in the Edo Period they had strict laws about this kind of thing..."[40]

In a prophetic essay called *Coming Up for Air*, George Orwell wrote in 1939:

> As soon as you think of fishing you think of things that don't belong to the modern world. The very idea of sitting all day under a willow tree beside a quiet pool – and being able to find a quiet pool to sit beside – belongs to the time before the war, before the radio, before aeroplanes, before Hitler. There is a kind of peacefulness even in the names of English coarse fish. Roach, rudd, dace, bleak, barbel, bream, gudgeon, pike, chubb, carp, tench. They're solid kind of names. The people who made them up hadn't heard of machine guns, they didn't live in terror of the sack or spend their time eating aspirins, going to the pictures and wondering how to keep out of the concentration camp.[41]

If coming up for air was difficult in 1939 and the peaceful civilization of Orwell's childhood nearly gone, the bleak postwar world was even worse than he imagined. The quiet pool under the willow tree may still have been there, but war has done something to people – whether in Europe or in Japan – that even Orwell's pessimistic vision did not quite anticipate. It is this dramatic shift in people's humanity that Ibuse explores in his first post-war fishing stories, setting it against the unchanged scenery of his native mountains and his river valley.

[40] During my visit at Ibuse's country home in Takamori, August 4–7, 1975.
[41] Orwell, George: *Coming Up for Air*. London, Secker and Warburg 1954, p. 76.

The title of this story and its theme of white hair versus black hair have a special significance in the context of Ibuse's writing. Any traditional culture will express respect for age and its wisdom, and in some languages we'll even find a saying to the effect: "Show some respect for white hair." In the patriarchal, agrarian traditions it is invariably the old man or the old woman who have seen more droughts, storms, bad years and good ones, and thus have amassed a greater store of valuable experience than the youngsters. Such traditions were mostly oral and transmitted personally, and so the figure of a wise old man or the knowledgeable white witch appears with fairly slight variations in most ancient cultures whose life and survival depended on green, growing things.

The figure of the wise old man has acquired special weight and a sophisticated articulation in the arts and the philosophical tradition of both China and Japan. We might point to the long line of Chinese sages from the Taoists Chuang-tzu and Lao-tzu to Master Confucius and Mencius, revered poets such as Li Po, Wang Wei and T'ao-ch'ien, or famous Zen masters – no matter how eccentric – like Hui-neng, Nan-yüeh, or Nan ch'uan. The sages of Japanese buddhism, Dôgen, Kûkai and Nichiren are also portrayed as venerable old men. There is the prominent role of the wise old man figure (*okina*) in Japanese folk tales and Noh plays.

We could even go a step further and claim that every great literary tradition has a favourite figure who best expresses his or her native culture's emotional depth, its wisdom and the unique quality that sets it

313

apart from other cultures. These are powerful, almost magnetic archetypes. Whether the individual writer's pen likes it or not it seems fatally drawn to this prevailing package of archetypal characteristics. So it is the young man that seems to dominate the heartland of American fiction from *Huckleberry Finn* to *Catcher in the Rye*. The American critic might argue that some very memorable old men can be found in his literature, for example Hemingway's Santiago in *Old Man and the Sea*. Yet the older one gets and the more of truly old men's writing one reads, the harder it becomes not to view Santiago as a young man in an old man's clothing. He keeps dreaming about lions, and cannot resist a life-and-death confrontation with a huge fish. In other words, he is still closer to what I'd call 'the Ahab mentality' than to the mellow resignation (*akirame*) of the Japanese old man and his inner quest. We notice that instead of going after the big ones, the old angler in "White Hair" tries to catch the smallest fish possible, fish that no fisherman normally pursues with hook and line:

> The old angler started out from crucian carp in his younger days, switching to killifish around forty; finally he took up *ayu* fishing and stayed with it till this day.
>
> Needless to say, the killifish is the smallest fish you can catch, and the fishing requires extreme skill. As the man explained, "No matter what you do, it is the pursuit of this ultimate skill that's so interesting." But nowhere did they sell hooks tiny enough and line thin enough to suit killifish, and so he had to make them himself. With watchmakers' glasses on his eyes and the finest file he could get, he crafted a minuscule hooklet out of a splinter

from a larger hook. To test how sharp it is, he touched its point on the tip of his own tongue. Since he couldn't weave a line thinner than a spider's web he begged the downy hair that grows over the forehead from some local maidens.[42]

Ibuse's favorite literary figure is just such a unique and somewhat eccentric old man. Of Japan's great modern writers, it is only Ibuse who almost exclusively concentrated on this particular type and kept developing it throughout his writing career. As Japanese critics have pointed out, the interesting thing here is that even his middle-aged or youngish men tend to speak with a mature timbre in their voices and reflect an old man's mentality in their thinking.

Ibuse's writing could be divided into two large thematic groups: the more accessible, popular type of stories and novellas represented by *Tajinko Village* or *No Consultations Today*, works whose technique is based on what the Japanese call *kikigaki* (writing as one hears), and on accurately rendered vivid dialogue; they seem more jovial and communal. Then there is the fairly exclusive and often less cheerful, more probing kind of writing like "White Hair." Though still humorous, it is less popular not only because it expresses a mature, sceptical point of view, but because it does so by focussing on a highly specialized activity and its particular lore, namely fishing.

When I translated this story forty-five years ago, I wasn't certain why it appealed to me; now I can see its place in the context of Ibuse's writing more clearly, but

---

[42] IM: "Shiraga." In: *IMZ IV*. Tokyo, Chikuma shobô 1974, pp. 231–232. Hereafter, bracketed numbers after quotes refer to page numbers of this edition.

I still feel one must tread very carefully along the banks of its river scenery to interpret it accurately.

At first sight it is a familiar scenery, and the viewpoint it's observed from an intensely personal one. The setting is very close to Ibuse's home ground, and though it is not a *watakushi shôsetsu*, it may be the most passionately personal among his fishing stories. We recognize the valley of the Shigawa, one of the two rivers of the writer's childhood, and from several remarks the narrator makes about himself we gather that his background is very close to Ibuse's own. He mentions that he'd spent a year in the suburbs of Kôfu and some two and a half in his native village in Hiroshima prefecture during the war, just as the author had done. The fishing scenery is closely modelled on the real setting of his place and the location of the fishing holes could most probably be traced on the local anglers' area map. The technical vocabulary of fishing is made very personal, almost unpleasantly so: the story opens with the narrator assessing the strength of the hair from above his forehead, at the back of his head, or his temples, and comparing it with various grades of fishing line. Thus his head almost becomes a repository of fishing tackle, and the memories of fishing, normally kept on the inside of a devoted angler's mind, are here visibly externalized. In the narrator's specialized and somewhat outdated 'fishing culture', psychic demarcation lines between real and imagined, outer and inner, were of course as strong as steel bars, but the youngsters who humiliate him by his favourite stream recognize no such subtleties. The sophisticated verbal culture in the older man's mind has no meaning for them, as they think everything important happens in the physical world outside.

While the first 'movement' of the story introduces the narrator and his 'bad habit' of compulsively pulling out his own white hair and joining it together with specialized fishing knots, the second opens as a recollection that leads us into the fishing scenery, where, as we learn, the 'habit' had its origin:

> But whenever I recall fishing in mountain streams, an irritating memory comes to my mind and makes me raving mad. I still find it hard to express just how unpleasant a memory it is. It's not an exaggeration if I say that my kindest feelings were most cruelly trampled on. And what's worse, it's a story that's bound to make laugh everyone to whom I might appeal about it. (220)

The unpleasant memory is that of meeting with two city youngsters at the narrator's favourite riverside. Although the older man does his best to share his intimate knowledge of the place with the boys, taking them to a clear spring in the thicket and explaining the intricacies of local fishing – something that any newcoming angler would be immensely grateful for – the youngsters seem to be completely engrossed in their mean little world and hardly listen to the narrator's small talk. While they are having lunch by the well, washing their salmon *sushi* down with generous amounts of whiskey and never offering a drink to the older man, they become increasingly envious of his previous fishing exploits. When they later discover they'd forgotten the main part of their tackle, the fishing line, the two get downright nasty. Trying to divert them, the narrator recounts one of his entertaining yarns about his childhood fishing when he used to pull white hair from a horse's tail and employed it as a perfect substitute for a fishing line. At that point the more arrogant of the two youths snaps:

> 'This guy's a real talker. Makes me sick – hey, old man, you do like shooting off your mouth, don't you?... How about sharing some white hair from your dear old head instead of the horse's tail, eh?' (226)

In an ironic reversal, the aging angler who narrates the story gets accused of being a windbag – a quality that most of Ibuse's old men lack. Their favourite mode of expression is the understatement, the oblique hint – the 'talkers' usually are the rude outsiders, the wheeler-dealers, in short the intruders into the self-contained little cosmos of their villages. True anglers do like sharing tales and little secrets, even a bit of gossip now and then. But it seems this fragile verbal culture of the older men was encoded in a special language, a unique *parole* which does not communicate to the youngsters. In a way then, the theme is similar to that of previous stories, mainly "Bridgeside Inn," but the contrast between the two orders, or between the older code and the new one, if you will, is here expressed more dramatically in terms of a brutal generation gap. The tranquillity, the luxurious and somewhat selfish solitude the traditional angler could enjoy through his 'contemplative sport' is ruthlessly disrupted by reality. The white-haired older man is not only prevented from telling his stories – a kind of attack on the natural dialogic, or polyphonic nature of Ibuse's text – but becomes a commodity, an available store of things. The youngsters not only lack manners and any sensitivity towards the older verbal code, speaking in an abrupt, cynical city language, they revert most readily to physical violence. Despite the older man's protestations, one of them holds him in a vise-like grip, while the other plucks white hair from his head – an act of rape rarely encountered in other Ibuse stories. In the countryside of rougher parts of the world one would naturally expect more physical, perhaps violent ways, but as we saw in the previous stories, in Ibuse's cultivated and fairly sophisticated southern village even punishment was a mostly verbal, nearly theatrical affair. Mr. Tange wouldn't have lifted a finger against his servant, and preferred to ridicule his bad habits in a rather exaggerated satirical harangue.

At a more subtle level then, this story is not just a lament about the psychic ravages of war and time in a general sense, but a probe into the changing ways in which the Japanese relate to their natural environment. From the very first encounter with the youngsters we feel there is a pronounced contrast between the way they see the river scenery and the way the narrator perceives it. They criticize everything they see, complaining about the fruit trees on the banks which make casting difficult, the considerable distance between this fishing spot and the nearest railway station, etc. The narrator, on the other hand, remarks how used he is to this river and how intimately he knows every spot on it, even going into the details of fishing tricks that must be used in its various fishing holes. But now, he says, it doesn't look that he'd be coming back and so he is willing to share his secrets with the newcomers. This is the story's tragic note: though he is more than willing to share his intimate knowledge of the place, its yarns, customs and even the practical fishing know-how that opens its secrets, the youngsters' ears are stone-deaf to any such message.

And perhaps, the author suggests in a sad and rather novel insight, the way in which his narrator relates to the place is already an anachronism, a fading nostalgia of the past. Time hasn't stopped even here and it keeps transforming the place, whether one likes it or not. It is significant that the narrator introduces the unpleasant episode with the youngsters by a recollection of a small shrine he decides to visit before leaving the valley for Tokyo. Though he'd often gone fishing to the Shigawa during his long evacuation during the war, he says, he never thought about visiting the shrine he'd known thirty years ago. Yet he did remember its scenery and sometimes even told his friends about the interesting Bizen oil jar and sake bottle he'd seen in a stone lantern there. This is how he describes the shrine after thirty years:

> I forgot whether the shrine was dedicated to the rice god Inari or the god Yakushi. Its tumbledown wooden structure stands amidst a cedar forest, and by its side stretches a line of fir trees and a granite night lantern. I could hardly believe my eyes: was this tiny little building the same shrine I had seen thirty years ago? There is no oil jar and no sake bottle in the stone lantern, just a darkish, sooty saucer and on its bottom a jewel insect's wings had stuck. But this is not the unpleasant incident I want to talk about. (220–21)

And yet unpleasant enough, the subtle suggestion goes. I think it is because he feels that the shrine is a focal point of the scenery and a bridge between his youth and his present, that the narrator feels he must say goodbye to it. Yet as always in such moments, the contrast between the magic scenery of youth and that seen by the adult eye is disappointing. But it is not only the usual disenchantment coming from the diminished size of things that we feel here. The shrine now gives an eerie feeling of being abandoned, and out of function. Moreover, the rainbow-coloured jewel insect, a fragile memento of the enchanted days of youth, has lost its wings, and they are 'imprisoned' in a darkish sooty saucer.

This is an effective image, placed with a great sense of rightness, almost inevitability. And yet when we go over the story carefully, we realize that next to the description of the narrator's fishing holes, it is practically the only vivid image symbolizing an emotional foothold within the scenery, sad and nostalgic as it may be. Ibuse's vantage point has obviously shifted here: while in the earlier stories he always had someone firmly rooted in the place – old Kuchisuke, Mr. Tange and other local characters – and the narrator, usually a younger man, most often the author's persona, was returning back to his place, here we meet a whole cast of outsiders. The narrator himself is becoming a 'castaway', and his view of the landscape is already a nostalgic one. While still rooted in some ways in the landscape, he is about to leave it; perhaps as he says, never to come back. When he is being tormented by the young thugs, he looks at the idyllic scenery of the valley, and spells out his mixed feelings: the more peaceful and beautiful the village looks, the more miserable it makes him feel. As much as he'd like to shout for help, he's afraid to be seen in this embarassing situation. And so he decides not to call for help, something the common villager would do most naturally. He's already in a kind of detached and compromised position and doesn't dare to appeal to the local villagers directly. Portraying a man who doesn't belong to the valley any more, but relates to it only through memory, Ibuse has decided not to put too many sentimental footholds in his text. He deliberately avoids images that might function as stepping stones into the scenery and enable his narrator to linger on in it. Eventually the story's events take him even farther away from the landscape, to a rather painful vantage point where he has to admit:

> Had it not been for this incident, I may have postponed my departure for Tokyo last summer and done some more fishing in my mountain stream. But the mere sight of the river gives me the shivers now and I can't stand its noisy murmur. (228)

The Japanese traveller-poets of old did not so much describe the landscape as invoke it and inscribe themselves into it. In the ancient animistic rituals, the natives invoked their gods using 'special' language, pleasing to the ears of the gods. From these ritualistic invocations, as many Japanese scholars believe, evolved the ornate 'poetic epithets' (*makurakotoba*) that evoke the essential poetic mood of a given scene. The local gods, those invisible presences saturating the scene's rivers, mountains, rocks and waterfalls, wrapped the locals into the familiar cloak of rooted identity. This spiritual communion between a 'native' and the gods of his landscape has been brutally disrupted here. Rather than simply becoming remote, or being veiled in a fading nostalgia, the landscape acquires downright hostile, irritating overtones.

Such a radical change of viewpoint must of course have influenced the language of the story. In most of the pre-war 'village stories' we have seen a meeting of standard Tokyo Japanese and the quaint speech patterns of the local characters. In "White Hair" nobody speaks with even a trace of the local dialect. The pattern is strangely and ironically reversed here: the ones who speak most colloquially – albeit in a rough and vulgar manner – are the two city youngsters. This too is a fairly novel thing in Ibuse's work, for colloquial Tokyo Japanese was rarely used to reveal a character from within in the earlier stories. Could we link this unpleasant fictional incident to Ibuse's formative experience of the frightening encounter with Tokyo language, spoken by a midnight prowler during his childhood? Perhaps, but only in a marginal sense. The robber spoke a thick, visceral downtown brogue, full of the pronounced narrow $\hat{e}$'s that gave his language a certain villainous warmth. In "White Hair" the emphasis is on the coldness and the brutal cynicism of the youngsters. The author avoids giving their speech any such endearing, visceral qualities. Colloquial, yes, but without any trace of individual originality or the linguistic inventiveness that so often marks Ibuse's lower class speakers. These young men may even have some education, and hardly come from a true downtown Edo family, for when they first meet the narrator, they use a smooth and polite standard language.

So the story does dramatize the theme of shifting identity, but its treatment is anything but simplistic. At first sight it may look like a straight confrontation of the young and the old and a kind of neat restatement of the pre-war world of tradition and custom expressed through the niceties of the attractive fishing lore. And yet the old angler whom the narrator meets on a bus at Izu – a charming figure in old-fashioned gaiters and straw sandals – has also made his compromise with the brave new world. Dying his snow-white hair – and thus concealing his true identity – he returns to the office post he'd held before the war. It is only during his private, fleeting and almost clandestine encounter with the narrator on the bus – in other words a place that really belongs nowhere – that he reveals his private world. It is a wonderful, almost magic world: he recalls having crafted nearly invisible hooks to catch the tiniest fish possible, and spins charming yarns about the strength of a virgin's downy hair and the brittle hair of those who don't observe celibacy. But it is also an extremely fragile inner world, and no matter how much the middle-aged narrator admires it there is little hope that it will provide a viable model of identity for him. Listening to the old angler, one can't avoid the feeling of a fairy tale or a myth in the making. One can also imagine how in a close-knit and firmly rooted river community these tales might grow into local legends and add to the distinct identity of the place and its habitués. Yet in "White Hair" it's not that easy. The two men are allowed no more than a fleeting encounter on the moving bus; they meet, communicate for a brief while and go their separate ways. I think Ibuse stresses the fleeting nature of this encounter by having the narrator say: "I wish I could have listened to the old angler a little longer" (232), but he loses him in the confusion on the bus. In the story's final line, an unusually urgent one for Ibuse, whose endings are most often on a peaceful, harmonious note, he vows: "This isn't a joke anymore. No matter what, I must get rid of this annoying tic of mine."(233)

Yet one fears that, like the Ancient Mariner, he is doomed to live on with his unpleasant memories, and continue his 'bad habit' of pulling white hair. And should he manage to forget, the brave new world that has penetrated the 'village' will provide ample reminders. In "Lieutenant Lookeast" Ibuse explored the inside of the village, its remaining codes of communication and its changing human networks and personalities. In "White Hair" he probes deeply into the meaning of its 'eternal environment' and more specifically, the meaning of his own native landscape as a source of verbal expression and identity. The familiar conflict of Country and City, presented rather playfully through the smooth dialogue of his earlier works, acquires not only unpleasant personal, but larger symbolic overtones here. The stylized dialect, so important in Ibuse's dialogic mode as a voice of his birthplace and Country in general, has been abruptly muted by an invasion of a cruder and simpler *lingua franca*.

The story contains a more universal meaning as well. In his best novel, *Fifth Business*, Robertson Davies has a wise Jesuit, Padre Blazon, say:

My own idea is that when He comes again it will be to continue His ministry as an old man. I am an old man and my life has been spent as a soldier of Christ, and I tell you that the older I grow the less Christ's teaching says to me. I am sometimes very conscious that I am following the path of a leader who died when He was less than half as old as I am now. I see and feel things He never saw or felt... All Christ's teaching is put forward with the dogmatism, the certainty, and the strength of youth: I need something that takes account of the accretion of experience, the sense of paradox and ambiguity that comes with years![43]

In *Too Loud a Solitude* the Czech writer Bohumil Hrabal, who studied Lao Tzu and had a remarkable rapport with Eastern thought, puts it in similar terms:

...I saw an angry young man, who wants to change the world, while the old master looks around in a resigned way and by returning to the origins lines his coat with eternity. I saw Jesus charm reality so it'd turn into a miracle, while Lao Tzu follows the laws of nature along his Great Way and only thus reaches wisdom in ignorance.[44]

By willingly renouncing 'white hair' and the time-proven ideal of oriental wisdom it stands for, and accepting a superificial imported cult of youth, Japanese culture signed its own death warrant. That Ibuse realized so clearly what the future spiritual orientation of his country would be more than fifty years ago is remarkable.

[43] Davies, Robertson: *Fifth Business*. Toronto, Penguin Canada 1996, p. 168.
[44] Hrabal, Bohumil: *Příliš hlučná samota*. Trans. Liman, Anthony. Praha, Odeon 1989, pp. 40–41.

*The wise man delights in water, the good man delights in mountains.*

Confucius, Analects VI, 21

"White Hair" was written in 1948, this story came out in November 1963. The mysterious name of the title's flower (*kotatsubana*), a plant that can't be found in any encyclopedia, immediately suggests a very different scenery from the familiar, mild and civilized Shigawa River valley. This story takes us deep into the more rugged valleys of Shinshû (Nagano Prefecture), surrounded by the lofty snow-capped peaks of the Japan Alps, a wilder scenery than the cultivated valley of the previous story and more remote from the genteel influence of the mainstream culture. Like most deep mountains, it has an ancient, almost primeval aura and its inhabitants – whether human, plant or animal – assert their existence in ways that baffle the city traveller's intellect.

The gorge of the Himegawa – Maiden, Princess River – is cool and narrow, the mountains along it soar into passing clouds. From the right to the left, the angler can see the Togakushiyama, the Kurohimeyama and the Amekazariyama, names which in the original add to the atmosphere of the place: The Door-Clouding Peak, The Dark Princess Mountain and The Mountain Adorned by Rain. In midwinter shy mountain goats come to the edge of the cliffs and stand there, as if frozen to the spot, for as long as a week; the local people call their strange behaviour "the frozen stand of the mountain goat" or *"kamoshika no kandachi"*. By the path leading down to the river stands a weatherbeaten monument to The Master of the Land (*Ôkuninushi*) of Japanese mythology, and side by side with it two stone lanterns and a statue of *Jizô* the Road Guardian. According to one rendering of an episode from the Izumo cycle of myths, called "Kuninushi Searches for a Bride" (*"Ôkuninushi kyûkondan"*) the mythical hero courted a maiden by the name of Nunakawa. Nunakawa or River of Jewels is often an imaginary river, not necessarily located in Izumo, but the Himegawa (Maiden River) of this area might be related to the mythical princess. It is also one of the very few locations in Japan where jade was found in pre-historic times.

The hearth flower of the title is introduced early in the story and helps create its unique atmosphere. Though the shape of its petals resembles a pink (*nadeshiko*), quite unlike it this flower has four pistils and a vermilion hue. It is casually displayed in a plain vase at the local barber shop, and when the narrator inquires whether it belongs to the pink family, the barber's wife simply replies: "It's a *kotatsu* flower." When I first visited Ibuse's summer home in Takamori, I asked: "*Sensei,* is there really a *kotatsu* flower or did you invent it?" He pointed to the *tokonoma*, where a single dark red flower stood in a slim vase and said: "There, have a good look at it!"

We know only too well the common fallacy of city-based literature that tends to discover dreamlands in the remote countryside and inhabit them with wonderful creatures of fantasy, whose romantic attributes are often simply the product of the writer's ignorance. But even on second or third reading this story retains its strong, *zuihitsu*-like authenticity; Ibuse's casual remark about "recording the fishing experience to practice his storytelling" in one of his memoirs[45] suggests how carefully he must have observed the natural detail of its background. Without such sharp observation, you might say, there can be no first-rate literature regardless of its cultural background. Yet in Ibuse's case we must also take into account the strange vividness with which fishing sceneries sink into the angler's mind. Moreover, this angler happens to be an artist of unique and consistent vision, who works most patiently on crystallizing a carefully circumscribed range of experience.

The castaways' chronicles do take his protagonists out of Japan, but there the focus is on their distorted, 'Japanese' perception of the alien outside world rather than its realistic portrayal. With writers like Greene or Conrad it matters less whether their major works are located in England or Africa, for the landscape of *Heart of the Matter* or *Heart of Darkness* is above all the inner landscape of the human heart. I am not saying that Ibuse's writing lacks such an intense inner quality, but I think it is always expressed through a precisely articulated, authentic description of the external world. As in the best works of photographic realism the soul shines through precisely because of the fine articulation of the detailed 'surface'; the heavier, kabuki-like 'make-up' of Ibuse's earlier stylization gives way here to a more subtle and careful stylistic presentation of the natural features. We have observed such vibration in unison between the inner and the outer landscape as early as in one of his debut stories, "Carp." But while in "Carp"

[45] IM: "Oboegaki." In: *Jisen zenshû VII*. Tokyo, Shinchôsha 1986, p. 406.

there were allusions, albeit ironic ones, to an external literary structure and its conventional symbols, in mature stories like "The Hearth Flower" the rich verbal texture has an almost deceptive verisimilitude of a realistic, symbol-proof surface. Yet we must bear in mind that it is above all a fine *verbal surface* that Ibuse so deftly creates, not a naturalistic reflection of reality. In "Making Sense" Jonathan Culler draws a fine and useful line between "naturalizing interpretation" and the appeal of "verbal surface" which applies to Ibuse's text:

> The poet or novelist succeeds in challenging naturalization not by going beyond the bounds of sense but by creating a verbal surface whose fascination is greater than that of any possible naturalization and which thereby challenges the models by which we attempt to comprehend and circumscribe it.[46]

"The Hearth Flower" clearly contrasts two ways of knowing and two distinct ways in which language absorbs 'reality'. The way the old man deals with the snakes, or the peculiar way people in the mountains call their local flowers, belong to the direct, intimate kind of knowledge based on long experience. When the narrator gets back to the city, he consults his encyclopedia, but he can't find any hearth flower (*kotatsubana*); to the abstract, encyclopedic knowledge of the city it simply does not exist. Knowledge must be watered down to fit into an encyclopedia, and the concrete, detailed awareness of place makes sense only within the narrow confines of its natural habitat and its special *parole*. It rests on an intricate network of lo-

[46] Culler, Jonathan: "Making Sense." *20th Century Studies* 12, 12, December 1974, p. 33.

cal connections where certain fish will take only one particular bait at a given time of the year: "If you don't use baby wasps on this river at this time of the year," says old Hogoden, "you're out of business." A writer of fiction, the Western critic might object, can weave any credible motif into his story as long as it works aesthetically; it matters little where he took it from. After all, does it make much difference whether you got the fish with an artificial, city-made lure or the local natural bait? The story's imagery suggests that Ibuse realizes both the value and the limits of such 'local knowledge'. Towards the end of "The Hearth Flower," his narrator moves on to another river in nearby Kôshû. But here in the next valley, the baby wasps he'd forgotten in his bait box are no more than an embarrassment. Most of them are dead anyway, and at best they'll provide chickenfeed for his landlady's poultry. Seeing the familiar hearth flower in his new lodging, the narrator then asks the woman if it's also called *kotatsubana* around here: "No, this is an *odenbana*."

The reason why Ibuse focused on this mountainous corner of Shinshû is not only that he had chosen his retreat in the same general region and observed it for more than two decades by this time. We have seen in "White Hair" that his own native valley can speak to his protagonist in a familiar, intimate voice, but it can also fill his heart with unbearable nostalgia and sadness. Though he brings to this new place the same meticulous 'grammar of perception' and the angler's patience for storing valuable experience, it is a less emotionally charged environment. Having been 'opened' and developed agriculturally much later than the fertile and accessible lowlands by the ocean, the soil of these rugged mountains has not accumulated as many cultural layers through Japan's history; for the same reason the most ancient strata are closer at hand. The deeper into the mountains one goes in Japan, the more basic the world becomes. We can observe this in examples as diverse as Sôseki's *Three Cornered World* (*Kusamakura*), Izumi Kyôka's *Demon Pond* (*Yasha ga ike*) or Fukazawa Shichirô's *The Ballad of Narayama* (*Narayama bushikô*) and many other works. Almost another literary convention of its kind, it is based on the belief that the farther away from the plains one gets, the more primeval is the world one finds. This belief is of course grounded in a solid geographic and historical reality, and it would seem that deep in the mountains the world is indeed clearer in its basic needs and aspirations. Shelter and nourishment become very central here, and we notice that they expand imaginatively into the natural world around. An elegant plant is called 'hearth flower' (*kotatsubana*) in one valley and '*oden* flower' (*oden* being a common peasant food) in the next; in both cases we can observe a direct link between life's practical necessities and imagination. In a sense then, imagination is less free in this meager climate, but to the observant eye it still offers a rare glimpse of its vital link with survival.

Throughout his writing career, especially from the mid-period on, Ibuse has been deeply concerned with themes of survival and identity. Though the word 'identity' doesn't exist in Japanese proper and the author himself might scoff at its somewhat grandiose implications, in his quiet, unobtrusive way he has been seriously and consistently questioning what it really means to be Japanese in a rapidly changing, difficult world. What are the characteristics that have sustained his race through the ages and might help them to survive in this confused century? Scores of flashy and narcissistic *nihonjinron* (theories of Japaneseness) have asked the same question, and given bolder answers. Other senior artists have searched for a suggestion of the answer in the mythical simplicity of different traditions, less cluttered by cultural sophistication and its many historical layers. In *Dersu Uzala,* the great film director Kurosawa imaginatively explores parallels between the mental world of a rugged, 'primitive' Siberian hunter and the most basic mythical *Weltanschauung* of the Japanese. Kurosawa's saga of a Goldi hunter obviously does not reflect so much the director's interest in remote primitive cultures as a vicarious search for Japanese roots. In recent years, as the green world and the natural identity of traditional Japan are being eroded, a nostalgic quest for some kind of 'basic' Japanese identity – an emotional *Heimat* in the pre-Yayoi Jômon culture – has become very popular.

I think Ibuse's story is one of the first such attempts and old man Hogoden of the Himegawa his 'Dersu Uzala'. Most of the text consists of the old man's character portrayal; it has much less of a plot than "White Hair". What 'story' it has, is provided by Hogoden's interpolated tales or recollections. At first sight, he looks like a "distracted old man" (the narrator's polite alternative for describing him as a somewhat dim-witted looking old fellow), but he is a true master of streamcraft. 'Hogoden' is really his nickname, and consists of an abbreviated part of his name, Denbei, and the word *Hogo*:

> I heard later from my host at the kiln that the old man, who'd turned seventy-seven this year, lived in comfortable retirement and that his real name was Denbei. To his face people were calling him 'Den sa', and behind his back 'Hogoden'. *Hogo* is an ancient word meaning a carefree life of indulging in one's own hobbies and receiving a cash allowance from the community instead of doing field or forest work. It seems that in the old days, when someone came back from town with a pocketful of money he'd made at the market or at a gamblers' den, people would say: 'He came back as a *hogo*.'[47]

The narrator does not say whether or not the word meant what it means now, namely 'wastepaper', or 'useless thing'. The old man must have a family name, but it is never mentioned in the story. Instead, he is referred to as "Hogoden from under the fire-bell" or *hanshôshita no Hogoden;* as usual in the Japanese countryside, it is his dwelling, his place in the village's physical space that defines him. The character for *den* is that of 'legend' or to 'hand down' and thus the nickname that might translate as 'Old Scraps' contains in a nutshell the old man's entire existence: to the frugal, hardworking village community he is a bit of a useless presence, but because of his extraordinary fishing skills he is also something of a living legend (*den*). He moves through his world with complete ease, aware of every creature and its habits, especially those of the depths, the large, salmon-trout (*yamame*) and the rainbows of

---

[47] IM: *"Kotatsubana."* In: *IMZ VIII*, p. 13. Hereafter, bracketed numbers after quotes refer to the page numbers of this edition.

his river, as well as the stinging, poisonous ones, like the vipers and the wasps. When the narrator brings worms, his usual – and most common bait – to the river, Hogoden glances at them and says: "These crawlers ain't no good 'round here. No crucian carp livin' in this river. There's just one bait that'll get you fish this time of the year, and that's baby wasps!... There are plenty of wasps' nests everywhere" (5–6), he explains casually to the visitor as he pokes under the cap of the nearby stone-lantern with the butt of his fishing rod. "See, every year the wasps build their nest under the cap of this lantern" (6) – and indeed, before the wasps have time to fly out, their nest drops to the base of the lantern. When the prudent narrator seeks refuge from the buzzing wasps behind the statue of the guardian *Jizô,* Hogoden teases him: "Listen, there's nothing like whistlin' if you want a powerful charm against these wasps." (7) But even before the wasps can sting the old man, he deftly weaves together a bundle of dry mugwort stalks, lights one end, and burns the adults, while keeping the nest with the young ones. Like a benign trickster, secure and at home in his realm, Hogoden likes to tease the newcomer, though he is equally generous with helpful advice. His easy familiarity with the environment shows again in his casual remark upon discovering a viper near the river, coiled "like a piece of filigree artwork" by a single hearth flower: "I have to get my tool to catch this guy. I keep it at the trout hatchery over there..." (8) He explains to the narrator that the snake won't move as long as someone keeps an eye on him. Typically, the city visitor does not see the snake, but offers to stay, since the snake "Wouldn't know that I really don't see it anyway. Comes to the same result, doesn't it?" The old man is a little surprised by this piece of city logic, and mumbles: "Hmm, if you say so…" (8) With a 'Y' shaped stick whose end is polished by long use like an old scythe-handle, Hogoden holds the snake's neck down and lets it bite into another piece of wood. Turning it softly in the viper's mouth, as if "kneading its gums," he then begins to break its poison fangs. The startled narrator asks:

'Isn't this viper a little bigger than usual? How old is it, do you think?'

'I wouldn't know its age, but I can tell you it has a bellyful of young ones.'

'A viper's teeth are very strong, aren't they? Can you pry them out like that?'

'On the contrary, its teeth're brittle; you can break'em off with no trouble. If you do it too rough, dirt'll get in the snake's mouth and it won't bring you a penny. One of these vipers'll fetch ya a good ¥650…. I'll be letting the young ones out of her belly now – have to skin'er anyway – so I'll need your blade. I'll wash and return it later.'

'As for my knife, use it as you like. But are you saying that you're going to cut the snake's belly and let out its brood?'

'That's right, must be done now.'

Watching the snake as it dangled in midair, the old man puffed on his cigarette… (10-11)

Seeing the old man prepare calmly for a vivisection is strong stuff for the city intellectual; grateful for the opportunity to linger on in the safer world of words for a while, he listens to Hogoden's explanation:

'When I catch a viper, I always let out her brood. The small ones are like sausages, shelterin' inside a pouch of thin skin. Two and two of the lil' sausages're linked together, and sometimes there's as many as twelve young ones in a single viper, would you believe that? People say when the young snakes hatch in their mother's belly, they'll bite their way out through the skin.'

'So there's something like a day-care centre inside her belly, isn't there?'

'That's it, she's got the ancient Sugaru's infant-chamber right in her tummy.' (11)

Few modern Japanese writers can blend descriptions of the more gruesome realities of life and humour with the same ease as Ibuse, a consummate skill that would serve him in good stead in the most challenging task of his writing career, *Black Rain*. From this text, old man Hogoden emerges as a far more complex figure than Ibuse's earlier old men. While sharing some of their characteristics – the fine tuning to the chthonic and aqueous rhythms – he is much less vulnerable and far more articulate than they were. Old Kuchisuke or Grandpa Isomatsu of "Bridgeside Inn" had the same instinctive rapport with their environment, and a good deal of traditional wisdom. But they were helpless *vis-à-vis* the pressures of the modern world, its ruthless utilitarian logic and the powerful new 'magic' of its intellectual, abstract word. Though tempered by humour, in Kuchisuke's portrayal there was still a lingering touch of the sentimentality with which the modern city-based Japanese author tends to portray his villagers. If in *Tajinko Village* Ibuse began lifting this sentimental veil, here he has stripped it off without trace.

Hogoden certainly shares his wisdom with the previous old men and his instincts are no less keen, but in addition he has a fairly objective awareness of things and a considerable skill with words. He is also a more practical survivor: if there are people in the city who believe in the magic properties of a viper's liver or its skin, he'll sell it to them and not worry whether their belief is a foolish superstition or not. He can play the city's game as well as he can play the visitor's verbal games. Note how skillfully he parries the narrator's smart remark about the 'nursery school' in the viper's belly: "That's it. She's got the ancient Sugaru's infant-chamber right in her tummy." (11) Sugaru is a rather obscure semi-legendary figure whom the Emperor Yûryaku (456–479 A.D.) asked to collect silkworms (*ko*). Mistaking this word for the homophone *ko* of 'little children', Sugaru gathered a bunch of infants and presented them to the Emperor. The ruler was amused by his servant's mistake and entrusted the children's education into his care. The same Sugaru is noted for his connections with legendary reptiles. According to the *Nihonshoki*, he was sent by the Emperor to capture a mighty serpent in the mountain of Himorodake. Hogoden certainly knows how to use a line from his classics, for nowadays even an educated Japanese of the younger generation wouldn't have a clue what the Sugaru reference means. At one point, the old man even offers his own charming explanation of the serpent's scary nature; it sounds like an anecdotal digest of Jungian theory:

'In any case, the snakes, who were called reptiles in the previous karma, seem to have tormented people a lot in their former existence. Perhaps they brought this feeling of 'how scary, how chilling' from the previous life into this one. Is there anybody who'd like snakes?' (16)

And yet one feels that Hogoden neither likes nor dislikes them; he does take the life of the parent-snake, but like a careful harvester he releases the young ones and makes sure they find a safe shelter that will enable their survival. His mind seems to be remarkably free from the uneasy pendulum of extreme attitudes towards animals, so typical for Western man. Yet he seems to show more sympathy for a water-snake than he does for the viper. The water-snake lives on the river, catching fish just as he does, perhaps even better:

'Listen, Grandpa, how come you get so many fish? Won't you teach me how to hook these salmon? There's some kind of secret to it, isn't there?'

'Don't ask me, just watch the fish. They'll teach you...'

'Now let me show you a true master of anglin,' he said, and though I hadn't finished my lunch, he reached among the boulders of the embankment and brought out a water-snake...

'As I say, this guy's a master of fishin'. If you wanna know about the right frame of mind, or the best posture of your body when fishin', you'd better let him teach you.'

'Come off it, Denbei san. Don't you see I haven't finished my lunch? This thing gives me the creeps...' (14–15)

A few days later, when the two men meet again by a smaller local river, the Kusugawa, Hogoden tells the narrator a longish story about another water-snake he'd observed here five years ago. It was on a summer day after a devastating typhoon and the usually clear stream had changed into a raging, muddy torrent; the snake was dangling precariously over the stream from a branch. Observing it closely for some time, the old man concluded that it was waiting for an auspicious gust of wind that would bring it nearer to the trees on the opposite bank. Feeling his way into the snake's mind, Hogoden tries to 'read' its intentions and at some point even talks as if he were the snake:

> 'The snake was doin' exactly what I was thinkin'! So I say to the snake in my mind, hey, pull yourself together, give it all you got!' (23)

Ibuse jokingly suggests Hogoden nearly possesses those magic qualities of the Jômon shaman that enabled him to mediate between the human and the natural world. Interestingly, the seemingly disproportionate length of this episode in an otherwise tersely written story approximates, by extending narrative time, the adjustment of the old man's mind to the flexible time-frame of the 'hunting mentality' where it is the animal that sets the pace. In a thoughtful essay on hunting, Ortega y Gasset calls the poacher "the municipal paleolithic man" or the "eternal troglodyte domiciled in modern villages,"[48] and hunting itself "the only occupation that permits him [man] something like a vacation from his human condition."[49] We may easily extend hunting to fishing and see Hogoden as the 'Jômon man' or the 'paleolithic man' of his village who can perceive, as he identifies with the fish or wild

---

[48] Ortega y Gasset, José: *Meditations on Hunting*. Trans. Wescott, Howard B. New York, Charles Scribner and Sons 1972, pp. 105–106.
[49] Ibid., p. 111.

animal, the landscape both in its smallest functional detail (the relationship between wind – branch – river's width etc.) as well as in its completeness and truly be within it. The farmer and the tourist, even the traditional poet, as Ortega points out, cannot, for they enter a cultivated, human landscape from which their eye selects only those features that suit their respective purpose. Elsewhere, the old man addresses the snake as he might a wanton female from the other end of the valley: "Impudent creature! Ain't you ashamed of yourself? What self-respectin' snake would show its white belly to humans?" (24)

The suggestion of the snake's erotic appeal also links the image to the long folkloric and literary tradition of the female snake, most vividly represented in the Dôjôji legend ("Red Heat" in the folktale version). Yet Hogoden's interpretation never strays too far from the sharply observed *gestalt* of the snake's actions. Throughout the story, his cautious, rooted imagination is contrasted with the more volatile speculations of the narrator:

> I wondered: does this snake [the viper] coil itself because it's the most steady posture? Or is it a most natural, most comfortable one? If it were human, would it be like lying on one's back face-up? (9)

The dialogic mode is more objectively refracted in this text: the direct, humorous banter of the two anglers points to a sharper contrast of their views and their perception than that of the early Kamo valley stories. How stubbornly Hogoden's mind rejects fanciful words and notions is humorously suggested towards the end of the story. When the narrator tells him that a certain fishing technique which is locally known as 'plover approach' (*chidorikake*) is also called the 'garden fence (*gâden fensu*) approach' elsewhere, he ignores this imported language. When the narrator meets him in his festive old fashioned costume on the night of the *obon* festival and asks him: "Enjoying the evening cool, are you?" (27) Hogoden grumbles that he's trying to memorize this year's *obon* song, but its words not only change from year to year, they now include foolish phrases like: "Our boy has half-a-horse-power, *sa-sa,* so we got two-and-a-half-horse-power…" (28) and similar nonsense. The intelligence that registers in minute detail what happened on the river five years ago and recreates it verbally is unable to digest a few words of an insipid song. It instinctively tries to stay close to the familiar first world of his village, and to those symbolic expressions and language forms that can cope with it. What his mind refuses to understand and his language can't denote (e.g. the imported notion of *garden fence approach* instead of *chidorikake*) is passed over as an extralinguistic, and therefore unimportant fact.

There is no question that on second or third reading a certain symbolic symmetry begins to emerge from the story. Or perhaps it is quite apparent from the very first and one's eye just dismisses it, for it is too fascinated with the rich and colourful detail of the text's verbal surface. The two kinds of serpents, one poisonous and the other benign, the old man's nonchalant familiarity with their secrets, his rapport with the mythical Master of the Land to whose statue he bows every time he goes down to the river, all these images have rich mythopoeic overtones. The old man obviously shares the snakes' vitality: "Hogoden had tucked up the sleeve of his shirt, and I could see the snake coiling around the surprisingly lustrous skin of his forearm."(15) Like The Master of the Land who sometimes appears in snake-form, he seems to have a power of life and death over these creatures of the 'lower world'. Wasps, snakes (and centipedes) were of course the inhabitants of the Japanese Hades, the *Yomi no kuni* or *ne no katasu kuni*. Among the trials of The Master of the Land was sleeping in a snake pit and in a chamber swarming with wasps. He also had a narrow escape from death in a burning grassy moor. We know that the old man is a superb master of streamcraft and thus has an intimate rapport with water, but we are also told that he is 'Hogoden from under the Fire-bell'; furthermore, we know that he had subdued the stinging wasps with fire. These images call for a Jungian interpretation. Clearly, old Hogoden has most of the archetypal attributes of Jung's 'wise old man' – crafty and benevolent at the same time, his advice always ambiguous and often without logical sense. Because he comes close to an archetypal, objectified psychic attitude, crystallizing the instinctive wisdom of his race, he provides an ideal inner meeting point of nature and civilization, or of the premodern and modern mind. Ibuse has little to do with naive 'back to nature' nostalgia, but rather tries to maintain a dialogue between the 'green centre' within our mind and the 'modern self' of the more urbanized mentality. Unlike the vulnerable old men of the earlier stories, Hogoden's trickster attributes are more apparent, and, despite his nickname, he most definitely does not come across as a pathetic relic of a bygone age.

343

In *Aion,* his study of the history of symbols, Jung points out[50] the great complexity of the serpent image, one of the richest and most ambivalent human symbols. Representing the lowest and the highest at the same time, it forms the linking principle between the darkness of the unconscious and spirit or wisdom; as a tree numen it can connect the vegetative and the animate world: we notice that the viper is coiled like "a piece of filigree artwork" next to a single hearth flower, suggesting a mysterious connection between the two. The Gnostic symbol of the Ouroboros, or the serpent biting its own tail, also expresses its essential ambivalence. When old man Hogoden dangles the viper in the air before "letting out her young ones," we could point to what Cirlot calls the "image of the crucified snake,"[51] or the chthonic and feminine principle being vanquished by the spirit.

From Warramunga and Yurlunggur, the snake deities of the Australian aborigines to the plumed serpent Kukulcan of the Toltecs and the Mayas, or Tlaloc, the serpent god of the Mexicans, snake worship belongs to the oldest expression of human religious feelings. Snakes have fascinated the human mind from its very dawn: by shedding their skin serpents get to be 'reborn' every year, having no eyelids they seem to have mesmerizing, even radiant eyes, dwelling in the ground they connect the earth's chthonic depths with its surface and thus can act as messengers between the

[50] Jung, Carl G.: *Aion, Untersuchungen zur Symbolgeschichte.* Zürich, Rascher Verlag 1951, pp. 273–274.
[51] Cirlot, Juan E.: *A Dictionary of Symbols.* Trans. Sage, Jack. London, Routledge and Kegan Paul 1962, pp. 275–276.

deified ancestors and the living, or become representatives of the ancestors themselves. The slithery, limbless form, so different from every other creature, the rich ornamental patterning of their skin, their undulating motion, the extraordinary length of their copulation, all these attributes are ideally suited for symbolic projection.

As Yoshino Hiroko argues in *Mountain Gods*[52] (*Yama no kami*) the snake was most probably also the oldest Japanese deity whose worship reached far back into the Jômon period. The name of the harmless water or grass snake, *yamakagashi*, that plays such an important role in this story may be related to the ancient spelling of *kagachi* that appears in the *Kojiki,* but also in place names where it may indicate a snake-shaped mountain range. Some local *matsuri* have preserved symbolic representations of the snake as the central mountain deity and there are several shrines where snake worship has survived to this day, most notably at Mt. Miwa (literally 'Three Coils') where the whole mountain is perceived as a large, coiled serpent. The Japanese reader, quite understandably, feels reluctant to spell out this underlying meaning, or the mythic and religious motifs under the finely crafted visual and tactile texture of Ibuse's 'verbal surface' and experience them more than subliminally. Yet the Western critic, whose perception of all the linguistic nuances is necessarily limited, should, I think, make an effort to become aware of them.

As always, a good deal of the story's tactile appeal will remain locked in the original text; what Ibuse had

[52] Yoshino, Hiroko: *Yama no kami*. Tokyo, Jinbun shoin 1989, pp. 19–31.

learned in the earlier works – portrayal by stylized dialect and personalized speech patterns – comes into full play once again here. Perhaps the stylization is even more skillful, for the writer has a more objective distance from the Nagano – Yamanashi mountain dialect than from his own native Bingo speech. Like a patient guide through unfamiliar territory, the narrator translates some of the more cryptic local speech-patterns; his bracketed explanations add objective diversity to the dialogic voices. As in the earlier Kamo valley cycle of stories, the old man's speech is touched up with carefully selected representative bits of dialect, not a faithful simulation of it. Its tone is characterized mainly by the narrow *ê,* similar to the Tokyo downtown pronunciation. Thus *hae* (fly) becomes *hê, hairu* (enter) becomes *hêru* etc. The old man ends most of his sentences with a question: *"Mamushi ippiki, 650 en de ureru ja nê ka?"* ("Doesn't a viper sell for 650 Yen apiece?") Probably a common sentence-ending of older people in the area, in the context of standard Japanese it acquires a charmingly involving, even a slightly condescending quality, as if saying: "Don't you know that a viper sells for 650 Yen apiece?" This question-like ending of Hogoden's sentences goes well with his role of trickster-advisor, or of a somewhat comical incarnation of 'The Master of the Land'. Interestingly, while it is the polite and neutral-sounding standard Japanese of the author's connecting description that looks like the proper and correct language at the outset of the story, towards its end it is the colourful, droll mutilation of the standard language in the old man's mouth that sounds far more appealing and natural.

Here is Bakhtin's 'double-voicedness' in action: while in "White Hair" it was the neutral, cold Tokyo speech that invaded the narrator's native valley and froze its genuine 'voice', in this story it's the warmth and the strength of the local *patois* that looms large over the standard speech. Ironically, the narrow *ê* of Edo's vulgar pronunciation, that had once offended Ibuse's southern ear, is the outstanding characteristic of this mountain dialect.

When the fisherman-narrator of "The Hearth Flower" comes back to Tokyo, he opens his encyclopedia and looks for the *kotatsu* and *oden* flowers he saw in the mountains. But all he can find are several pink family (*nadeshikoka*) plants that only resemble the real thing. In our world, not only are thousands of living species dying out, we are also losing their poetic names, our language grows poorer, people's minds approach the digital uniformity of computers. A world without a *kotatsubana,* we realize, is a poorer world. The clues to their original humanity which all men share cannot be found back in Tokyo in the generalities of an encyclopedia and its limited verbal potential. One must look for it somewhere higher upstream, closer to the springs of a nation's unique imagination and language. The higher we go, the more the languages may differ, but we might be getting closer to an essential human experience that can be shared. After all, genuine communication can only take place between genuine identities. The man who knows and can name *kotatsu* and *oden* flowers has more identity than the one who knows only that there is something like a pink family.

Having crystallized and put into perspective in his own mind the vital issues of identity and survival, Ibuse and his craft were finally ready for the great trial by fire: a major novel about the atomic bombing of Hiroshima.

*"And if thou wilt, shalt thou arouse the blasts, And watch them take their vengeance, wild and shrill… Thou shalt change Black Rain to drought, at seasons good for men…"*

Fragments of Empedocles

In taking up the crushing theme of *Black Rain* – the atomic ordeal of Hiroshima – Ibuse undoubtedly accepted the greatest challenge of his writing career. He needed all twelve volumes of his complete works to prepare for this masterpiece, and a great amount of documentary research. In an interview with Kawamori Yoshizô[1] he talks about the overwhelming volume of documentary material he had to go through on Hiroshima. The tenor 'voice' of the novel, Shigematsu, is said to have taken on a double, or even a triple liability in Yasuko. In his own way, Ibuse has taken on an even heavier burden.

Why did he subject his style and his whole artistic past to such a hazardous trial by fire? Certainly not just because "the bomb was there." Critics have suggested that with *Black Rain*, Ibuse paid off an outstanding debt to the native Chûgoku he had left half a century earlier to take up a writing career in Tokyo. Although he

[1] Kawamori, Yoshizô: *IM zuimon.* Tokyo, Shinchôsha 1986, pp. 11–12.

was not born in the city of Hiroshima, but in a village nearby, this novel is a symbolic return to his birthplace in a wider sense of the word and to his most consistent theme: in an instant half a million people are reduced to castaways floating on an ocean of non-sense. The people of Hiroshima have lost their 'village' in a faster flash than the young boy in *Waves* or *John Manjirô: A Castaway's Chronicle*, for they live in a more advanced age. The task of rebuilding their village is far more formidable. They will have to reach for the oldest gestures of village mutuality, the bits and pieces of superstition and half-forgotten village remedies, the memories of life-celebrating *matsuri,* the branches and fruit from the old trees of their *furusato,* and significantly, a special kind of 'remembering' and organizing their experience: Shigematsu's chronicle, the village headman's way of putting things down for posterity.

In broader traditional terms one might call the novel a kind of *chinkon no uta.*[2] It is not only the bomb as such that has wounded Ibuse the village boy's vulnerable sensibilities, but the attitudes both of his fellow Japanese and of the flag-waving delegations of foreign mourners of the dead. No amount of "their damned anti-bomb rallies"[3] can soothe the "voice of those hundreds of thousands of souls – seemingly welling up from beneath the earth." (12) What must have made Ibuse particularly sick about the whole thing is that all the political prancing and shouting about the bomb

[2] Requiem mass of Shinto.

[3] IM: *Black Rain*. Trans. Bester, John. Tokyo, New York and San Francisco, Kôdansha International 1969, p. 30. Hereafter, bracketed numbers after quotes refer to the page numbers of this edition.

and its victims makes so little sense in Japanese terms. Everybody seems to have forgotten the real thing. People unthinkingly flock to the rallies either because 'everybody does', or because they seek a tangible affirmation that they are gloriously alive and the 'precious victims' safely under the ground. But in either case, it means a frightful numbing of the traditional sense of life-continuity. For the age-old Japanese attitude toward the souls of the dead never stresses merciful forgetfulness, but on the contrary, clear remembrance. The memory must be carried on, be it ever so painful for the survivors. Through the act of direct, personal identification with the dead, the living carry on the spark of their lives in memory. One does not have to be an occultist to perceive the psychic reality of that ancient form of *chinkon* ritual called *tamafuri*[4] or "binding to our own being the souls coming from outside (*gairaikon*)." Through a close link with a living being, the 'outside souls' were believed to beget vital energy. Interestingly enough, this vital energy itself was called *musubi* (link or connection, in modern Japanese).

In a typical Japanese fusion of subject and object, self and other, the ritual reinforces *belief* in life; for if a dead person's spirit can be roused with painful clarity in one's mind, it is not dead. It remains a meaningful

[4] I am using Jean Herbert's interpretation of these terms in his *Shinto: At the Fountain-Head of Japan*. London, Allen and Unwin 1967, pp. 88–89: "*Tama-furi*, as practiced in the Iso-no-kami-jingu, aims at binding to our own being a great soul from a higher world (Takama-no-hara), a *gai-rai-kon*, which has strength and energy and can give them to us... When thus linking themselves closely with man, the *gai-rai-kon* (souls coming from outside) beget vital energy, i.e. *musubi*." A very useful discussion of *tamafuri* etc. can be found in Ebersole, Gary L.: *Ritual Poetry and the Politics of Death in Early Japan*. Princeton, Princeton University Press 1989, pp. 54–55 and 83–85.

part of the identity of the living, who hope for the same share of life after death. But *tamafuri* may be taken even more literally: *tama o furu*, or 'to stir up souls'. It may be very painful and even personally insulting to the souls of the dead. But it is good and beneficial as long as it can jolt their souls back into some kind of shared life with the living.

Now if we put these images of a premodern personifying mentality into practical modern terms, we can talk about the intense awareness of reality, and the carrying on of vitally important memories, in a way that makes sense in the context of the culture. Waving paper doves and shedding crocodile tears over the fate of all our precious victims is neither too painful personally nor very meaningful culturally; one could even draw a frightening parallel between the impersonality of these massive rallies and the abstract mega-logic of the bomb itself.

This very mega-logic of the bomb has by now spread out into a world-wide obsession with 'numbers of people incinerated', 'numbers of acres razed to the ground', 'numbers of degrees in the epicenter' and so forth. It is this megalomanic obsession with meaningless numbers that Ibuse counters with a passionate emphasis on the personal, the individual. And he gently leads the 'writer' Shigematsu to realize this:

> Without exception, they talked of the bombing. Each told what he had seen or heard as an *individual*, without relation to the others, so that even synthesizing their stories it was *impossible to get an overall picture* of the disaster. Even so, I have set some of them down here *just as I remember them*. (116; italics mine)

To find a proper way to pass on important individual memories is what story-telling, and particularly this novel are all about. Ibuse's immense restraint and his carefully low-keyed presentation of documentary material may give us the impression of a realistic writer who says: Look, this is what *really* happened. True, Ibuse modelled his protagonist, Shizuma Shigematsu, on an existing personality: Mr. Shigematsu from the actual village of Kobatake. The only concession to fiction he made was to switch the order of family (Shigematsu in reality) and given names (Shizuma in reality). The real Mr. Shigematsu did keep a diary, recording his memories of the bombing. I have seen a part of it and was impressed by its lively, expressive style. In the novel, Shigematsu goes fishing with his friends, just as in reality Ibuse used to go fishing with Mr. Shigematsu. When they became good friends and Ibuse heard the sad story of Mr. Shigematsu's niece, he asked him if he could look at his diary. Mr. Shigematsu not only lent the writer his diary, he urged Ibuse to make the story of his niece into a novel. This was probably what originally inspired Ibuse to write the novel the way he did, as a montage of diaries. The documentary aspect of Ibuse's novel has become the focus of recent critics, some of whom claim that the borrowed parts outweigh the imaginative ones.[5] Comparing the Shigematsu diary in the novel with

---

[5] As Toyota Seishi does in *Kuroi ame to Shigematsu nikki*. Tokyo, Fûbaisha 1993. In a recent study (*IM ron, zenshûsei*. Tokyo, Chûsekisha 2004) Matsumoto Tsuruo sums up these arguments in a chapter called "Is *Black Rain* a Stolen Work?" making an obvious conclusion that even the work of most creative writers (e.g. Goethe) relies on plots, stories, motifs and images that were used by previous authors.

the actual diary of Mr. Shigematsu reveals a thorough imaginative and stylistic reworking of the original text. Besides the indomitable Dr. Iwatake, Ibuse introduced several characters who are real personalities and appear under their actual names, most notably the policeman Satô. Mr. Satô Susumu, a friend of Ibuse's, has spent his life in Hiroshima and served as a respected member of the prefectural parliament. Unquestionably then, the novel has a solid documentary groundwork, although many survivors have told me that the reality of the bombing and its aftermath were far more hellish than the 'facts' Ibuse presents. But it is crucial to realize that in fact the author is only saying: "Look, I am presenting to you a handful of *memories* of what really happened." And memories, as everybody will agree, are not objective, technical photographs of real events. Dealing with a memory, the mind always emphasizes some aspects of the event and forgets others. In fact, there is a mythmaker at work in each of us once we start recreating our memories. Memory is a form of personal myth, for it selects what is most *important* to one's identity and one's survival. It selects the most meaningful sources of one's personal history, not the most *real* in the objective sense. Communal or racial myths on the other hand are individual memories passed on, polished and enriched by numbers of people from generation to generation. Critical, objective history reflects what we think we know about ourselves; myths tell us directly what we are. And what we are is invariably more than what we know. As Shigematsu tells Shigeko:

'... I haven't got down on paper one-thousandth part of all the things I actually saw. It's no easy matter to put something down in writing.'

'I expect it's because when you write you're too eager to work in your own theories.'

'It's nothing to do with theories. From a literary point of view, the way I describe things is the crudest kind of realism...' (60)

The 'writer' within the narrative realizes that from that vast, horrendous holocaust he will have to filter out only the most important facts; he will pass them on as painful but often ennobling memories that cannot and must not be forgotten. If he calls his way of putting things down 'the crudest kind of realism', he is not talking the same language as critics. It is rather the condensed, existential crudeness of a folktale or myth that Ibuse suggests here, not the objective, photographic realism critics usually have in mind.

But the writer Ibuse, too, must be honest with his memory. He cannot be expected to forget his whole artistic past, or to violate his view of the world, which emerged as his 'poetic cosmology' from stories such as "The River", "Isle-on-the-Billows," or "The Hearth Flower." It is ultimately the question why Ibuse the storyteller had to take up all these memories, blend them with his own and weave them into a work of art that is most relevant. Could he possibly have picked this most difficult of themes out of the blue? The themes in a good writer's work always represent his basic preoccupations; they always show a certain continuity with the images and symbols, in short, the whole style that an author uses to tell his story. We have seen the theme of volcanic eruption in "Isle-on-the- Billows," and it can be found in several other stories by Ibuse. But how frequently do themes of cataclysmic change, of natural disasters and large-scale destruction appear in Japanese literature generally?

As a matter of fact, the strange absence of these very themes in Japanese writing is puzzling. The fires described in, say, the *Ten Foot Square Hut* (*Hôjôki*) or in *Essays in Idleness* (*Tsurezuregusa*) cannot be really included in the disaster theme as they represent an established Buddhist formula for the impermanence of the fleeting world. Of course, there are numerous *emakimono* with frightening pictures of fiery Hells, and several Noh plays, such as *Motomezuka* or *Utaura*, whose florid descriptions of blazing hell-fire might have indirectly influenced Ibuse's vocabulary when he dealt with the fire images in *Black Rain*. But again, these passages are really figurative expressions of a basic Buddhist message in the plays, and I would hesitate to consider them genuine disaster themes.

How is it possible then, that the perennial earthquakes, landslides, typhoons, floods and particularly volcanic eruptions which have plagued and frightened the Japanese race for thousands of years did not find their way into literature? One might accept the answer closest to hand: the Japanese literary tradition, both in poetry and prose, is predominantly lyrical and as such avoids gross and unpoetic themes. The Japanese sensibility, one might further argue, is always concerned with the minute details – falling cherry petals, fluttering butterflies; it selects the smiles and tears from nature's face, rarely the rages and tantrums. Still,

Japanese poets never felt that, as men, they lived in a world much different from wild nature.

It is precisely because Ibuse Masuji struggles to maintain his deep belief in the ultimate rightness of the natural course and man's belonging to it, that he tries to expand the narrowness of traditional poetic vision. The traditional Japanese lyrical picture of nature – both in poetry and prose – is too genteel, or sentimental if you wish, to accommodate images of cataclysmic change, not to mention brutal modern images of massive destruction. Ibuse's long process of ironic disenchantment with conventionally perceived nature found its first clear expression in "The River", led to the engagement of violent natural forces in the dramatic catharsis of "Isle-on-the-Billows," and finally to a sceptical, mature re-assertion of the 'natural identity' of a Japanese old man figure in "The Hearth Flower." Without it, the fine realistic balance of *Black Rain* could never have been achieved. Throughout Shigematsu's diary we see powerful images that suggest the emptiness of conventional poetic emotions and symbols in the face of the blast:

At one end of the bridge, a body lay face up with its arms stretched out wide. Its face was black and discolored, yet from time to time it seemed to puff its cheeks out and take a deep breath. Its eyelids seemed to be moving, too. I stared in disbelief... swarms of maggots [were] tumbling from the mouth and nose and crowding in the eye sockets; it was nothing but their wriggling, that first impression of life and movement. Suddenly, a phrase from a poem came back to me, a poem I had read in some magazine when I was a boy: 'Oh worm, friend worm!'

it began. There was more in the same vein: 'Rend the heavens, burn the earth, and let men die! A brave and moving sight!'

Fool! Did the poet fancy himself as an insect, with his prating of his 'friend' the worm? How idiotic can you get? He should have been here at 8:15 on August 6, when it had all come true: when the heavens had been rent asunder, the earth had burned, and men had died. (160–161)

What infuriating hypocrisy, thinks Shigematsu. How can a man who hasn't seen the voracious appetite of the 'jellyfish cloud' throw around flowery language like that? How could he possibly have the right to wallow in such sentimental rhetoric when he wasn't there? And maybe the author recalls his own past imaginative flights, the smooth ease with which he had blended human death into the greater order of nature in stories like "The River", and says it's not easy to accept the wriggling maggots as life and movement here; it's awfully hard to sympathize with nature's healthy appetite at close sight.

As Shigematsu wanders through scenes of cruel desolation with Yasuko and Shigeko, they come to a place where an imposing mansion with a beautiful traditional garden used to stand. Nothing remains now but the blackened skeletons of three large pine trees, a scorched granite rock and a tall pillar of stone:

Why it alone should have remained standing was a mystery.... It was somewhat over ten feet tall, and instead of the usual long inscription it had the single character "Dream" carved on it, about two and a half feet from the top. Some high-ranking priest was said to have written the original, and the effect was doubtless considered stylish and rather sophisticated in its day, but at present, style and sophistication alike failed utterly. (103)

Anything tender and fragile like the pine trees or reaching up in symbolic gestures of style and refinement, was razed to the ground. Only the most basic things – the muddy earth and the rocks – remain. And the scorched rock seems to announce that it was all a "Dream."

And yet, though the bomb may have shocked Shigematsu nearly out of his mind, it did not kill all his tender feeling for nature. Or should I say the genius of his language does not let him forget it? Let us compare the English translation, "Rock though it was, a thin layer had been burned away all over it" (103), with the original: *"Ishi wa ishi da ga, yaketadarete hitokawa mekurete iru"*[6] – "Rock though it was, it was burnt (hurt) and one layer of its skin peeled off!"

So a little bit more than the scorched rock survived. A fraction of Ibuse's characteristic sympathy with *all forms* of existence withstood the blast and lit up in Shigematsu's eye as soon as it met with the rock. But it is terribly difficult to see life and affection in the death-dominated inferno around. When Shigematsu passes a badly burnt horse, standing by a corpse in gold-spurred boots, he tells himself:

The horse must have been a favorite of the soldier's. Though it was on the verge of collapse, it still seemed – *or was it my imagination?* – to be yearning for some sign from the man in the spurred boots. How immeasurable the

[6] IM: *Kuroi ame*. Tokyo, Shinchôsha 1966, p. 109. IM: *Kuroi ame*. Tokyo, Shinchôsha 1966, p. 109.

pain it must have felt, with the west-dipping sun beating down unmercifully on its burned flesh; how immeasurable its love for the man in the boots! But pity eluded me: I felt only a shudder of horror. (109; italics mine)

Significantly, the original has 'just a shudder', *mi-burui bakari,* not 'a shudder of horror'. A shudder of horror is a well-defined feeling, while Shigematsu's 'shudder' is one of *utter bewilderment,* utter confusion. He cannot begin to make any sense of the horrible scene that is presented to his confused sensibility. He even questions the existence of the affection his eye seems to perceive. It must have hurt Ibuse to put down these lines, but he simply does not have any answers at the moment. The reader, too, is left on his own at this point – is there some old-fashioned affection around, or is everything cold efficient brutality? Will the horse become just so much rotting organic garbage, or does its mute suffering suggest far more eloquently than any human pain that a precious form of communication has been irrevocably lost? Here is a life so different from ours, Ibuse seems to say, yet it has given us everything it had and we have left it terribly alone. Who will remember its love, who will carry on its memory? Is the horse *lost* in the most essential sense of the word? This age-old poetic image of the warrior and his horse seems to be contrasted with the crazy age of the bomb, where emotions are stunned by ugliness too great to be beautified by the wildest stretch of one's imagination.

Might the fragile and sensitive center of the traditional imagination itself have been stunned by the blast? There is a suggestion of this in a passage that precedes the scene with the seared horse. Shigematsu remembers how he had caught fish as a child in the country by hitting rocks in the stream with a sledge-hammer:

> There would be a great clang of metal on stone, and a gunpowdery smell, and at the same instant the fish would emerge from under the rock and stop quite still, stupe-fied, in the water... their nerves had stopped functioning for the time being, paralyzed by the shock.
>
> I, though... had registered nothing with my senses apart from the ball of light and the blast. That fish should die, great granite posts be blown down, and walls be broken through, yet human beings on the ground come through almost unscathed, was beyond my understand-ing. (87)

Ibuse's favourite fish image is used most effectively here. But unlike the paralysed fish, Shigematsu keeps moving. He drags his feet through the ashes, trying to get Yasuko, Shigeko and himself to safety. Yet his feeling that human beings came through almost unscathed must be a kind of delusion at this point. Although he felt nothing apart from the light and the blast, some vital centers of his being must still be in shock. Just as he is unaware of the lethal radiation at this moment, he is also not aware of the extent to which the blast impaired his imaginative power to relate to the hellish mess around him and make sense of it.

As usual, Ibuse has placed this crucial image of the stunned fish very casually. But it contains a wealth of further suggestion: that there can be no substantial break between the past and the present; that one's own little history cannot be separated from the greater historical event. No matter how pretty they look in the veils of memory, that distant tiny spark and the bang of the hammer against the rock have a power over the life of fish similar to what the bomb has over ours.

Whether that small explosion could someday grow into a gigantic blast, did not depend on the whim of some supernatural or inhuman deity; it depended entirely on the whims of nature in Shigematsu's heart. In his social encounters, Shigematsu may use words like "unimaginably beastly" or "act of a vicious bully" about the bomb, but never does he refer to it as inhuman or unnatural.

These words have no place in Shigematsu's vocabulary. Not that Ibuse would be unfamiliar with them. We saw that he did use similar words for satirical purposes in his early stories, and we know he realizes how large they loom in the vocabulary of postwar, Western-inspired 'humanists' in his country. But with his characteristic honesty, Ibuse refuses to step inside that neat magic circle of purity that the modern humanist has drawn around himself: everything that is inside the circle (with him) is human and therefore natural; what is outside is inhuman, unnatural and has nothing to do with the real him.

As could be expected, the August 6 entry in Shigematsu's diary not only takes up almost half of the novel, but makes up its core. It can hardly be a coincidence that all the passages where Shigematsu's emotional and imaginative reactions are most bewildered fall into this part of the diary. As the dazzling flash of white light recedes into the depths of memory and time, very slowly, almost invisibly the stunned imagination starts coming to:

In the playground of the First Prefectural Middle School in the city – one of them said – there was a reservoir of water for fire-fighting purposes. Around it, hundreds of middle school students and voluntary war workers lay dead. They were piled up at the edge of the reservoir, half-naked since their shirts had been burned away. Seen from a distance, they looked like beds of tulips planted round the water. Seen closer, they were more like the layers of petals on a chrysanthemum. (154)

Although Ibuse prudently describes this scene through the mouth of a woman in the crowd, we cannot miss his unmistakable touch: his eye refuses to see ugly corpses and still holds on to the living beauty of the children. It is most fascinating to watch the fine tremors of the awakening imagination of Shigematsu and the other survivors at this point; by the time he copies his diary he is already safely out of the inferno, dosing himself with tolerable amounts of the experience and thus disarming it.

And this is the main source of the stoic beauty in Ibuse's novel: like the slow, almost invisible motion of the Noh actor's feet gliding over the stage, his imaginative gesture starts out carefully restrained. It is a groping in the dark. The blazing light of the bomb has destroyed that cherished poetic twilight where dimly lit objects of everday life lose their sharp edges and change shapes freely. It has mercilessly ripped apart the curtain of shadows that alloved phantasy to roam freely. That blinding light that outshone the sun must be followed by a deeper darkness.

Shigematsu's hardy persistence in fighting radiation sickness, and his later concern with various life projects such as raising carp, are moving and admirable and have not been missed by critics. But what excites me most about him has not been stressed at all: his remarkable reluctance, almost inability, to recognize death even when surrounded by its overpowering presence. Let me quote just a few examples:

> Other bodies came floating in steady succession along the river. Every so often, one of them would catch on the roots of a riverside willow, swing round with the current, and suddenly rear its face out of the water.... Or another would swing round beneath a willow tree and raise its arms as though to grasp at a branch, so that it almost seemed, for a moment, to be alive. (107)

> And occasionally the shock of hitting the ground would do something to the joints of a corpse, so that it reminded me of Pinocchio, in the children's tale, with all the pins removed from his wooden limbs. If even Pinocchio, poor plaything of wood and metal pins, was supposed to have felt pain in his own wooden way when he barked his shin against something, what of these the dead, who had once been human beings? (162)

It is this dimension of Ibuse's vision that for some strange reason puzzles many Japanese critics. To quote just a few lines from one of the novel's critiques: "So one might say that the real hidden motive of this novel is to depict the overwhelming number of 'corpses' rather than the countless 'deads'."[7]

This is very misleading. The real motive of the novel is most certainly not to depict 'deads' and much less 'corpses', but rather to give us a wonderfully direct insight into the nature of staying alive! And for Shi-

[7] Takada, Kinichi: "Ibuse Masuji ron." *Mita bungaku* 60, August 1973, p. 82.

gematsu to be fully alive, to be fully himself, he must carry on living memories that are vitally important to his survival and his identity – just like carrying on the living memory of the dead in the *tamafuri* ritual – whether society likes the twist of these memories or not. And these memories are just as important to those whom they concern as to the one who carries them on. Sometime, someone will come and listen, just as the writer Ibuse came and listened carefully to what the actual Shigematsu or the real Dr. Iwatake had remembered.

Even when Shigematsu can do nothing to help, at least he does not offend by useless charity; he can detect a spark of life in the most despairing situations and respect it. As he and his family trudge through the ruins, they see a little girl playing with her dead mother's breasts. At first, they feel an irresistible urge to pick up the child, take it away from the corpse and help it somehow. But Shigematsu wisely resists this urge. Maybe he realizes that to the child, the mother is not a corpse, but still her mother. It would be infinitely more cruel to drag the girl away at *this particular moment,* because she would not understand why. Left alone, the child will cling to its mother's breast and probably get one more peaceful sleep in her arms.

It has been suggested that the minor key in Japanese music usually carries death themes, while life themes are invariably expressed in the major key. One might say that these two 'keys' dominate any symbolic expression of the culture; Lady Murasaki and Kawabata obviously write in the more sophisticated minor key, Lady Shônagon and Ibuse in the robust major. One might argue that in the best works, these two keys blend and complement each other. I often have the feeling, however, that two totally different attitudes co-exist side by side here: one flirts with death, trying to probe imaginatively behind its face; the other recoils from it, or simply refuses to understand it.

It might be too neat a solution to subsume all the morbid and macabre leanings of the Japanese mind under Buddhist influences and all the positive, life-affirming qualities under the more basic layer of Shinto attitudes (although Buddhism does take care of all the death rites, while Shinto performs all the life rites). Let us just say that the Japanese, like other peoples, have their own colourful collection of unique memories (or archetypes) that sustain life or attempt to make sense of both life and death. It may appear that an individual artist selects from the collection whatever suits his taste, but it is rather his basic nature that makes him choose the dominant key of his work.

Ibuse Masuji impresses me as being in touch with some very ancient bedrock of feeling about death. The way Shigematsu's mind recoils from any abstract awareness of 'Death' reminds me of that primeval level of the Japanese mentality and language which did not know the words 'die' or 'death'. Before these concepts were imported from China, words like 'to withdraw' (*mi-makaru*), 'to rise up' (*kamu agaru*) or 'to hide' (*kakureru*) were used. The nether world itself was often identified as existing in remote countries 'over the ocean' and was called the world of hiding (*toko-yo, kakuri-yo*) or country of the roots (*ne no kuni*). But sinister and horrible though the place may have been, the Japanese imagination could never conceive of a dead world where life force could be totally annihilated. True, some of the *Kojiki* myths will refer to *yomi no kuni* as a horrible place of disintegration. Yet in some passages, for example, when Susanoo meets his son Kuninushi, the Master of the Land, there are not only wasps, centipedes and serpents, but also helpful mice, a vigorous ruler and a beautiful maiden full of energy. When Izanagi lets his comb fall to the ground, it sprouts into young bamboo shoots. Even in Hades life triumphs over death.[8]

The lethal blackness of rain may have frightened Ibuse as an ugly break in the natural cycle: how can something as right, as life-giving, as rain return to earth bringing black death? Interestingly enough, Robert Lifton stresses the scientific inaccuracy of this and other motifs in the novel; the 'black rain' really contains less harmful beta-radiation and could not effect Yasuko as it does here. But there may be deeper symbolic or cultural connections which Lifton does not realize; perhaps it is just an interesting coincidence, but old texts did call death 'black pollution' or black *kegare*. The word *kegare*, nowadays translated as pollution, contamination or ritual impurity, probably comes from the stem *ki* (life force, *élan vital*) and *kare* (withering, wilting). The way Shigematsu sees people's life force fading away confirms this view: "Those who forced themselves to work gradually wilted, like a pine tree transplanted by a bungling gardener, until finally they expired." (14) It is the withering of the life force

---

[8] Throughout the passage on *Yominokuni,* I am using Donald Philippi's translation of *Kojiki*. Tokyo, University of Tokyo Press 1968, pp. 65–86.

that is to be avoided while we are alive, not physical, moral or aesthetic impurity. And this is exactly how Shigematsu strikes me: he is searching neither for truth, nor for refined beauty. He cannot afford to be a perfectionist or a purist during his trial, for purism of any kind always ends up punishing life; he can only make use of what is real and practical, or in short, life-sustaining. If some of the cultural symbols, myths or superstitions can help him to make sense of the given situation, Shigematsu will hold on to them:

> Concluding that my eyes hurt because I had too much blood in the head, I had Yasuko give me the treatment they used to give children who had a nosebleed. It consisted of no more than pulling out three hairs from the back of the head, but it helped the pain a little. (104)

Shigematsu is so often at his wits' end that he cannot afford the luxury of questioning the rationality of these superstitions. And again, maybe they contain a memory of something very real and useful:

> I don't think anybody actually taught me to do so, but when I was a child I always made sure to gargle three times before drinking from a well or spring on unfamiliar territory. The other boys said *they* always gargled three times first. Besides preventing upset stomachs caused by drinking strange water, it was supposed to be a mark of respect for the water god who dwelt in the well or the spring. (48)

But these beliefs, too, have a situational validity. Some of these 'memories' do not make it through the fire-trial; yet it is dangerous to forget them:

> I leaned over the bucket... and, thrusting my face in as a dog does, drank ecstatically till I had had my fill. By

now I had forgotten that one should take three separate mouthfuls first: I *just drank*. It was very good... Quite suddenly, though, *all the strength drained* out of my body... (77–78; italics mine)

I am often told by Western readers: "This Shigematsu sure doesn't waste helpful gestures on the critical day of August 6!" But can he really afford to become emotionally involved with, say, the helpless little boy who walks with them for awhile? What else can he do for the boy other than let him share their silence? He is honest about his own survival – *all* the energy he can summon is needed to get himself and his immediate family out of the fireflood. But just a day later, as soon as they reach Furuichi, Shigematsu is ready to do what he can: he forgets the crushing fatigue and his own burns, learns Buddhist sermons and performs funeral rites for the dead. He shows an almost obsessive interest in the available details of each dead person's background, no matter how trivial these details may seem:

*Possessions Found on Deceased by Person who Tended Her* A large leather purse containing nine ¥10 notes, twelve ¥5 notes, twenty-two ¥1 notes, and ¥3.49 in coins. One old cotton towel and an imitation leather commuter's pass holder containing photographs of her husband in army sergeant's uniform and her son in a short-sleeved shirt. (141)

The reason Shigematsu gives for his concern with these details looks practical enough: the woman's name, address, status, and the names of any relatives must be recorded, so as to prevent complications later. Yet the very laconic listing of the dead woman's worldly possessions – some precious, some trivial – provides the painfully touching personal 'memory' which Shigematsu must be in touch with if he is to perform the rite well. Again, his serious involvement in the service for the dead reminds me, above all, of the ancient *chinkon* ritual. This rite performed for humans, also echoes another rite – the Mass for Dead Insects – earlier in the novel when Shigematsu and his neighbours make rice dumplings as an offering to the souls of the deceased insects they had inadvertently trodden on as they worked in the fields. The image of an enormous force haphazardly killing insects reflects what the bomb did to the unsuspecting population of Hiroshima. And indeed, several times the refugees have been likened to insects:

> Along the railroad tracks there stretched a long train of refugees like a trail of ants... in the distance, the hill in the park was like nothing so much as a great pale bun with ants swarming all over it. (47)
>
> The refugees... were going up the hill... in a long procession as though being steadily sucked up toward the higher parts. In two or three places higher up the hillside, forest fires were visible... To walk in droves in the direction of a hill fire reminded me terribly of moths dashing themselves against a lamp at night. (56–57)

These refugees have become insects in the full sense of the metaphor: they are running toward the hills from the alluvial plain of the frequently flooding river where the city was built, away from the 'disaster' that ages of experience have taught them to associate with flood. Their instinct itself is stunned and they do not realize that they are rushing from one firestorm into another.

Although I doubt Ibuse sees these human refugees as 'reduced' to insects – for every form of life is precious to him – he may be suggesting they deserve to be especially remembered, not because they are human and therefore more important, but because the blast robbed them of the precious gift that *most insects* have, the infallible survival instinct itself.

Shigematsu recites Buddhist sermons during the funeral rites because they are the handiest and most obvious thing to use in the given situation and because some sound nice, being written in a beautiful and homely Japanese. But he could not care less about doctrinaire Buddhism. This is only what the situation demands from him, and he, the situational man *par excellence*, delivers. And just because he is a *protean* man, he is also a pure man. There is all the difference in the world between the purist and the pure man: Shigematsu is pure because he remains in touch with his shattered body and mind and with the precious signs of life in his ravaged environment. His self is 'spread out' and immersed in his environment, though little remains of it. Less profound and maybe less exciting than Ivan Karamazov, Captain Ahab or Kawabata's Shûichi, he is a more broadminded and less dangerously human man. He is not consumed by the blazing inner flame of all these profound seekers, who are so narrowly self-absorbed, so busy exorcizing their personal demons that they have no time to look around. Compared to Shigematsu who seldom indulges any personal quirks and is only mildly interested in any deep problems he may have, these modern heroes strike one as dangerous monomaniacs. The trouble with the flame that rages inside their souls is that it can so easily spread out into a much bigger conflagration. One might even say that a literary figure like Captain Ahab owes his existence to the same metaphysical stretch of imagination that searches for the mystery of matter, to try and solve it or defeat it. The bomb is so typically human because it personifies one important route of this metaphysical quest – and its dead end, too. The most powerful shift in the natural flow of matter ever made, this greatest victory of the human spirit over matter, is ironically one of its last. To compound ironies, one of the least Promethean of peoples, the Japanese, had to pay the fire-thief's toll – be struck by the mighty firestorm. Doomsday images of Armageddon proportions, or simply future-oriented millennial moods, play an important role in the Christian imagination; the Japanese mythical script on the other hand insists on the validity, even the sacredness of everyday existence. If Shigematsu looks for salvation, he does so through the detail and the chore of everyday life. What we witness here then, is not only a confrontation of the Bomb and the Japanese *shomin's* vitality, but by extension a clash of the two mythical scripts.

Ibuse realizes the futility of isolating the lone Hero under harsh spotlights, and he does not try to delve deeper and deeper into the psyche of his people for the 'truth' of their being. Like in many of his previous portrayals of common men of the crowd, the reality of Shigematsu's being in the world is there to be seen by everybody: it can be found in his actions, in the way he relates to people and things, which in turn reflect and 'make' him. He is pure because his inner feeling is in harmony with his outer actions. Being capable of throwing himself, body and soul, into a situation, he can perceive its whole context correctly and choose instinctively the right course of action. But he is no fanatic of blind action at any cost like some of Mishima's favourite heroes. Like a homing bird, or a running fish, he seems to be directed by a quiet, natural sense of orientation. One has a feeling that his whole being is always there, in touch, doing the right thing at the right moment. He might occasionally do the wrong thing – for example, dragging Yasuko through the radioactive ruins – yet he does not torture himself over things that cannot be undone. He did what he thought best at the moment and leaves the rest to take care of itself. If Shigematsu has any morality, it is the morality of present action. His past memories and experiences and his relationships all gravitate to one center, the present.

It seems to me that somewhere beneath the Japanese mind's obsession with images of purity there must lie a similar source: 'purity' must have originally meant being in touch with living, present reality, being tuned in to life through the senses and thus being intuitively capable of immediate, decisive action. All the modern interpretations of purity do not make sense to anybody who has lived in Japan for a while: ethical standards there are flexible to the utmost, attitudes to cleanliness schizoid to say the least, and aesthetic purism ultimately suffocating. There must be something more vital hidden in this obsessive image of purity, something more life-sustaining in the long run. It is a mistake to underestimate the imaginative power of the premodern mind, because it often makes much bolder unconscious connections than we do. Could not ancient expressions of purity such as *jôsui* (clean water) and *jôka* (clean fire) symbolically embody this dynamic concept of action? It could very well be that they express the absence of a split between inner motivation and outside behaviour. We are only too ready to brush off these symbols as obsession with ritual impurity, but what do they really mean? It might be a total misinterpretation of the original unconscious intuition of pure *life-sustaining action* to associate the white garments of Shinto priests, or the ancients' worship of white wood, white flowers, white chrysanthemums (*shiraki, shirabana* or *shiragiku*) with moral or aesthetic purism, or worse, with hygienic cleanliness in the modern sense.

As I pointed out before, one of the main reasons why Shigematsu's sense of being in the world is not destroyed, or even tainted by his immersion in death, is his remarkable inability to recognize death. But he has another, equally important stronghold that helps him survive – a healthy, almost primitive trust in the ultimate rightness of his physical reactions. After all, it is the basic response of his body that assures him he is alive, rather than any complex imaginative response of his mind:

> I slept a while, and awoke with the cry of an owl ringing in my ears... To imagine owls crying was nonsense. In fact, I found, I had woken because my feet were cold. (153)

He accepts even the ugly burn on his cheek as something belonging to his body and almost caresses the pain that reassures him of his identity:

Taking one end of a curled-up piece of skin between my nails, I gave it a gentle tug. It hurt a little, which at least assured me that this was my own face... The action gave me a strange kind of pleasure, like the way one joggles a loose tooth that wants to come out, both hating and enjoying the pain at the same time. (143)

What Ibuse had learned from the careful stylistic exploration in his first survival story, *John Manjirô: A Castaway's Chronicle*, comes in very handy here. The earlier experiment in laconic storytelling not only taught him how vital physical reactions become in an extreme survival situation, but how much their skillful description can embody metaphorically. There is hardly any split between Shigematsu's mental and physical reactions. He always thinks very viscerally; just as one's stomach expels an offending substance it does not like, when he says: "How I hate the war", one has the feeling that his mind has instinctively thrown up something that disgusted it.

But is this uncomplicated, modest and unobtrusive old man by the name of Shizuma Shigematsu a contemporary Japanese everyman or Mr. Average as Arthur Kimball suggests in his article on *Black Rain*?[9] I believe Shigematsu is too positive, too essential to be a realistic portrait of Mr. Average. It is Ibuse's skillful handling of his character Shigematsu's matter-of-factness, his lack of eye-catching individualistic quirks that makes us accept him as Mr. Average. But in reality, I do not think too many Shigematsus walk the streets of contemporary Japan.

[9] Kimball, Arthur: "After the Bomb." In: *Crisis in Identity and Contemporary Japanese Novels*. Vermont and Tokyo, Charles E. Tuttle 1973, p. 56.

Shigematsu shares all the qualities that his name suggests: sturdy as a pine, his roots firmly planted in the ground, he bends to the winds of change with the same pliant strength and patient resilience. In fact, his lack of colourful personal phobias and idiosyncrasies, in short his very 'everyman' likeness, enables us to accept his wisdom and strength without falling for him as a Hero. This simple-looking old man is not only intelligent, but also *remarkably wise;* we should not miss his occasional nonchalant remarks, which usually begin: "In olden times people used to say..." Ibuse does not let Shigematsu put on this mask of classical poise too often, but when he does, then the voice behind it really rumbles from the bottom of the earth:

> Some of the skulls gazed fixedly at the sky with empty eye-sockets, others clenched their teeth in angry resentment. *In olden times,* I suddenly recalled, they used to refer to skulls as 'the unsheltered ones.' (138; italics mine)
>
> *In olden times, people used to say* that in an area badly ravaged by war it took a century to repair the moral damage done to the inhabitants... (149; italics mine)

I do not hear the voice of a contemporary Mr. Average in these lines. Rather, Shigematsu is the living memory of his race at these moments, voicing its deep wisdom and its conscience. I think this is what the author really wants to get across through Shigematsu's modest portrait: here is a precious memory of our people's essential strength and vitality which we have already started to forget. The baffled response of many younger Japanese critics to his wise old man proves only too clearly how right he may be. Quite a few Japanese visitors to the West have told me that they really discovered Ibuse far away from Japan. Summed up, their comment would be: "Somehow, he makes us feel good about being Japanese."

I believe such visitors needed distance to select a lasting, real memory of their Japanese identity, as opposed to the obvious reality of being Japanese that they are confronted with day after day. Maybe at a distance they realized that Ibuse's characters embody this important, lasting memory of the essential life force that has made and sustained them through the ages. The memory may be carried by a less thrilling figure than Kawabata's Shingo, Shiga's Kensaku or Tanizaki's mad old man whose exciting personal demons and obsessions provide the material from which psychic drama is made, but what if the going really gets rough? What if the race loses its vitality and only one mythical memory of its strength should remain? The subtleties of the psychic drama might then provide an elegant epitaph; the living memory of the Japanese *shomin's* basic strength would have to be shouldered by a more robust carrier, someone like Shizuma Shigematsu.

It is hardly suprising that a down-to-earth man like Shigematsu does not go in for easy poetic metamorphoses, or wild flights of fantasy. With one definite exception, of course: he cannot forget the lingering glow of the dazzling flash and the imprint of its looming mushroom-cloud in his mind. When Yasuko first tells him about her symptoms of radiation sickness, he 'sees' the cloud right there in his living-room:

> When she first told me about it... there was a moment when the living-room vanished and I saw a great, mush-

room-shaped cloud rising into a blue sky. I saw it quite distinctly. (219)

This is no time to bother suffering people with idle literary fancies, Ibuse seems to suggest; the only thing one has a right to imagine at a moment like this is the blast and nothing but the blast. Its dazzling light is perhaps also reflected in the white rainbow that Shigematsu glimpses on the eve of the Emperor's surrender broadcast:

> Glancing back for no particular reason, I suddenly saw a white rainbow, stretching across the morning sun that gleamed dully in the thinly clouded sky. A rarity of rarities. (288)

Yet strangely enough, his factory manager has seen one too, when he was in Tokyo, on the day before the February 26 Incident. His rainbow, like Shigematsu's, had crossed the sun horizontally. The manager, a practical down-to-earth businessman, is convinced that a white rainbow in the sky cutting across the middle of the sun is an omen of something very unpleasant. The link between the February 26 Incident, the bomb and the Emperor's broadcast is a simple and realistic one. But the link between the dazzling white light of the bomb which seems to reflect onto both the white rainbow that precedes it and the one that follows it, transcends 'realism' in the drab sense of the critical label. Ibuse couches the image in an aura of antiquity by having someone say that "a white rainbow that pierces the sun" was a sign from heaven. Apparently a quotation from the life of someone in the Chinese *Book of History*, it portends armed disturbance. Again, we have a skillfully placed strategic image: the gleam of the sword-rainbow that pierces the body of the sun is one with the dazzling flash of the bomb.

I have suggested that an author's style must have enormous power and broad poetic scope to match a theme of the bomb's caliber. Ibuse had experimented with disaster themes such as storms, earthquakes and volcanic eruptions in previous stories (*John Manjirô: A Castaway's Chronicle*, "Isle-on-the-Billows" etc.), but here the connection between his earlier fire themes and the 'bluish white flash' image in *Black Rain* is of a direct, stylistic kind. It seems that Ibuse approached the fire theme in careful steps trying to feel it out from different angles. In 1941 he published a collection of essays and sketches, entitled *The Mountain Inn* (*Yama no yado*) which included a short, five-page sketch called "The Day of the Eruption at Miyake Island" (*Miyakejima funka no tôjitsu*). It is a fairly realistic collection of factual material about the eruption: newspaper reports, a letter from Ibuse's local friend, Mr. Asanuma, who collects the islanders' notes and observations about the eruption, and a few references to the local superstitions, mainly concerning Gojinka, the local God of Fire. There is even a little chart in the sketch, dated 1940, which shows the location of the 1940 eruption and of four previous craters.

In 1943 Ibuse published a longer story under this very title of "God of Fire" (*Gojinka*), which deals with the volcanic eruption at Miyake Island in a far more imaginative way than the original sketch. Comparing the two, we can see a remarkable poetic transformation. A similar imaginative expansion of the documentary material must have taken place with the original Shigematsu diary. The newspaper reports and Mr. Asanuma's letter to the writer are still here, inserted in the story without much visible change – one of Ibuse's characteristic touches that add authenticity to his story. But the God of Fire and all the superstitions surrounding him are made much more important here than in the original sketch. When I read some of the fire descriptions in "God of Fire," I could hardly believe my eyes. Could the remarkable similarity between these descriptions in a story published a full two years before the bomb and those of the bomb's flash be just accidental? The point I am going to make is important, so original quotations must be used. First, let us have a look at several descriptions of the bomb's flash in *Black Rain*:

> ...*sono toki kitsunebi no yô na aojiroi hikari ga hirameite, monosugoi bakuhatsuon ga todoroita...*[10]

...in that moment a bluish-white light flashed like lightning and an enormous explosion was heard...

> ...*sono toki kôgai de aojiroi hikari ga sugoku hirameita... Hiroshima shigai no hôgaku ni soratakaku kemuri ga tachinobotte ita... Kazan no fun'en no yô ni mie... tonikaku tada naranu kemuri de aru...*[11]

...then a bluish-white light flashed fiercely in the suburbs... In the direction of the city of Hiroshima smoke was rising as high as the sky... it looked like a volcanic eruption... in any case, it was not ordinary smoke...

> ...*tsugi no shunkan, inazuma no yô na shiroi hikari arui wa tairyô no magnesium o ichiji ni moyashita yô na senkô wo kanji... dôji ni, monosugoi jihibiki o kiita...*[12]

[10] *Kuroi ame*, p. 26.
[11] Ibid., p. 16.
[12] Ibid., p. 265.

...in the next moment we perceived a white flash like lightning or as if someone had ignited a great amount of magnesium in an instant and at the same time we heard a dreadful rumbling of the earth...

Now let us compare them with the description of the bluish flash that accompanies the volcanic eruption at Miyake Island, in "God of Fire" (*Gojinka*):

*Minna umi no hô wo mita. ...wannai ni, aomi wo obita honoo ga hira-meite ita. Inazuma to mo chigai, funka to mo chigau kaen no hirameki de, sono kaen kara kokuen ga tachinobotte ita.*[13]

All of us looked at the ocean. ...In the bay a blaze with a bluish tinge flashed. It was a flash of a flame different from lightning, and different from a volcanic eruption, with black smoke rising from it.

*...sorekara murajû ni, watto iu koe ga shita. Sorekara bakuhatsu no shunkan ni, pistoru o utsu yô na oto ga kikoeta desu nê.*[14]

...then shouts resounded throughout the village. And then in the moment of the explosion, we heard a noise as if someone had fired a pistol.

The fascinating thing here, besides the nearly identical lines about the "bluish (or bluish white) blaze (light) flashing," is that the flash in "God of Fire" does not come from the volcano, but occurs over the ocean! Note that the author perceives it as being 'different from lightning', as well as being 'different from a volcanic eruption', the very metaphors he will use years later to express the bomb's flash and smoke. Significantly enough, it is the commander of the Japanese fleet anchored nearby who tries to explain the strange light phenomenon away as electric discharge and the

[13] IM: "Gojinka." In: *IMZ III*, p. 150.
[14] Ibid., p. 151.

ear-splitting sound that follows it as "cracking concrete in the embankment." "But sir," suggests his second-in-command, "there is no metal on the surface of the sea, so how could there be electric discharge?"[15] Of course, the local people have their own way of 'knowing'. When toward the end of the story, more rumbling is heard, a rustic charcoal burner (*sumiyaki*) asks: "Master, couldn't the bottom of the earth forgive us? It should be through with its thing by now..."[16]

And the story ends with this line:

> And if someone had given an order to this *sumiyaki* – go ahead and pray – he would have probably fallen to his knees then and there and begged the God of Fire for mercy...[17]

Now I am not saying that Ibuse identifies with the islanders' way of knowing reality or that he is trembling with fear as the God of Fire shakes the bottom of the island. But he respects their way of knowing as much as, if not more than, the superficial, rationalistic explanations of the fleet commander.

What a startling transposition of images! An unknown phenomenon of some strange, perhaps technological, nature flashes into the author's imagination at a time when his mind can only vaguely grope for such a cataclysmic event through the mythical image (maybe as a gesture of the raging God of Fire), but not express it verbally through the available natural metaphor—'not lightning', 'not an eruption'. Then this strange imagined light, unexplained and mysterious

[15] Ibid., p. 150.
[16] Ibid., p. 165, translation mine.
[17] Ibid.

(*fushigi na hikari*) becomes an apocalyptic reality, only to return to the mind and be absorbed by it through the very familiar, archetypal kind of metaphor: "... a flash, bluish-white like a will-o'-the wisp..." (31), "Black smoke rose up over the city of Hiroshima *like a volcanic eruption*" (17) "... there was a white flash like *lightning...*" (242; italics mine).

So there is more to this than an interesting transposition of imagery. If only the lines about the bluish white flash were identical, I would be satisfied with the explanation that the author has a certain limited vocabulary at his command and certain stylistic preferences which make him express a similar experience in a similar way. But the emphasis on the difference of this strange event in "God of Fire" from currently known natural phenomena, and the fact that it is always called "mysterious light," convinces me that we have to do here with a genuine mythical insight of an amazing intensity.

Just like the reflection of the white flash on the rainbows, the mythical insight works both ways, linking past and future to the present. But even if we say that true mythical insight is timeless, our rational minds tend to ask: is this uncanny insight, which is not only poetic but *real*, a 'memory' or a foresight of the bomb?

Is it useful at all to talk about linear divisions into past and future when dealing with the deeper workings of a mind like Ibuse's? His imagination works through space rather than through time; there are strange time lapses and tense shifts in a number of his earlier stories. Even in *Black Rain*, where the various diaries seem to be so well ordered chronologically, it is rather subjective time, the *temps durée* that really matters. Time is often condensed or expanded:

> Still Shigematsu continued the transcription of his "Journal of the Bombing." This month, he reflected, was a succession of festivals. The Mass for Dead Insects had gone by already; the Rice-Planting Festival came on the eleventh, and the Iris Festival, by the old lunar calendar, on the fourteenth. On the fifteenth there was the River Imp Festival, and on the twentieth the Bamboo-Cutting Festival. (101)

Even with the local variations it seems impossible that all these festivals could take place in one month. Far from having a strong awareness of chronological time, or being controlled by it, Ibuse *uses time* as a stylistic, technical device to order his narrative.

But even if Ibuse is not a cut-and-dried realist, neither is he a prophet, nor a mystic. A modern skeptical man in many respects, he just has an uncanny, almost primeval feeling for the greater shifts in the cosmic setting, or, as we can witness in "God of Fire," for the exact moment when 'nature's disposition' is being born:

> *Taimei, hayaku yo ga akekiru to ii no ni nâ... taiyô ga nobottara, nani ka zenbô ga akiraka ni naru ka mo shirenu. Sô sureba, nani ka shizen no shochi ga umareru yô na kimochi ga suru...* (153)
>
> "Mr. Taimei, I wish that the day would break soon... after sunrise, the whole situation should make more sense. One feels as if all nature's disposition were being born afresh then."

It is this initial moment, invisible to the insensitive eye, when nature's disposition is being formed that has always attracted and fascinated Ibuse. His eye is so finely tuned to the greater rhythm of nature that it can discern the birth convulsions of its new disposition before it becomes obvious. He seems to perceive natural change, be it on a gigantic or minute scale, as a kind of sudden shift; so he will often refer to massive disasters as the 'convulsions of nature', and even use the adjective convulsive (*hossateki*) about the split-second rush of a tiny fish or about the sobbing of a woman in a hysterical fit. In his eyes, there is no substantial difference between such slightly mystifying bursts of emotion – they all signal the birth spasms of forms of being, forcing their way into existence.

Ibuse has actually offered us a clue to his spatial understanding of time in the novel, but for some inexcusable reason the translator chose to omit the very crucial lines that contain it. Maybe they really make sense only in Japanese:

> *Boku no kyôri de wa 'asagarasu wa man ga yoi' to itte iru. Asagarasu wo mita mono wa, sono hi wa un ga waruku nai to iu imi da. Dôshokubutsu no shikisai no chôwabi wo ôka shite iru no de wa nakatta ka? Boku wa tsutomehajime no koro, ryômatsusho no toshoshitsu de 'man ga yoi' no 'man' to iu no wo shirabete mita. 'Man' wa 'ma' no tenka de, 'un' 'meguriawase' 'shiawase' de aru.*
>
> *Sore ni tsukete mo Hiroshima no machi wa kiwamete 'man'ga warukatta.*[18]

In my old home at the country they used to say 'the morning crows bring a good *man*'. It meant that those who saw a crow in the morning would have good luck on that day. Didn't they praise the harmony of colours of animals and plants? When I started working I looked up

---

[18] *Kuroi ame*, p. 186.

at the library of the war supply office the word *man* of *man is good*. *Man* is a variation of *ma* and means fate, destiny. In that sense, Hiroshima's *ma* was extremely bad.

Ibuse never had much patience with the modern trust in the neat linear causality of events. Note that he does not say: Hiroshima's destiny or Hiroshima's fate was bad; rather, its position in the spatial context of things, its *ma* or *feng-shui* in the Chinese sense was bad. It was destroyed not so much as a result of a causal chain of events that logically followed one another in time, but rather because it was, cosmically speaking, *in a bad place*. The lines about Hiroshima's *ma*, its spatial context or cosmic setting, being extremely bad are preceded by this passage:

> …the broad stretch of rice fields and the lotus pond that lay between Asahi-chô and Midori-chô were old friends. Every day on my way to work my eyes were delighted by the sight of crows settled on the dew-damp path between the fields. The glossy black sheen of crows' plumage in the morning blends well with the green of the rice plants, and equally well with the rice fields after they have started to turn yellow. The sight is indescribably pleasant; at daybreak on a really fine morning it is enough to set your heart beating faster. (171)

And this is the passage that follows the lines about the *ma* of Hiroshima:

> But today, even the lotus pond had a dead body lying in it. Beside the pond, I noticed a white pigeon crouching in the grass. I went gently up to it and took it in my hands, but it was blinded in its right eye, and the feathers above its right wing were slightly scorched. For a moment, I felt a sudden desire to eat it broiled with soy, but

I let it go, tossing it up and away from me into the air. It managed to flap its wings quite well, and flew off just over the tops of the lotus leaves, describing a horizontal parabola that curved steadily towards the left. But then, as I watched, it lost height and plunged into the waters of the pond. (171)

Yet despite the drastic difference between the two contexts or nature's 'dispositions', and the way things are related within them, Shigematsu's memory links the two scenes. His memory of the harmonious blending of the various natural patterns in the first *ma* actually guides his action through the second. This one is far from the harmonious scene he first contemplated, enjoyed and blended into, and yet he chooses the less obvious course of action: he does not eat the pigeon, but helps it to do the one thing it was made for – to fly. That the bird does not make it after all is not the most important thing here; at least it had its chance. But the crucial thing for Shigematsu's identity at this moment is that his *memory* of the other, gentler *ma* became a small part of the brutal scene, the changed *ma* around.

While the shift in the whole context of the two scenes here is obvious and visible to the naked eye, in "God of Fire" it required a prepared mind to see the change, although all the ingredients for the bomb were already given in the spatial context of the situation. It required a mind that is fully at home in the world of its language and its mythical images – the tools it must use to reveal itself and the world around. A poet who does not have this power of true mythical insight can hardly cope with a simple traffic accident, let alone the absurd mess of an atomic holocaust. It is not the objectifying power of his naked eye that helps him order this chaotic 'reality', but rather the objectifying power of his poetic vision. It is characteristic of Ibuse's mature poetic vision that it does not seek fancy, startling symbols or outlandish mythical images. Over the years he has established a modest 'poetic cosmology' and a small homely world of favourite images throughout his work. He does not need much more to tell his full story. Although the blaze in *Black Rain* seems to loom so large over his earlier life-size imagery, the author has made the acquaintance of the raging God of Fire (*Gojinka*) before: his old images make it through the fire trial after all. A little less innocent and some painfully burned, but they are all there: the ponds (*sensui*), the streams and canals, the pine and *kenponashi* trees, the sucking whirlwinds and whirlpools, the rocks, the rustic people with their superstitions and amusing yarns, and above all the fish. Note how Shigematsu's mouth caresses the flavour of these fish names: *sunahami*, *sunamuguri*, *gigi*, *gigichô*; no wonder that they all resist translation. But there is a world of difference between these little fish and an awesome literary symbol like the mysterious white whale of Captain Ahab.

I would call these things the novel's *existential elements* (or what Lotman calls *sujet* realities) rather than its symbols; they are too ancient and basic to conceal enough meaning to warrant critical delving. And just because Ibuse is so much in touch with these existential elements of his work, they make sense in the context of his story while they might look terribly naïve and conventional elsewhere. He has an amazing gift of making common words convey meaning in their most fundamental sense. And it is for the same reason that they look so genuinely Japanese and at the same time are so easily recognizable to any human being. Does this mean that they arouse no symbolic and mythical echoes in the reader's mind? I would suggest that the behaviour of these existential elements in the novel is just as flexible and protean as Shigematsu's; sometimes they symbolize something, sometimes they don't. In some places they evoke mythical echoes that add an important dimension to factual reality, elsewhere they fail to do so. Ibuse does not insist on symbolic meaning and mythical depth throughout *Black Rain*; some things behave strangely when they start dancing in the blast, but if their actions suggest a deeper meaning, it is between us and them. For example, we know that Shigeko prayed "for the briefest of moments" facing the pond (*sensui*) and that the family stores its most precious belongings there; if we wish to believe that the ancestral tablets came flying all the way through the powerful blast to seek the safety of the primal waters to escape the fire – and this thought must have crossed Shigematsu's mind – we are free to do so. But we might as well accept his improbable guess that the tablets were pulled back by the backdraft following the blast, or simply that "some things... refused to make sense, either in scientific terms or in terms of common logic." (146)

There is no single meaning in Ibuse's world, just as there is no single dominant will in it, be it Satan's or God's. Meaning itself is situational, and an immense variety of 'wills' exists in nature. The blast has terribly upset the interrelationship between these wills and tipped the balance between different forms of existence. It has played havoc with the life force itself, changing the unique rhythm of life that every individual form of being possesses, forcing the normally sleepy rhythm of plant life to run wild and accelerating the breeding pace of insects. But Ibuse does not suggest a neat mythopoeic exchange here – that human life is wiped out, but flies and plants celebrate an orgy of growth. On the contrary, Shigematsu cannot help wondering: if a surplus of such a beneficial element as water can cause structural weakness and the withering of rice plants, how could this massive fire-shock be life-sustaining in the long run?

Fire has always frightened and fascinated the human mind by the rapid substantial transformations it can cause; what "fire has caressed, loved, adored, has gained a store of memories and lost its innocence."[19] The bomb has ripped apart the familiar world at its seams and consumed a number of lofty traditions, sometimes leaving nothing but shadows behind. But the blaze cannot be all-powerful. Even if the images of fire loom so large through many chapters of the novel, they do not dominate the whole book. Mind you, Shigematsu is literally at his wits' end many a time; his conscious mind often cannot accept the frightening power of the blazes. Yet we must watch the nuances of his language and his choice of metaphor very closely if we want to know how his deeper mind absorbs the shock. A metaphor he will use here and there has often cleared the doubt and the remorse

[19] I am here paraphrasing Gaston Bachelard: *The Psychoanalysis of Fire.* Trans. Ross, Allan C. M. Boston, Beacon Press 1964, p. 57.

in his mind long before he evaluates the situation consciously.

For example, it is very important to realize that Shigematsu's eye first takes in the 'animal vitality' of the jellyfish cloud and only after that does he decide that "it was an envoy of the devil himself." (55) Ibuse's characters always show a sound respect for the dynamic flow and the animal vitality of natural forces, even when they are very frightened:

> ...the next moment it [the fire] would surge *forward in a great wave*. With the pointed tongue of its flames, it licked at the windows of the larger Western style buildings.
>
> "Look –," said Miyaji in a shaking voice, *"the tips of the flames are like snakes* – they flicker their tongues in at the windows first, then they crawl right inside." (81–82; italics mine)

Like most of us, Shigematsu does not like too drastic changes in his life. He may be just as conservative as any other man, but his choice of metaphor reveals that his deeper mind ultimately accepts destruction as the flow of change in things; if change means that it will rain flesh and blood from time to time, rain it must. Shigematsu's eye also perceives the power of the raging fire and smoke:

> A truly huge column of fire (*ôkina, ôkina hibashira*), it sucked together the smoke and flames gushing from different parts of the district, and fashioned them into a single great whirling pool...
>
> Although the wind did not seem to change direction, the flames from time to time would creep out over the roofs of buildings. At one moment, the fire would stretch out as though a huge rope were being twisted out of the

flame, then the next moment it would surge forward in a great wave (*ônami*). (81)

Elsewhere, we read:

A tremendous column of smoke was rising from the direction of the city hall. Here and there, other smaller clouds of smoke were rising. (145)

A great fire was still raging to the northeast, around Yokogawa, and *huge columns of flame* were swirling up into the sky. (99; italics mine)

A consistent pattern begins to emerge: a powerful upward surge of energy always perceived as a column or pillar (*hashira*) is accompanied by a more gentle downward or horizontal motion seen as a wave, cloud, sea, pool, or river. We might sum up these forces into a rising force (*tatsu chikara*) and flowing force (*nagareru chikara*). The 'leg' or *hashira* of the mushroom cloud after swelling up to five or six times its original size, becomes "no more than a shadow of its former self, seemed to have little power left to do anything" (78) and begins to float away. But note that it was a 'column of cloud' even at the height of its power. The twisting flames would suck together smoke and fire and, surging forward in a great wave, would spread out into a 'sea of flames' and a 'sea of charcoal'. The columns of smoke, too, would creep low over the surface of the river and vanish on the other bank. People's eyes became 'crimson pools of blood'.

There are numerous other *hashira* that were standing before the atomic mushroom opened and before the columns of fire surged to the sky. Some of them withstand the brutal power of the blast and offer protection. Here is Shigematsu:

My eyes shut, my body wedged in a wave of humanity (*hitonami*), I took one, then another step forward and found myself up against something hard again. Realizing that it was a pillar, I clung to it, scarcely aware of what I was doing. I wrapped my arms about it tightly, but still I was torn and buffeted mercilessly. Pushed to the right, thrust back immediately to the left, many times I came close to being torn loose. Each time, my arms were squashed, my body and chin ground against the pillar till it seemed that my shoulders must give way with the pain. I knew I had only to let go and join the wave of humanity, yet every time the wave beat against me, I clung desperately to the pillar so as not to be swept away. (38)

Again we can see the same pillar and wave pattern, or *tatsu chikara* and *nagareru chikara*. Of the ruined mansion, nothing remains but a tall pillar of stone. It had been standing for many generations, and instead of the usual longer inscription it has a single character – "Dream" – carved on it:

Some high-ranking priest was said to have written the original, and the effect was doubtless considered stylish and rather sophisticated in its day, but at present, style and sophistication alike failed utterly. (103)

Style and sophistication were indeed a sort of cultural dream, but the naked power of the rock withstood the blast. To underscore its strength, there is another, gentler rock at its foot that was hurt.

The stone on which Shigeko and Yasuko [Shigematsu's wife and niece] were sitting was almost certainly a rock from the garden inside the grounds. Rock though it was, a thin layer had been burned away all over it.

"That rock's granite, you know," I said, "I expect it was covered with moss only this morning." (103)

So some rocks and some trees survive and offer shelter, but not all pillars do:

> The posts [of the bridge] were of granite – a foot square and about four feet high, I should say. They had stood at intervals of some six feet, each capped with a block of stone about twice the area of the post itself. There had been dozens and dozens of these massive posts, and they were all blown down or blown away. (83)

Let us note that the end-posts of bridge railings called *o-bashira* were originally placed to prevent the passage of evil spirits in positions that commanded thoroughfares. These and other pillars lose their guardian power:

> The fire seemed to be spreading steadily. Concluding that she [Shigeko] should get out, she went first of all to get the silk bag containing the family ancestral tablets, but it was not hanging on its usual pillar. Nor was it on the pillar in the next room. (145)

There seem to be three kinds of pillars or *hashira* in the novel: the bomb with its fire and smoke has concentrated the most energy. It threatens the second type of pillar, the stationary ones. The third kind of *hashira* is trees, natural and alive. As one of the central images of this novel they are extraordinary trees:

> The camphor trees at the Kokutaiji Temple, which must have been easily six feet in diameter, had all three been uprooted and had fallen to the ground, where they lay, burned through and carbonized but still preserving the shape of trees, with their roots thrust upwards into the air.... The camphor trees were said to have been more

than a thousand years old, but today they had finally met their fate. (99)

Note that these 'guardians' of time and history were uprooted by the larger force of the bomb's *hashira*. Elsewhere 'skeletons' of three pine trees are mentioned. The top of the pine tree in Shigematsu's garden is also spurting flames. There are a *kenponashi* and a gingko with which Shigematsu has a special relationship. The *kenponashi* stands in the garden of his country home, and, in his words, it is a 'noble tree' with great emotional significance for him and for his entire family. Thinking that the Shigematsus must be dead in Hiroshima, his mother in Kobatake said:

> If you're going to Hiroshima... I'll trouble you to take some incense, at least. And some water and fresh leaves from the village. You can burn the incense on the place where the house was, and sprinkle the water and scatter the leaves there for them. And while you're about it, take some *kenponashi* nuts for Shigematsu – he was always fond of the *kenponashi* trees. (183)

It is these fresh leaves that Shigeko and Yasuko find lying beneath the charred remains of their pine tree and these incense sticks that they find by the pond, stuck in the earth together with the nuts and the water from the well. There is little doubt that this tree is a sacred guardian of the family's life and its most important events. It is only here, under the protective branches of their great 'tree of life', that Shigeko summons the courage to break the sad news to Shigematsu about Yasuko's radiation sickness.

This tree is also a guardian of the family's history. Its roots reach literally into the 'land of roots' or land of the dead (*ne no kuni*), linking past generations with the present and the family's small world with the world at large. In their storehouse the family keeps an old letter to which Shigematsu's great-grandfather seems to have attached great importance. It is from an early Meiji government inspector and acknowledges the gift of some *kemponashi* seeds that might be used as seedlings to line the avenues of Tokyo.

The other all-important tree is a gingko in old Kôtarô's garden:

> ...the pine had gone for the national effort during the war, and so had the gingko tree at Kôtarô's, which people said had been the same height. On sunny mornings in late autumn and on into the winter, the shadows of the pine and the gingko tree would reach out all the way to the foot of the hill on which Shigematu's house stood.
>
> As a boy, Shigematsu had seldom come to the flat rock to play, but he had often been to play under the gingko tree at Kôtarô's place. (74)

Both trees link past and present, or dead ancestors with living people. Both have (or had) impressive trunks and both offer precious gifts. In Japanese cosmology the function of the Tree is similar to that of the Heavenly Pillar (*ame no hashira*). The Tree also connects the three cosmic regions: from the middle ground its branches reach to the sky and its roots go down to the underworld. Like the pillar with its inner core or opening, it offers a possibility of communication between the three cosmic realms – Underworld, Earth and Heaven. Or it can transport a spirit from profane time into sacred time. The image of the whirling gingko leaves lifts Shigematsu's mind from the contaminated present to the grace and innocence, indeed the Heaven, of childhood:

> When the frosts came and the gingko tree began to shed its leaves, the roof of Kôtarô's house would be transformed into a yellow roof, smothered with dead leaves. Whenever a breeze sprang up, they would pour down from the eaves in a yellow waterfall, and when it eddied they would swirl up into the air – up and up to twice, three times the height of the roof – then descend in yellow whirlpools onto the road up the slope and onto the oak grove.
>
> This always delighted the children. As the wind dropped and the leaves came dancing down, the boys would stretch up their hands to clutch at them, and the girls would catch them in their outspread aprons. (74)

This image of an eddy surging in one powerful 'column' (*hashira*) and then gently floating down in yellow whirlpools clearly echoes and counters the other whirling columns of flames and smoke, and perhaps that of the bomb. The emotional force of this gentler whirlpool is at least equal to the power of the circling fire. We notice that elsewhere the author talks about a "big whirlwind of a flame" and in "God of Fire" about a "whirlpool of ashes." I have analyzed the oft-quoted passage of capricious whirlpools that play with a dead girl's body in "The River" elsewhere. This image of a whirling, dynamic natural force, usually a whirlpool or a whirlwind, sucking in things and people and thrusting them forth again, is another key image of Ibuse's poetic vision. It expresses his essential intuition of the dramatic flow of life's creative energy in an iconographically dense form and reminds us of the ancient

Chinese image of creative chaos. The great gingko lives on in Shigematsu's memory, even when its powerful trunk has been sacrificed for the war effort. But this fascinating old tree had still more to offer:

> During the war old Kôtarô's family had given up the great gingko tree ... for the sake of the war effort. As they were digging up the stump, they had uncovered the jar, an enormous affair in Bizen ware of the type once used for storing rice. (60)

Kôtarô directs water through a bamboo pipe into the jar and keeps fish in it. Shigematsu talks about it with Shigeko:

> 'There's always something in the jar at old Kôtarô's place, isn't there?'...

> 'When I was over there at the end of last year, he had seven or eight live eels in it,' said Shigeko. 'You never know what's going to come out of that jar. It's a kind of cornucopia.' (60–61)

Again we notice the familiar union of the rising force as exemplified by the tree trunk (*tatsu chikara*) and the flowing force from the life-giving jar (*nagareru chikara*). Since these forces are cyclic, we can see small eels coming out of the jar long after the tree is dead. The fire had been compared with snakes; the water gives life to eels. A snake's body, hard and pliant at the same time, can rise or 'flow' in its motion; the eel, a benign form of water 'snake' also combines the 'pillar' and 'wave' quality. By using the image of a myriad tiny baby-eels battling their way upstream to restate the union of the rising and the flowing force near its end, the novel transcends the conflict between the two leaving us with a strong impression of a wholesome and untainted life-force. This fusion of wave and column is also repeated in the rainbow image that closes the novel.

This is the basis of the novel and its mythopoeisis. Different forms of the pillar or rising force surge, expand, and clash, but they all contain the gentle wave of the flowing force since the very conflict between them is manifested by a wave of this force. One onomatopoeic word that Ibuse uses to describe the bomb's mushroom cloud expresses this coexistence very well: *mukuri-kokuri* – wavy and solid, soft and hard. The rain of the title is a falling, flowing force. But we know that heavy rain in Japanese can have 'legs'– (*ama-ashi*) and that a rain can be a 'rising rain' or *yudachi*. Thus, it includes both forces in its cyclic motion. The same dynamics is encoded in Shigematsu's name. He is not only a pine (*matsu,* i.e., rising force), but also a *shigeru matsu.* The *shige* of his name is written with the character for *kasanaru,* to pile up, store up. So the emphasis in *shigeru* is on the onflow, or piling up of experience, strength, and wisdom, that grow and pile up in waves just as a tree's years.

If the bomb wiped out his pillar-like qualities – his private sexuality and narrow ego – it also released the all-embracing wave of his cosmic consciousness. The mythical Heavenly Pillar (*ame no hashira*) has a secret core, a cosmic opening through which one can look into the Underworld or into Heaven. The deep wound that the bomb, a modern version of the *ame no hashira,* inflicted in Shigematsu's mind is also a beneficial cosmic opening, through which he can glimpse Hell and Heaven, and perhaps the true nature of life and death.

It is at the level of these fine stylistic ambiguities and tensions that Shigematsu's eye most betrays its affinity with Ibuse's earlier poetic cosmology as expressed in "Isle-on-the-Billows" and other stories. This is where Ibuse's style dances on the subtle line between realistic and mythical expression, and awakens dormant resonances in us. And if the image of fire looms so large throughout the novel, so does that of its counterpart, water. Water is the source of things, it has the safe depths and the purity that alone can restore the innocence of things, that was lost in the fire. Let us again recall the images of old Kôtarô's jar, found at the roots of the gingko tree, from which a cornucopia of life comes – eels, sweetfish, trout, or "anything else one can fancy". Even tiny minnows seem to know that in water "there is shadow, there is safety". Yasuko and her companions creep out "like fresh-water crabs" from behind the rocks, where they hid during the explosion. Shigematsu and his family walk to safety through the river. The baby-eels struggling against the stream toward the end of the novel should have been killed in the boiling waters downstream, but they made it, for the fire could not get at the bottom of the river. It tries to lick its way through into the water all the time:

> I knew from experience that the flames from a fire tended to sweep over the surface of rivers... the whole area had become a *sea of flames,* and I myself saw people who had been burned to death as they floated in the water. (244; italics mine)

Or as it says elsewhere in the original: *"Kaen wa kawazura wo nameru no da"* (267): "The blaze is licking the water's face!"

Do we feel a polarity between water and fire at this level, or rather a strange mutual attraction? Do these 'opposites' meet when they come full circle and become almost interchangeable? After all, many languages still talk about burning ice or the icy whiteness of intense heat. To the premodern mentality it was clear that these forces were not enemies; life could not exist without both of them. The existence of this link between fire and water does not puzzle Shigematsu's deeper mind. It is the upset balance, the overwhelming abundance of one of these forces that bothers him. This is why virtually all sun images in the novel have unpleasant overtones. Ibuse's landscape, unlike Kawabata's or Tanizaki's nocturnal scenery, is usually flooded with sunshine. But in this novel, the bright sun of his birthplace is too much, only adding to the suffering of the scorched country. Some of the fire-images not only suggest the archetypal proximity of the two elements, but also the two different contexts in which they operate. If there are funeral fires in the dried-up river bed, there are also the memories of other fires kindled in a similar river bed, over which young Shigematsu's friend Chûzô used to bake delicious bamboo shoots. Again, there is no substantial difference between these fires, but rather a shift in their entire cosmic context (their *ma*).

Ibuse plants these and other important images as tiny seeds early in his narrative, only to let them grow and gain weight. Thus, the image of dryness sucking at water, that works together with both the whirlpool imagery and the overall fire-water dynamics of the novel, is casually introduced early in the novel:

Everything on the second floor of the storehouse, which was dimly lit and smelt of dust, was *so dry* that it seemed to *suck at the very moisture* in their bodies. (42; italics mine)

It is interesting that in the letter to his grandfather, which Shigematsu finds in the dry storehouse, seeds of *kenponashi* trees are mentioned; the thirst of these seeds combines with the faded ink of the letter to underscore the image of sucking dryness.

The image keeps recurring: a long procession of refugees is sucked into the mountains by the hillfires only to be burned like moths who dash themselves against a lamp at night. Still they cannot quench the terrible thirst of the fires. But other fleeing crowds keep rushing to the hills and this time Shigematsu perceives them quite differently:

Yet here too, the fleeing crowds were pressing on with one idea of getting to the hills. I remembered what I had heard of *tidal waves* – how they *ooze on in muddy swirls*, on up to the higher ground beyond.... (57; italics mine)

The myth of the world-wide blaze must come to mind here: the fireflood can only be quenched by a powerful deluge or a mighty tidal wave, otherwise the very existence of the world may be threatened. Here the people of Hiroshima themselves have become the swirling flood water that cannot fail to quench the insatiable thirst of the blazes. But the thirst of the fires must be quenched within as well. If there is one lust remaining in Shigematsu's body – for he feels no pain, no hunger and no sexual urge – it is the burning lust for water:

I rolled onto my belly, and... drank. It was a heaven-sent nectar. I had had no idea that water was so good. The ecstasy was touched, almost, with a kind of pride. (110)

Water is life, life is thirst. Some language groups have preserved the archetypal proximity of these basic urges; for example, the word *zhizn* means life in Russian, but *thirst* in some other Slavic languages. The human wave may have quenched the thirst of the fires, but this is still not enough. The bomb has created a powerful vortex that sucks in people and things; the survivors must do more if they want to get away from its terrible sucking force. We will note that Shigematsu's recollections begin at the railway station, about 2–3 kilometers from the explosion. As we read on, we have a feeling of closing in on the ruins and on the stream of refugees, a feeling of being sucked into the bomb's whirling core. This is where Ibuse's imagery matches exactly what psychologists call the 'illusion of centrality'; one cannot help sharing Shigematsu's feeling of being pulled right into the centre of the blast.

But as we get to the second part of the novel, especially to the last 'inserted' narratives – the diaries of Dr. Iwatake and his wife – the feeling grows that we are being distanced from the bomb's power. As the main stream of the narrative meanders away from the epicentre toward the other important 'centre' of the Iwatake story, we notice that other little episodic streams are rushing in the same direction along the Hesaka-Hosokawa railway line. The episodes are all linked through a series of chance meetings. For example, Shigematsu meets his old childhood friend Teiko on the railroad tracks; Teiko knows the Hosokawa clinic, which in turn takes us into the Iwatake story. Shigematsu himself met Shigeko and Yasuko by mere chance, at a moment when he was setting about a completely different course of action in order to find them. Dr. Iwatake is being transferred from Hesaka to Shôbara, when he spots a girl at Miyoshi Station who happens to have been the ward of his aunt; thanks to this meeting, Iwatake feels he should be able to contact his friends and relatives. Mrs. Iwatake too, when she is searching for her husband in the ruins of the 2nd Army Hospital, just by chance happens to meet a man who directs her to Hesaka, where her husband had in fact gone. She had two or three different choices; she could have gone to Kabe, she could have gone out to the Geibi line, and yet she goes to Hesaka and Shôbara and finds her husband. On the train she happens to meet a man who knows the Fuchû branch of the Hosokawa clinic, and he takes a message to Dr. Hosokawa in Yuda, who is her elder brother.

All of these chances have been gifts received by people who were desperately concerned with one another. They always seem to be rewarded: Mrs. Iwatake is rewarded with finding and saving her husband, and Shigematsu finds Yasuko and Shigeko before the fires get to Sendamachi. These people have survived not by chance and their will power alone; there are sinews binding them with others that the bomb's fiery heat and blast has not been able to sever. Once again, it is the ancient meaning of *musubi* as vital energy shared that applies here; they would not have made it if it were not for the effort and kindness of those who cared and *remembered*.

As Ibuse carries his narrative forward, this technique of linking episodes keeps its pace and gives the novel a kind of increasing concentration and, indeed, of a brevity that otherwise would not have been there. As the physical distance from the explosion increases, the narrative distance begins to change as well. The different voices and memories – eyewitness accounts, official reports, rumors and wild tales – echo each other, but never repeat themselves, although they always refer to the central event of the blast. There is a feeling that the colourful tales are beginning to fill the gaping hole that the great explosion ripped in the social fabric.

Much has been said about Ibuse's cruel way of describing some of the scenes of horror. Yet these scenes are actually quite few and always very carefully selected. Let us look at the two most grotesque ones:

> In the tank was a human figure with the head alone reduced to a skull and the rest of the body beneath the water, on the surface of which floated viscous, greasy brown bubbles. As the laborers reluctantly approached the tank with their corrugated iron sheets, the skull, without warning, suddenly tilted forward and sank amidst the bubbles. (166–167)

> A length of more than three feet of large intestine had sprouted from the buttocks of one of the women, who floated upside down; it was swollen to about three inches in diameter, and floated in a slightly tangled ring on the water, swaying gently from side to side like a balloon as the wind blew. (159)

Exposed to a bizarre spectacle of this kind, one's eye often shies away, although it is tempted to steal a glance. Or should I say one's conscious morality forbids the eye to see what it is offered? In a fraction of time, before any moral 'evaluation' of the scene can occur, the incomparably older 'visual brain' has already grasped the scene. The eye has its own morality; what it sees may be horrible and grotesque, but it is thoroughly fascinated nonetheless. After all, it is with this innocent savagery that children look at gruesome reality. But there is more to this: these shocking images, too gruesome to look at directly, gradually grow into grotesque tales. By retelling these stories the mind not only gets rid of the horror, but makes a kind of shift in context. Anybody who has grown up in the country as Ibuse has, must remember how important to village people are the gruesome tales that enliven their sleepy, monotonous lives. Maybe the way Ibuse presents his vignettes of horror shifts them back into this older context of normal life, into another, gentler *ma*. It may sound paradoxical, but it seems to me that he humanizes the absurd, multiple brutality of these scenes by transforming them into vivid well-integrated tales.

When we get to the end of the novel, all these colourful yarns and episodic streams seem to swirl together and merge in an inevitable confluence. Just as the bomb created its own vortex, the narrative elements all flow together as Ibuse brings them to one center, and we have a definite feeling of a narrative whirlpool sucking everything in, right to the end of the novel. But the interesting thing is that, rather than opening the narrative with this swirling concentration, he puts it at the end. And this is where it belongs. This whirlpool of human voices and memories cannot play around as innocently as the capricious whirlpools in "The River"; its will must always be equal to the sucking power of the blast's vortex.

The fiery heat of the blast can only change the substance of something weaker than itself. Dr. Iwatake miraculously survived because his will was as strong as the bomb's, and the thirst for life in his body was equal to its monstrous appetite; through the blast his body was tempered and some parts of it made new. Yasuko is rather like the wounded pigeon – she may be too gentle to pull through. Yet Shigematsu did his honest best to give her a chance. He knows he will have to live on with her memory and his own radiation sickness; yet if he feels no triumph, he also does not feel defeated. The Emperor's surrender broadcast is mentioned in the last entry of Shigematsu's diary, not so much for its importance, but rather to show how little it concerns him at this point. Another man who wasn't there is trying to tell him something, but he's had enough. Instead, he turns away and walks toward the clear stream of the canal where he finds countless numbers of baby eels, battling their way upstream. With them he can talk, for they seem to smell the fresh water of their home higher up the stream. This is just what Shigematsu wants to do; he feels relieved that the madness is over and he can begin to recover the debris of his wrecked emotional 'home'. That is why he suddenly recalls the relief he had felt as a little boy when he ran back home to his mother, away from the local half-wit who used to tease him. He had not wept in front of this lout, but ran home instead, badgered his mother into baring her breast for him, and only then burst into tears; he remembers the salty taste of her milk to this day.

In the end, Shigematsu seems to feel very much at home among all the chores that keep him busy: he must read over and put a cardboard cover on his diary, he must go and have a look how the *aiko* in the pond are coming along and, once there, he cannot miss the slender stalk in the water on which a small, dark purple flower blooms. In the midst of death and destruction, a man upholds precious images of life and creation. What is more, his deeper mind perceives – though frightened and confused at times – that very death-dealing force as a part of life's indomitable energy.

There is no doubt that *Black Rain* is a work of central importance to Ibuse's *oeuvre*. The Western critic might be tempted to overemphasize the grimness of its theme, according it a little more weight within the context of Ibuse's entire output than the author himself. Extrapolating from *Black Rain* a grand design that would counter the bomb's Faustian implications and reading the more cheerful, lighter work in its shadow, we might get a more 'significant' Ibuse.[1] Instead of a writer who has sidestepped all generalities and structures we'd have one who is morally committed to an intelligible metaphysical system. Like some of our great artists, he might then become a man who seeks wholeness and yet keeps depicting disintegration. This particular Japanese artist was able to maintain a wholesome vision of life through the darkest of times, not because he inserted a magic screen of words between himself and reality, but precisely because writing – no matter how polished – is no more and no less to him than one of life's meaningful chores, an activity firmly rooted in the everyday flow of his people's historical existence.

[1] As John Treat does in his *Pools of Water, Pillars of Fire*. Seattle and London, University of Washington Press 1988. See my review in *Monumenta Nipponica* 44, 1, Spring 1989, pp. 115–119.

Ibuse did not favour any particular religion or philosophy, although he had a great respect for the humanistic teachings of Confucius. During our discussions, he often made an admiring remark about the Chinese sage: "Well, after all they had Confucius…" ("*Yappari Kôshi-sama ga ita, nê*").[2] In the interview with Kawamori Yoshizô he dismissed any Christian influence on his writing and when we talked about Nobunaga and his dislike of Buddhist bonzes, Ibuse expressed a fairly strong critique of the Buddhist establishment, saying: "Well, the only kind of religious structure I can take, is a small Shinto shrine (*hokora*) in the woods…"[3] Because of the pressures of orthodox leftism in the twenties, he was not sympathetic to marxism, although he had good personal relationships with many of its followers (Sata Ineko, Nakano Shigeharu and others).

As Japanese literature becomes more urban and cosmopolitan and writers like Murakami Haruki catch the international reader's attention, Ibuse's meticulous concern with local colour and nuances of rustic dialect may look like relics of the past. Yet if we look for a genuine sample of Japanese identity before the mixed blessings of globalization, for writing that springs from the very essence of its time and its culture, then reading Ibuse is perhaps even more enlightening today than at the time of the stories' conception.

It has become fashionable to talk about orientalism – most recently about the self-orientalization of

[2] During my visit at Ibuse's home in Ogikubo, in the spring of 1972.
[3] During my visit at Ibuse's country house in Takamori, Nagano prefecture, in the summer of 1975.

the Japanese – cultural constructs etc. and it is true that contemporary Japanese intellectuals are far more consciously aware of the symbolic structures that inform their native culture than Ibuse's generation, yet we must bear in mind that to artists of his background and his time cultural identity was something intuitively shared, not objectively analyzed. That is also the reason why the contemporary reader may feel that their attitude to, say, the Japanese war effort was too docile and not critical enough.

Ibuse never travelled outside his country (except when forced to Malaya by the military during the war) and when I invited him for a fishing trip to Canada, he replied politely: "Thank you very much, but I don't know my own country well enough yet..."[4] His profound knowledge of Japan's history and folklore was not of an academic kind, rather a magnificent collection of stories and yarns, not necessarily logically organized. He had an intimate rapport with the imprint of historical lives in concrete places. So on a walk through a mountain gorge in Shinshû he pointed to its narrowest point and casually remarked: "That's Shingen's escape route..." (*"Are wa Shingen no nigemichi da..."*).[5]

Once we talked about his favourite Russian novels and he praised Goncharov's *Frigate Pallas* for the extraordinary precision of its description: "A *bakufu* official comes to the harbour to question the Russian sailors, sits down and taps his knee with his fan... The preci-

---

[4] Ibid.

[5] Ibid. Takeda Shingen (1521–1573), the great warlord whose home territory were the mountains of Shinshû. Shingen subdued the entire Shinano Province, defeating even the famed Uesugi Kenshin. He also masterminded one of the most ambitious projects of the 16th century, the damming of Fuji River.

sion of that description is awesome."[6] Such faithfulness to accurate detail may not be considered an important characteristic of writing in a world where the appearance and meaning of things are ever more uniform.

More than anything else, Ibuse's literary achievement is based on an inimitable authenticity of setting and a sophistication of its stylistic expression; few other modern writers have expressed as convincingly what it means to be Japanese in a difficult century.

[6] During my visit at Takamori.

## 1. PRIMARY SOURCES IN JAPANESE

Ibuse Masuji: *Bamen no kôka*. Tokyo, Daiwa shobô 1966.

— *Chôyôchû no koto*. Tokyo, Kôdansha 1996.

— *Dazai Osamu*. Chikuma shobô 1989.

— *Hana no machi*. Tokyo, Bungei shunjûsha 1943.

— *Hito to hitokage*. Tokyo, Mainichi shinbunsha 1972.

Trans. Ibuse Masuji: *Hôgen monogatari; Heiji monogatari; Gikeiki*. Tokyo, Kawade shobô 1974.

— *IM zenshû*, vol. I–XIV. Tokyo, Chikuma shobô 1974–1975.

— *IM zenshû*, vol. I–XXX. Tokyo, Chikuma shobô 1996–2000.

— *IM shû*. Tokyo, Shinchôsha 1960.

— *IM shû*. *Nihon bungaku zenshû 19*. Tokyo, Kawade shobô 1965–1966.

— *IM shû*. Tokyo, Chikuma shobô 1966.

— *IM. Nihon bungaku zenshû 41*. Tokyo, Shûeisha, 1967.

— *IM, Kanbayashi Akatsuki shû*. Tokyo, Chikuma shobô 1970.

— *IM. Gendai nihon bungakkan 29*. Tokyo, Bungei shunjû 1970.

— *IM shû. Shinchô nihon bungaku 17*. Tokyo, Shinchôsha 1970.

— *IM shû*. Tokyo, Yayoi shobô, 1982.

— *IM taidansen*. Tokyo, Kôdansha 2000.

— *IM taidanshû*. Tokyo, Shinchôsha 1993.

— *IM zentaidan*. Tokyo, Chikuma shobô 2000.

— *Jisen zenshû*, vol. I–XIII. Tokyo, Shinchôsha 1986.

— *Kawatsuri*. Tokyo, Iwanami shinsho 1975.

- *Kawa to tanima.* Tokyo, Sôgensha 1946.
- *Kuroi ame.* Tokyo, Shinchôsha 1986.
- *Natsukashiki genjitsu.* Tokyo, Kaizôsha 1930.
- *Nanatsu no kaidô.* Tokyo, Bungei shunjûsha 1958.
- *Nihon no yakimono.* Tokyo,Yomiuri shinbunsha 1974.
- *Ogikubo fudoki.* Tokyo, Shinchôsha 1982.
- *Sazanami gunki.* Tokyo, Sakuhinsha 1980.
- *Shuzai ryokô.* Tokyo, Shinchôsha 1957.
- *Sugareoi.* Tokyo, Chikuma shobô 1977.
- *Teihon Wabisuke.* Tokyo, Seiga shobô 1970.
- *Tomonotsu chakaiki.* Tokyo, Fukutake shoten 1986.
- *Tsuribito.* Tokyo, Shinchôsha 1970.
- *Yakimono zakki.* Bunka shuppankyoku 1985.
- *Yofuke to ume no hana.* Tokyo, Shinchôsha 1930.
- *Yomu.* Tokyo, Sakuhinsha 1985.
- *Umiagari.* Tokyo, Shinchôsha 1981

## 2. SECONDARY SOURCES IN JAPANESE

Fukuda, Kiyoto and Matsumoto, Takeo: *IM*. Tokyo,
    Shimizu shoin 1990.

Hagiwara, Tokushi: *IM kikigaki*. Tokyo, Seikyûsha 1994.

Hasegawa, Izumi and Tsuruta, Kinya (eds.): *IM kenkyû*.
    Tokyo, Meiji shoin 1990.

*IM no sekai. Kokubungaku kaishaku to kanshô, tokushû* 50, 4
    Shibundô 1985.

*IM. Kokubungaku kaishaku to kanshô, tokushû* 59,6 Shibundô
    1994.

*IM-Fukazawa Shichirô. Nihon bungaku kenkyû shiryô sôsho*. Tokyo,
    Yûseido 1977.

Isogai, Hideo (ed.): *IM kenkyû*. Hiroshima, Keisuisha 1984.

Iwasaki, Fumito: *Hitotsu no suimyaku*. Hiroshima, Keisuisha
    1990.

Karatani,Kôjin: *Nihon kindai bungaku no kigen*. Tokyo, Kôdansha 1980.

– *Imi to iu yamai*. Tokyo, Kawade shobô 1975.

Kasei, Tadao: *IM no hakubutsushi*. Tokyo, Rindôsha 1995.

– *IM, rekishi bungaku no kenshô*. Tokyo, Rindôsha 1988.

– *IM shiron*. Tokyo, Rindôsha 1985.

– *IM to sono jidai*. Tokyo, Rindôsha 1986.

– *Shijin IM*. Tokyo, Rindôsha, 1991.

– *Tabibito IM*. Tokyo, Rindôsha 1993.

– *Tsuribito IM*. Tokyo, Rindôsha 1989.

Kawamori, Yoshizô: *Ibuse san no yokogao*. Tokyo, Yayoi shobô 1993.

– *IM zuimon*. Tokyo, Shinchôsha 1986.

– *Sakka no sugao*. Kyoto, Shinshindô 1972.

Kawashima, Masaru: *Sayônara dake ga jinsei*. Tokyo, Bungei shunjû 1994.

Kôno, Toshirô: *IM*, Tokyo, Nihon tosho sentâ 1999.

Kumagai, Takashi: *IM, kôen to taidan*. Tokyo, Hato no mori shobô 1978.

Matsumoto, Takeo: *IM, henshû hyôden*. Tokyo, Shinchôsha 1994.

– *IM, hito to bungaku*. Tokyo, Bensei shuppan 2003.

– *IM, nenpu kô*. Tokyo, Shintensha 1999.

– *IM, shukuen no bungaku*. Tokyo, Musashino shobô 1997.

– *IM, shukuen e no manazashi*. Tokyo, Tôkyôdô shuppan 2003.

Matsumoto, Tsuruo: *IM, nichijô no moteifu*. Tokyo, Chûsekisha 1992.

– *IM ron*. Tokyo, Tôjusha 1978.

– *IM ron, zenshû shûsei*. Tokyo, Chûsekisha 2004.

Mori, Hideto: *Chôgyo taizen*. Tokyo, Kadokawa shoten 1979.

Murô, Saisei: "Ayu." In: *Ayutsuri no ki*. Tokyo, Sakufûsha 1984.

Nagata, Ryûtarô: *IM bungaku shoshi*. Tokyo, Nagata shobô 1972.

Nakano, Yoshio: *Gendai no sakka*. Tokyo, Iwanami shoten 1962.

Ôkoshi, Kashichi: *IM no bungaku*. Tokyo, Hôsei daikgaku shuppankyoku 1980.

Okuno, Takeo: *Bungaku ni okeru genfûkei—harappa dôkutsu no gensô*. Tokyo, Shûeisha 1972.

– *Gendai bungaku fudoki*. Tokyo, Shûeisha 1976.

Orikuchi, Shinobu: "Mizu no onna." In: *Orikuchi Shinobu zenshû II*. Tokyo, Chûôkôronsha 1984.

– "Kyaku to marebito." In: Orikuchi *Shinobu zenshû III*. Tokyo, Chûôkôronsha 1984.

Satô, Kôseki: "Deshi jiman." In: *Ayutsuri no ki*. Tokyo, Sakufûsha 1984.

Satô Tsuguo: *IM, sanshôuo to kaeru no sekai*. Tokyo, Musashino shobô 1994.

Shimizu, Shôzô: *IM, sono bungaku to sekai*. Tokyo, Sojûsha 1984.

Sôma, Shôichi: *IM no kiseki*. Hirosaki, Tsugaru shobô 1995.

Sugiura, Minpei: *Gendai nihon no sakka*. Tokyo, Miraisha 1964.

Tôgô, Katsumi and Terayoko, Takeo (eds.): *IM ron, Shôwa sakka no kuronotoposu*. Tokyo, Sôbunsha 1996.

Tôgô, Katsumi: *IM zenshû sakuin*. Tokyo, Sôbunsha shuppan 2003.

Toyota, Seishi: *Kuroi ame to Shigematsu nikki*. Tokyo, Fûbaisha 1993.

– *Shirarezaru IM*. Tokyo, Sôyôsha 1996.

Umehara, Takeshi: *Nihonjin no ano yo no kan*. Tokyo, Chûô Kôronsha 1989.

Wakuta, Yû: *IM jiten*. Tokyo, Meiji shoin 2000.

– *IM no sekai, shôsetsu no kôzô to seiritsu*. Tokyo, Shûeisha 1983.

— *IM wo meguru hito-bito.* Tokyo, Rindôsha 1991.

— *IM, sakka no shisô to hôhô.* Meiji shoin 1986.

— *Shichû IM.* Tokyo, Meiji shoin 1981.

— *Zusetsu IM, sono hito to sakuhin no zenbô.* Tokyo, Yûhô shoten shinsha 1985.

Yanagita, Kunio: *Nihon no matsuri.* Tokyo, Kadokawa shoten 1966.

Yasuoka, Shôtarô: *IM den.* In: *IM. Gendai nihon bungakkan 29.* Tokyo, Bungei shunjû 1968.

— *Tôno monogatari.* Tokyo, Shinchôsha 1973.

— *Senzo no hanashi.* Tokyo, Chikuma shobô 1975.

Yoshino, Hiroko: *Yama no kami.* Tokyo, Jinbun shoin 1989.

## 3. SECONDARY SOURCES IN ENGLISH

Cohn, Dorrit: "Fictional versus Historical Lives: Borderlines and Borderline Cases." *The Journal of Narrative Technique* 19, 1, Winter 1989.

Davies, Robertson: *Fifth Business.* Toronto, Penguin Canada 1996.

Ebersole, Gary L.: *Ritual Poetry and the Politics of Death in Early Japan.* Princeton, Princeton University Press 1989.

Fowler, Edward: *The Rhetoric of Confession.* Berkeley, University of California Press 1988.

Goossen, Theodore (ed.): *The Oxford Book of Japanese Short Stories.* Oxford and New York, Oxford University Press 1997.

Herbert, Jean: *Shinto.* London, Allen & Unwin 1967.

Karatani, Kôjin: *Origins of Modern Japanese Literature.* Trans. Bary, Brett de (ed.) Durham, Duke University Press 1993.

Keene, Donald: *Travellers of a Hundred Ages.* New York, Columbia University Press 1999.

— *Landscapes and Portraits*. Tokyo and Palo Alto, Kôdansha International 1971.

Kimball, Arthur G.: "After the Bomb." In: *Crisis in Identity and Contemporary Japanese Novels*. Vermont and Tokyo, Charles E. Tuttle Company 1973.

La Fleur, William: "Introduction." In: *Mirror for the Moon*. New York, New Directions 1978.

— *The Karma of Words*. Berkeley, University of California Press 1983.

Lee, Ou-fan Leo: *The Romantic Generation of Modern Chinese Writers*. Cambridge, Harvard University Press 1973.

Lifton, Robert J.: "Black Rain." In: *Death in Life: Survivors of Hiroshima*. New York, Vintage Books 1969.

Liman, Anthony: "Ibuse's Black Rain." In: *Approaches to the Modern Japanese Novel*. Tsuruta, Kinya and Swann, Thomas (eds.). Tokyo, Waseda University Press 1976.

Liman, Anthony: "Carp." "Pilgrim's Inn." In: *Approaches to the Modern Japanese Short Story*. Tsuruta, Kinya and Swann, Thomas (eds.) Tokyo, Waseda University Press 1982.

Liman, Anthony: "The River: Ibuse's Poetic Cosmology." In: *Essays on Japanese Literature*. Takeda, Katsuhiko (ed.). Tokyo, Waseda University Press 1977.

Maupassant, Guy de: "The Two Friends." In: *Selected Short Stories*. Trans. Colet, Roger. Harmondsworth, Penguin Books 1986.

Miyoshi, Masao: *Accomplices of Silence: The Modern Japanese Novel*. Berkeley, University of California Press 1974.

Nagashima, Yoichi: *Objective Descriptions of the Self: A Study of Iwano Hômei's Literary Theory*. Aarhus, Aarhus University Press 1997.

Poulton, Cody: *Spirits of Another Kind: The Plays of Izumi Kyôka*. Ann Arbor, The University of Michigan 2001.

Rimer, Thomas J.: "Tradition and Contemporary Consciousness: Ibuse, Endo, Kaiko, Abe." In: *Modern Japanese Fiction and Its Traditions*. Princeton, Princeton University Press 1978.

Shiga, Naoya: *The Paper Door and Other Stories*. Trans. Dunlop, Lane. San Francisco, North Point Press 1987.

Symons, Arthur: *The Symbolist Movement in Literature*. New York, E. P. Dutton and Co. 1958.

Treat, John W.: *Pools of Water, Pillars of Fire*. Seattle and London, University of Washington Press 1988.

Ueda, Makoto: *Literary and Art Theories in Japan*. Cleveland, Western Reserve University Press 1967.

## 4. GENERAL LITERATURE CONSULTED:

Auden, Wystan. H.: *Enchaféd Flood*. London, Faber and Faber 1951.

Bachelard, Gaston: *L'Eau et Les Rêves*. Paris, Librairie Jose Corti 1942.

— *The Poetics of Space*. Trans. Jolas, Maria. Boston, Beacon Press 1969.

— *The Psychoanalysis of Fire*. Trans. Ross, Alan C. M. Boston, Beacon Press 1964.

Bakhtin, Mikhail: *The Dialogic Imagination*. Four essays. Trans. Caryl Emerson and Michael Holquist. Holquist, Michael (ed.). Austin, University of Texas Press 1981.

Barthes, Roland and Duisit, Lionel: "An Introduction to the Structural Analysis of Narrative." *New Literary History*, 6.2, Winter 1975.

Barthes, Roland: *Empire of Signs*. Trans. Howard, R. New York, Hill and Wang 1982.

— *The Pleasure of the Text*. Trans. Miller, R. New York, Hill and Wang 1975.

– *Writing Degree Zero.* Trans. Lavers, Anette and Smith, Colin. London, Jonathan Cape 1967.

Blacker, Carmen: *The Catalpa Bow: A Study of Shamanistic Practices in Japan.* London, George Allen and Unwin 1975.

Bloom, Edward A.: *The Order of Fiction.* New York, The Odyssey Press 1964.

Boyle, Robert: "Upon Fishing with a Counterfeit Fly." In: *Occasional Relections upon Several Subjects.* London, Henry Herringman 1669.

Burroughs, John: "The Halcyon in Canada." In *Locusts and Wild Honey.* Edinburgh, David Douglas 1898.

Camus, Albert: *Carnets, 1942-1951.* Trans. Thody, Philip. London, Hamish Hamilton 1966.

Cassirer, Ernst: *Language and Myth.* Trans. Langer, Susanne K. New York, Dover 1953.

Cellini, Benvenuto: *Autobiography.* Trans. Symonds, John Addington. New York, Garden City Publishing 1932.

Cirlot, Juan Eduardo: *Dictionary of Symbols.* Trans. Sage, Jack. New York, Philosophical Library 1962.

Cohn, Dorrit: "Narrated Monologue: Definition of Fictional Style." *Comparative Literature* 18, 2, Spring 1966.

– *Transparent Minds: Narrative Modes for Presenting Consciousness in Fiction.* Princeton, Princeton University Press 1978.

Culler, Jonathan: "Making Sense." In: *20th Century Studies.* 12, December 1974.

Dillard, Annie: "To Fashion a Text." In: *Inventing the Truth: the Art and Craft of Metaphor.* Baker, Russel and Zinsser, William (eds.). Boston, Houghton Mifflin 1987.

Drabble, Margaret: A *Writer's Britain: Landscape in Literature.* London, Thames and Hudson 1979.

Elbaz, Robert: *The Changing Nature of the Self: A Critical Study of the Autobiographical Discourse.* London and Sydney, Croom Helm 1988.

Eliot, Thomas Stearns: *The Four Quartets.* In: *The Complete Poems and Plays of T. S. Eliot.* London, Faber and Faber 1969.

Fiedler, Leslie A.: *Love and Death in the American Novel.* New York, Stein and Day 1966.

Forster, Edward Morgan: *Aspects of the Novel.* Harmondsworth, Penguin Books 1968.

Freedman, Ralph: *The Lyrical Novel.* Princeton, Princeton University Press 1963.

Frye, Northrop: *Anatomy of Criticism.* Princeton, Princeton University Press 1957.

— *Fables of Identity.* New York, Harcourt, Brace and World 1963.

— "Literature and Myth." In: *Relations of Literary Study: Essays on Interdisciplinary Contributions.* Thorpe, James (ed.). New York, Modern Language Association 1967.

— *The Great Code: The Bible and Literature.* Toronto, Academic Press 1983.

Girard, René: *Mensonge Romantique et Verité Romanesque.* Paris, Editions Bernard Grasset 1961.

Girardot, Norman J.: *Myth and Meaning in Early Taoism.* Berkeley, University of California Press 1983.

Goldsmith, Oliver: *A History of the Earth and Animated Nature.* Vol. 2. Glasgow, Blackie and Son 1840.

Heidegger, Martin: *Sein und Zeit.* Tübingen, M. Niemayer 1963.

Herendeen, Wyman: *From Landscape to Literature: The River and the Myth of Geography.* Pittsburgh, Duquesne University Press 1986.

Hughes, Ted: *Poetry in the Making.* London, Faber 1967.

Jung, Carl: *Aion, Untersuchungen zur Symbolgeschichte.* Zurich, Rascher Verlag 1951.

— *Psychology and Religion: West and East*. Trans. Hull, R. F. C.
  Princeton, Princeton University Press 1969.
— *The Archetypes and the Collective Unconscious*. Trans.
  Hull, R. F. C. Bollingen series, vol. 9. New York,
  Pantheon Books 1966.
Kaplan, Harold: *The Passive Voice: An Approach to Modern Fiction*.
  Athens, Ohio University Press 1966.
Katô, Shûichi: *Form, Style, Tradition*. Trans. Bester, John.
  Tokyo, Kôdansha 1981.
Keith, Thomas: *A History of the Modern Sensibility*. New York,
  Pantheon Books 1983.
Lao Tzu: *The Way of Life*. Trans. Blakney, Raymond B. New
  York, New American Library 1955.
Lukacs, Georg: *The Historical Novel*. Trans. Mitchell, Hannah
  and Stanley. Harmondsworth, Penguin Books 1969.
Melville, Herman: *Moby Dick* or, *The Whale*. Mansfield, Luther
  S. and Vincent, Howard P. (eds.). New York, Hendricks
  House 1952.
Moreau, Reginald Ernest: *The Departed Village: Berrick Salome
  at the turn of the century*. London, Oxford University Press
  1968.
Mumford, Lewis: *The City in History*. New York and London,
  Harcourt, Brace, Jovanovich 1961.
Ortega y Gasset, José: *Meditations on Hunting*. Trans. Wescott,
  Howard B. New York, Charles Scribner and Sons 1972.
Orwell, George: *Coming Up for Air*. London, Secker and
  Warburg 1954.
Pascal, Roy: *Design and Truth in Autobiography*. London,
  Rutledge and Kegan Paul 1960.
Pavel, Ota: *Veliký vodní tulák*. Praha, Čs. spisovatel 1980.
Pilling, John: *Autobiography and Imagination*. London,
  Routledge and Kegan Paul 1981.

Profumo, David, and Swift, Graham (Eds.): *The Magic Wheel.* An Anthology of Fishing in Literature. London, William Heinemann and Pan Books 1985.

Renza, Louis: "The Veto of the Imagination: A Theory of Autobiography." *New Literary History* 9, 1, Autumn 1977.

Richards, Ivor A.: *Practical Criticism: A Study of Literary Judgement.* London, Routledge & Kegan Paul 1978.

— *Principles of Literary Criticism.* London, Routledge & Kegan Paul, 1955.

Ricœur, Paul: *The Rule of Metaphor: Multi-Disciplinary Studies of the Creation of Meaning in Language.* Toronto, University of Toronto Press 1977.

Rimmon-Kennan, Shlomith: *Narrative Fiction: Contemporary Poetics.* London and New York, Routledge 1989.

Robb, James: *Notable Angling Literature.* London, Herbert Jenkins 1947.

Sartre, Jean Paul: *Nausea.* Trans. Alexander, Lloyd. New York, New Directions 1964.

Schapiro, Meyer: *Paul Cezanne.* New York, H. N. Abrams 1962.

Spencer, Herbert: *An Autobiography.* Vol. 2. London, Williams and Norgate 1904.

Spender, Stephen: *The Struggle of the Modern.* Berkeley, University of California Press 1965.

Steiger, Emil: *Grundbegriffe der Poetik.* Zürich, Atlantis Verlag 1963.

Thomas, Keith: *Man and the Natural World.* Harmondsworth, Penguin Books 1984.

Thomas, Lewis: "A Long Line of Cells." In: *Inventing the Truth.* Zinsser, William (ed.). Boston, Houghton Mifflin 1987.

Todorov, Tzvetan: *The Poetics of Prose.* Trans. Howard, Richard. Ithaca, Cornell University Press 1977.

Walton, Izaac: *The Compleat Angler.* Harmondsworth,
    Penguin Books 1985.
Weber, Max: *The City.* Trans. Martindale, Don and
    Neuwirth, Gertrud. New York, The Free Press 1958.
Weir, Robert F. (ed.): *Death in Literature.* New York,
    Columbia University Press 1980.
Wellek, René: *Concepts of Criticism.* New Haven and London,
    Yale University Press 1963.
Welty, Eudora: *One Writer's Beginnings.* Cambridge, Harvard
    University Press 1984.
– *Place in Fiction, Three Papers on Fiction.* Northampton, Smith
    College 1962.
Williams, Raymond: *The Country and the City.* London, Chatto
    and Windus 1973.
– *Keywords: A Vocabulary of Culture and Society.* New York,
    Oxford University Press 1976.
Wilson, Edmund: *Axel's Castle.* New York, Charles
    Scribner's Sons 1969.
– *The Wound and the Bow: Seven Studies in Literature.* London,
    W. H. Allen 1952.
Wimsatt, William K.: *The Verbal Icon: Studies in the Meaning of
    Poetry.* Lexington, University of Kentucky Press 1967.
Woolf, Virginia: "Fishing." In: *The Moment and Other Essays.*
    London, The Hogarth Press 1947.

IBUSE MASUJI: A CENTURY REMEMBERED
ANTONÍN LÍMAN

Published by Charles University
in Prague, Karolinum Press
Ovocný trh 3–5, 116 36 Praha 1
http://cupress.cuni.cz
Prague 2008
Vice-rector-editor
Prof. PhDr. Mojmír Horyna
Layout by Zdeněk Ziegler
Typeset by MU studio
Printed by PB tisk, Příbram
First English edition
ISBN 978-80-246-1452-6